W9-DFC-871

China in the twenty-first century

This book is based on a symposium held in commemoration of the 120th anniversary of the founding of Aoyama Gakuin, Tokyo. The symposium was sponsored by Aoyama Gakuin University and the United Nations University.

China in the twenty-first century: Politics, economy, and society

Edited by Fumio Itoh

**United Nations
University Press**

TOKYO · NEW YORK · PARIS

H-Y LIB
(W)

ENCHING LIBRARY
HARVARD UNIVERSITY
2 DIVINITY AVENUE
CAMBRIDGE, MA 02138

YANKEE
07/07/1999

HC
427.92
.C3278
1997

© Aoyama Gakuin University, 1997

The views expressed in this publication are those of the authors and do not necessarily reflect the views of the United Nations University.

United Nations University Press
The United Nations University, 53-70, Jingumae 5-chome, Shibuya-ku, Tokyo 150, Japan
Tel: (03) 3499-2811   Fax: (03) 3406-7345
Telex: J25442   Cable: UNATUNIV TOKYO

UNU Office in North America
2 United Nations Plaza, Room DC2-1462-70, New York, NY 10017
Tel: (212) 963-6387   Fax: (212) 371-9454
Telex: 422311 UN UI

United Nations University Press is the publishing division of the United Nations University.

Cover design by J.-M. Antenen, Geneva

UNUP-946
ISBN 92-808-0946-6

Contents

Preface

On 16 November 1994, Aoyama Gakuin (comprising the University and affiliated primary and secondary schools) celebrated its 120th anniversary. In contemplation of that occasion, Aoyama Gakuin University gave careful consideration to the mission of the University as it moves toward the twenty-first century. Consequently, as a commemorative event, the University planned that the least it could do would be to contribute to the learned world by holding an international symposium entitled "China in the Twenty-first Century." With the contributions to the symposium serving as the background, this book, after appropriate editing, was created.

As is widely known, trading between China and Japan has flourished. During the 300 years between the Nara era and the Heian era, Japan assimilated China's culture, but by modifying it in a manner that would cause it to be consistent with, and to enhance, its own original ways. Thus, the continental culture of China has had a tremendous impact on the formation of the Japanese culture. However, the Sino-Japanese War, the Manchurian Incident, Japan's aggression, and the unfortunate history of events between China and Japan after World War II have sometimes produced friction between the two countries, making it difficult to sustain a good and viable relationship. However, normal relations between Japan and China were restored by the historical establishment of diplomatic relations in November 1972. Especially in the field of economic relations, Japan has become China's largest trading partner, and China, surpassing Indonesia, has become Japan's largest investment target in Asia. The mutually dependent relations between the two countries have grown closer and closer.

During the 2,000 years of the past, China had achieved the world's highest level in terms of technology and income. However, looking back to the past two centuries, China has become weak when compared with certain other countries. Internally, China has suffered a kind of separation, and the people have had to live in economic poverty. But the reform and liberalization beginning in 1979 has been a catalyst, and China's economy has developed far more rapidly than that of Korea, Taiwan, Hong Kong, and Singapore. During the 1980s, China's economy grew at the rate of 9 per cent per year.

China's policy of reform and liberalization and its economic development have now reached a significant position in the world, significant in the sense that China, a member of the East Asian region, has become the world's "Development Centre." It is also significant in the sense that China is shifting from a planned economy to a market economy. As China's economic development changes its politics, so it is also changing the Asian economy. Furthermore, it is also about to change world politics.

After World War II, Asia was impacted by the East–West Cold War, followed by the Korean upheaval, the Viet Nam War, and the Cambodian conflict. With a huge population, China became a nation characterized by an extreme ideology. It experienced internal strife (called the "Cultural Revolution") and, in the area of foreign relations, China was in conflict with the Soviet Union over the motivating forces of socialism and its true nature. In the 1990s China began a historical reconciliation with the Soviet Union. In addition, it normalized diplomatic relations with Viet Nam, Indonesia, India, Mongolia, and Singapore. Moreover, China normalized diplomatic relations with South Korea, which had been an opponent since the Korean War. These recent moves by China have created a feeling of stability in the other Asian countries. Also, China has built an atmosphere that enables it to concentrate on its economy.

The tense international relations in the world were alleviated when the Cold War structure collapsed after the Soviet Union was broken up. However, a new world order has not yet been established, and the world is still experiencing chaos and instability. How can an orderly world environment be created and sustained? Asia has 60 per cent of the world's population, with China occupying 21 per cent of that population, or 1.2 billion people. It is imperative for China's economy to grow continuously in an orderly fashion. The world must understand the significant potential of China as the nation that will become the core of the Asian region.

It was based on this understanding and recognition that the University held the international symposium, "China in the Twenty-first Century." The objective of the symposium was to achieve comprehensive recognition of the "light and shadow" of China's present and future. This book is a recorded account of the symposium, participated in by knowledgeable persons from home and abroad, as they discussed China's future from various points of view. It will certainly deepen our understanding of China's present condition. We are convinced that we have presented a valuable opportunity for considering whether the world can understand and adjust to China's expectation of coexistence.

The international symposium was held for three days, from 29 to 31 October 1994. It was co-sponsored by Aoyama Gakuin University and the United Nations University, and supported by the Ministry of Foreign Affairs, the Embassy of the People's Republic of China, and the *Yomiuri Shimbun* (newspaper). The first part of the symposium was devoted to keynote speeches. Research presentations and panel discussions occupied the second and third parts, respectively.

To obtain insights from China and abroad, Mr Rong Yiren, Vice-President of the People's Republic of China, the founder of China International Trust and Investment Corporation (CITIC) and the former Chairman of the Board of CITIC, spoke on "China in the Twenty-first Century" from an inside view of China. Mr Rong played a central role in introducing foreign capital to China, which was the main factor in China's incredible economic growth. He appealed for support in sustaining valid world relationships by saying: "In the twenty-first century, China's situation will affect not only the fate of the more than 1 billion people of China, but also the world development and peace process."

Speaking in terms of an external view of "China in the Twenty-first Century," the next speaker was former Chancellor of the Federal Republic of Germany, Helmut Schmidt. He was born in 1918 in Hamburg, is sympathetic to Japan, familiar with things Japanese, and he wrote his graduation thesis on the reform of Japanese currency. As Chancellor of the Federal Republic of Germany he contributed greatly in relieving the tensions of East–West relations. He said:

Twenty years from now, there is a possibility that China's GNP will surpass that of not only Japan, but also the United States. However, in that case, five conditions [see his keynote speech] must be met. The United States and the European countries should make every effort to understand and show respect to the Asian countries, and at the same time, the Asian countries should do the same for the United States and the European countries. By doing so, conflicts of civilization can be an avoidable matter.

The "Presentation of Research" session consisted of three segments: (1) "The Chinese Economy in the Twenty-first Century"; (2) "Chinese Management in the Twenty-first Century," and (3) "Chinese Politics and Society in the Twenty-first Century." A total of eight sessions were conducted, three of which addressed political and social problems, three the economic crisis, and two management problems. For these sessions, three people – one Japanese, one Chinese, and one from outside these two countries – constituted a group; one person presented the problem and two debated the problem. A presentation and debate forum was conducted so that the problems related to the theme of the research could be studied from a global perspective from within Japan, and from perspectives of neighbouring countries and other countries. By and large, enthusiastic presentations and questions and answers addressed the problem of how economic development, political democratization, and the task of modernization will be closely connected.

The panel discussion was conducted by eight panellists: Liu Guo-guang (Adviser, Chinese Academy of Social Sciences, China), Chen Qimao (former President, the Shanghai Institute for International Studies, China), Shigeru Ishikawa (Professor Emeritus, Aoyama Gakuin University), William Cline (Senior Fellow, the Institute for International Economics, USA), Susan Strange (Professor, University of Warwick, UK), Byung-Joon Ahn (Professor, Yonsei University, Korea), John Wong (Professor, National University of Singapore, Singapore), and Fu-chen Lo (Principal Academic Officer, The United Nations University Institute of Advanced Studies). By considering the content of the keynote speeches and the "Presentation of Research," they actively debated the evaluations made on the political strategies of the revolution and liberalization that have brought a rapid change in the Chinese economy and society. They also discussed both security and regional cooperation amongst the Association of South-East Asian Nations (ASEAN) countries.

The contents of the symposium were very much related to peace and the process of development in the world for the future, and it was an event that should have been made available to all the people around the world. The Organizing Committee believed that it would be expedient for the results of the research of the symposium to be published and made available throughout the world as public property, and we felt that it was our duty to do so. Hence, we have decided to publish the proceedings of the symposium in Japanese, Chinese, and English.

At the time of editing this book, the entire keynote speeches of the Vice-President of the People's Republic of China and of the former Chancellor of the Federal Republic of Germany were included. The presentations of the research for each session and the comments made by the debaters were included as the "Presentation of Research." Also, the valuable comments made by the chairman of each session were put together as a "Summary." For the panel discussions, some repeated opinions were cut in order to make the discussions clear.

The content of the international symposium was interpreted simultaneously in English, Japanese, and Chinese. Hence, the keynote speeches, the presentation of research, and the opinions of each presentation for the panel discussions were transcribed, then translated. Additional alterations were made for corrections and additions by each presenter. This manuscript was finally edited by the Editing Committee in order to maintain consistency throughout the book. For the Japanese edition, the Simul Press Inc., and for the English edition, the United Nations University Press, have undertaken the work of publication. The details of the Chinese edition are still being discussed with a publishing company.

Publication of the Japanese edition is through the kind offices of Satoshi Amako (Professor, School of International Politics, Economics, and Business [SIPEB], Aoyama Gakuin University [AGU]), Shizuka Ide (Professor, SIPEB, AGU), Ken-ichi Senba (Professor, SIPEB, AGU), Takashi Oshimura (Associate Professor, SIPEB, AGU), Kumiko Kobayashi (staff member of the Office of the Graduate School, AGU), and Nanako Shinagawa (staff member of the Office of SIPEB, AGU). They cooperated greatly through their untiring work and efforts related to management of the international symposium, especially as far as the publishing of this book is concerned and, at the same time, also by being members of the Editing Committee.

Without the devoted collaboration of the members of the Committee, neither could I have achieved the success of the international symposium nor could I have had the opportunity to have this book published. I would like to express my deep gratitude and appreciation to each member of the Committee. Also. the realization of this book's publication was the result of the warm consent of the United Nations University Press to publishing it. In addition, I am more than thankful to Amadio A. Arboleda and to the rest of the staff at the publishing office.

Lastly, this book was published as the result of the realization of the international symposium, which was made possible by a great deal of help from various organizations and many people. I received tremendous help from the United Nations University, the Japanese Ministry of Foreign Affairs, the Embassy of the People's Republic of China, and the *Yomiuri Shimbun*.

I am especially grateful to many persons of Aoyama Gakuin University: Yuji Hasaka, Masanobu Fukamachi, Minoru Yoshida, Shouichi Naito, Shigeru Ishikawa, Mitsuru Yamamoto, Kunizo Kasai, Teruaki Fukumoto, and Katsuhira Suzuki. I am grateful to people of the United Nations University: Heitor Gurgulino de Souza, Tarcisio Della Senta, Takeo Uchida, and Fu-chen Lo. My deep thanks go to the staff of the Japanese Ministry of Foreign Affairs: Tadashi Ikeda, Ichiro Fujisaki, Yoshio Nomoto, and Nobuyuki Watanabe. I am grateful for the help of people of the Embassy of the People's Republic of China: Xu Dunxin, Wang Taiping, and Qiu Guo Hong. I extend my thanks to the *Yomiuri Shimbun*: Tsuneo Watanabe and Yoshinori Tandoh.

I want to acknowledge the special debt I owe to Yoshihiro Nakayama (the former Japanese Ambassador to France and former Professor, AGU), Lee B. Hughes (former Professor, AGU), Du Jin (Associate Professor, Kita Kyushu University), and Li Wei (Chief of the Asian and African Division of the Foreign Affairs Bureau, Chinese Academy of Social Sciences).

On this occasion, I would like to express our deepest appreciation and gratitude to all, and especially to the School of International Politics, Economics, and Business for all its unending support in conducting the international symposium and for its effort related to publishing this book. I will be most fortunate if this book provides the reader with some insights into the significance of "China in the Twenty-first Century," especially within the context of Asian solidarity and, indeed, solidarity of the world itself.

Fumio Itoh, Dean, SIPEB
Aoyama Gakuin University

Rong Yiren   Helmut Schmidt

Helmut Schmidt and Rong Yiren

Panel discussion

Keynote addresses

China: Moving towards the twenty-first century

Rong Yiren

Mr Chairman, Ladies and Gentlemen:

I am very happy to have the opportunity of coming to Aoyama Gakuin University, with its long history and galaxy of talent, to discuss, together with so many eminent politicians and scholars, the development problems to be confronted by China in the twenty-first century. This symposium will certainly play an active role in further understanding China and strengthening communication between other countries and China. Here, I would like to express my lofty respect to all our friends who are concerned with the reform and development of China. And I would also like to express my cordial thanks to the symposium organizers, Aoyama Gakuin University and the United Nations University.

As the turn of the century approaches, how to summarize the past seriously, construct the present actively, and plan for the future scientifically has become a common problem faced by all mankind. China is a large developing country that has one-fifth of the total population of the world. The situation in China in the coming twenty-first century will be related not only to the fortunes of the over one billion Chinese people but also to the progress of world peace and development. Therefore, the significance of problems discussed in this symposium is definitely not limited to China.

In the history of human development, the Chinese nation has made many brilliant contributions to world civilization. In modern times, however, China was reduced to a colony and semi-colony for a time, as a result of the decadence and incompetence of the government as well as the aggression and bullying of imperialist big powers. Consequently, China lagged behind the developed countries in economic development, science and technology, culture and education, and so on. By the middle of this century, after over one hundred years of extremely arduous and difficult struggles, the Chinese people finally achieved a revolutionary triumph under the leadership of the Chinese Communist Party. Since the foundation of the People's Republic of China, large-scale economic reconstruction has taken place. These generally acknowledged achievements have been made in spite of experiencing some setbacks. They have laid a preliminary foundation for the realization of the industrialization and modernization of China.

Since 1979, China has entered a new historic period of implementing reforms and creating an open-door policy to carry out the construction of modernization. Under the guidance of Deng Xiaoping's theory of establishing a socialist country with Chinese characteristics, China has generated unprecedented achievements in economic development and other fields.

China is a large country within which the peasants constitute the absolute majority of the total population. The rural economy and the peasants' condition are directly associated with national economic development and social stability. The reforms in China started in the rural areas. By implementing policies for the "household responsibility system" and by developing rural enterprises, the initiative of millions of Chinese peasants was aroused and the rural economy then grew quickly and contributed to the great changes happening in the rural areas. The success in rural reform has pushed forward both national economic development and urban reform. Starting from the year 1984, the emphasis of economic reform in China turned to the urban regions and a series of reforms were progressively enacted. On the basis of active exploration and practice over 10 years, a general goal of reform has been established – that is, to build up a socialist market economic system. At present, the price of Chinese commodities has essentially been set free, and commodity pricing depending on market transactions accounts for more than 90 per cent of total industrial goods, more than 85 per cent of total agricultural and sub-sidiary products, and over 80 per cent of total industrial production materials with factory prices. This year, the Chinese government has taken decisive steps in macro-management system reforms involving finance, taxation, banking, foreign currency, and foreign trade. The results expected have been realized. From next year, while continu-ing to perfect the macro-management system reforms, government emphasis will be placed upon state-owned enterprise reforms, which are planned to be finished within a few years. These reforms are expected to inject new vigour into the economy of China.

Opening the door to the outside world is a basic national policy of China. The open areas have gradually developed from the newly established special economic zone to the coastal area, the area along the Changjiang River, the boundary area, and the interior with the provincial capital as a core. Nowadays, an all-orientation, multi-level and multi-form opening pattern has been formed in China. Those fields open to abroad have been consistently increasing. With the progressive improvement of the investment environment and the completion of laws and regulations concerning foreign affairs, more and more foreign investors have come to China. Foreign trade is growing very quickly. Import and export trade volume has increased from US$20.6 billion in 1978 to US$195.8 billion in 1993. This open-ing has not only brought about a great advance in the economy of China but also promoted wide and broad communication and co-operation between other countries and China.

The economic reconstruction of China that started in 1979 is intended to achieve the goal of modernization in three steps: first, doubling the size of the 1980 gross national product (GNP) and attempting to solve the problems in feeding and clothing the pop-ulation; then, by the year 2000, further doubling the GNP achieved in the first step and affording the Chinese people a *xiao kang* (better-off) level of life; thirdly, taking several decades more to reach a level compatible with the middle class in developed countries, and essen-tially achieving modernization by the middle of the twenty-first cen-tury. The objective of the first step was essentially realized in the 1980s, and we are now devoting ourselves to the realization of the goal set for the second step. Judging from actual developments, we are confident of accomplishing this goal. On the other hand, we clearly recognize that, as a large country with weak foundations and a huge population, China will still be a developing country for a long time, irrespective of achieving the goals set for the first two steps. We

5

hope to be able to accomplish this modernization through great struggle and effort in the decades to come.

Choosing the correct way for development is of great significance for achieving the twenty-first century development objectives of China. I myself have experienced most of this century's Chinese history and know well the difficult struggle for state independence and the great endeavours for a prosperous and powerful country achieved by the Chinese people over the past one hundred years. I deeply believe that, following the path of Deng Xiaoping's theory on establishing a socialist country with Chinese characteristics, the modernization of China will be accomplished successfully, as expected.

We will persist in the reforms and the open-door policy firmly and unshakably. According to the existing plan, a preliminary socialist market economic system will have been created by the end of this century and then, on the basis of this newly established system, a more mature and finalized system will be generated following a further 20-year effort. We will continue implementing actively the opening process, promoting economic and technological communication with other countries, and forging mutual links with the world so as finally to move the development of China forward. We welcome investments from foreign businessmen. From now to the end of this century, the total import and export trade volume of China will be not less than US$1,000 billion. Such a large market will surely contribute actively to the development of the world economy. While conducting the economic reforms, China is also actively performing political reforms to perfect further the system of the National People's Congress, the system of inter-party cooperation, and the Chinese People's Political Consultative Conference led by the Communist Party of China, as well as to develop socialist democratic politics with Chinese characteristics. While pushing forward with the reforms and the opening-up policy, we have tried to deal appropriately with the relationship between reform, development, and stability. China is a developing country whose society is in transformation. Therefore, keeping that society stable is of special importance.

We will make great efforts to maintain a sustainable, rapid, and healthy increase in economic development. China has many favourable conditions for rapid development. As for the conflicts and difficulties due to rapid economic development, the Chinese government has solved these problems by strengthening and improving macroadjustments and controls. There currently exists a promising trend for economic development in China. In light of the condition of – and trends in – economic development, the economy of China will be able to continue increasing rapidly for a relatively long period.

China will make an effort to generate sustainable development through the collaboration of its population, economy, society, environment, and resources. The sustainable development strategy is the correct choice for humanity to achieve twenty-first century development objectives. The policy we are adopting is not only actively to accelerate economic development, but also to try hard to protect the ecosystem and the environment. How to cope appropriately with the relationship between social development, population increase, and environmental protection has become an important worldwide issue. Our government has already published a White Paper entitled "China: the Twenty-first Century Agenda" in which the objectives, policies, and measures for the development of the population and the environment in the twenty-first century have been systematically planned, and a strategy for continuous development has been proposed. Carrying out this strategy will allow China to achieve greater development in the twenty-first century and to make its due contribution to the development of the world.

We are also dedicating ourselves to the establishment of a spiritual civilization in addition to the material civilization. The twenty-first century must be a more civilized century. China has put the development of science, education, and cultural undertakings in an important position, and is paying attention to the study of the theory of establishing socialism with Chinese characteristics, patriotic training, law, and discipline, as well as the study of traditional Chinese culture. My experiences over the past several decades have taught me that the several thousand years of cultural development in China and the traditional Chinese virtues, combine to make up the modern civilization with Chinese characteristics. Dealing well with the relationship between traditional culture and modern civilization will be helpful for both the modernization and development of China in the twenty-first century.

China is a unified multi-ethnic country. The China that is moving towards the twenty-first century will make great efforts to develop unity among its various nationalities and to push forward with unifying the country peacefully. Our country has adopted a policy of actively supporting economic and cultural development in minority nationality areas in addition to the less developed areas, so as to reach a level of common prosperity among all the nationalities and to consolidate and improve the great unification efforts of our various

7

nationalities. Taiwan, Hong Kong, and Macao are all inseparable parts of China. To accomplish the task of unifying the country is the common wish of all Chinese people, including those who live in Taiwan, Hong Kong, Macao, and overseas. China will assume control in Hong Kong in 1997 and in Macao in 1999. Moreover, China has both the determination and the ability to maintain the level of prosperity and stability in both Hong Kong and Macao. At present, contact across the Taiwan Strait has been increasing day by day. In light of the policy of "Peaceful Unification and One Country with Two Systems", we are striving to unify the country as early as possible. The Chinese government and people will never remain indifferent to, nor accept, any attempt to divide China.

Ladies and gentlemen, the current international society is experiencing a fundamental and complicated change. Peace and development are still the two most important issues in the world. An open, economically developed, and stable China is an important force for promoting world peace and development. On the other hand, China also requires a peaceful and stable international environment to strengthen contacts and cooperation with other countries for development. We will steadfastly pursue an independent peaceful foreign policy, and will make all efforts to establish a peaceful and stable international environment together with other governments and people as part of our active contribution to world peace and development.

Economic development is the problem with which various governments and people are most concerned. The end of the Cold War has provided a new opportunity for world economic development. Economic considerations now play a more important role in dealing with international relations. Various countries have come to pay more attention to international economic cooperation while emphasizing their own economic developments. However, it has to be pointed out that, in international economic relations, trade protectionism and discriminatory policies still exist and have led to difficulties for many developing countries and sharper contradictions between the North and South. This situation is harmful not only to developing countries but also to developed countries. I think that regional economic and trade cooperation and worldwide multilateral trade arrangements should be open rather than closed and should be pursuing the principles of equality and mutual benefit. The developed countries have the responsibility to take active measures to help solve the problems in developing countries by opening their markets, providing financial support, transferring advanced technology, and decreasing the debt burden of the developing countries. This will be helpful not only to the developing countries but also to the further progress of the developed countries.

Although a general relaxation seems to be prevailing with respect to international relations, attempts at hegemony and power politics still exist. Regional hot-spot problems arise one after another, and many unstable factors continue to exist; the world, therefore, is far from achieving real peace. International society is currently discussing how to establish a new post-Cold War international relationship so as to ensure that the twenty-first century will become a century of real peace, development, and prosperity all over the world. The new international relationship should be established on the basis of following strictly the United Nations Charter and other well-recognized principles of international relations – for example, mutual respect for territorial integrity and sovereignty, mutual non-aggression, non-interference in other nations' internal affairs, equality and mutual benefit, and peaceful coexistence. Altercations and disputes between countries should be solved in a peaceful way through dialogue and negotiation between the countries concerned. Interfering in other countries' internal affairs, exerting pressure, or implementing sanctions – and even employing military force – not only will be useless for fairly and reasonably solving problems but also will make the problems more complicated, thus increasing the level of difficulty in arriving at resolutions.

To develop friendly relationships with neighbouring countries has taken on a special meaning in the foreign policy of China. China and Japan face each other across the sea, and friendship between the people of the two countries goes back to ancient times. Since the normalization of diplomatic relations between the two countries in 1972, China and Japan have made considerable progress in friendly communication and cooperation in various fields through joint efforts by both governments and private citizens. Reflecting on the past in light of the present, we truly feel that the Sino-Japanese Joint Declaration and the Sino-Japanese Treaty of Peace and Friendship are the political bases and fundamental principles for standardizing and developing relations between the two countries. The practice has verified that, whenever we insist on and uphold the fundamental principles of the Declaration and Treaty, the Sino-Japanese relationship can develop smoothly. Whenever we have ignored or even violated these fundamental principles, the relationship between the

9

two countries has become disturbed or even fallen into a relapse. Regardless of the past, present, and future, scrupulously abiding to the principle and spirit of the Declaration and Treaty – meaning that there is only one China and that Taiwan is an inseparable part of the People's Republic of China – and seriously performing the respective responsibilities and obligations, are the guarantee of improving friendly Sino-Japanese relations.

The Sino-Japanese relationship is entering a new stage of development and an important characteristic of this is the new level of mutual economic and trade cooperation. At present, Japan has become China's largest trade partner while China has become Japan's second-largest trade partner. The total foreign trade volume of the two countries is expected to exceed US$40 billion this year. This fact shows that China and Japan are good cooperative partners now and will not become antagonists in the future. To establish an overall cooperative Sino-Japanese relationship with equality and mutual benefit has become the general trend. The further strengthening of Sino-Japanese friendly relations will be not only in keeping with the aspirations and benefits of the people of the two countries but also helpful for peace, stability, and prosperity in the Asia-Pacific region and all over the world. I believe that, as long as both China and Japan can insist on the various principles stated in the Sino-Japanese Joint Declaration and the Sino-Japanese Treaty of Peace and Friendship, keeping both positive and negative experiences and lessons of history firmly in mind, and by going beyond the differences in social ideology and systems to collaborate frankly with each other in a long-term perspective, the scale of economic relations and the collaborative level of the two countries will be able to increase continuously in making active contributions to both the modernization of China and the lasting prosperity of the Japanese economy. And thus the strenuously obtained Sino-Japanese friendly relationship can be consolidated and developed. If a peaceful, stable, developed China has a long, friendly, neighbourly relationship with a Japan continuing to persist in peaceful development, it is certain that the two countries will be able to make their respective contributions to the establishment of a more prosperous twenty-first century.

Ladies and gentlemen, the new century is moving towards us. An amazing future is waiting for us to build it. I believe, with the joint efforts of people all over the world, that humanity's twenty-first century will be the most brilliant and magnificent yet.

Thank you all.

China in the twenty-first century

Helmut Schmidt

Mr Vice-President of the People's Republic of China, President Naito of Aoyama Gakuin University, Ladies and Gentlemen:

In the first place, let me express my gratitude for being invited to address this impressive audience of this 120-year-old institution and to do so at the side of Vice-President Rong Yiren.

Of course, you will have to understand that I am speaking in a totally private capacity, as a private observer, and not on behalf of any authorities of my country.

I have been travelling a lot to Japan, to China, to other countries in East Asia and South-East Asia, and I have been learning a lot about different cultures and mentalities, and I'm still learning. But, in the same process, I have become a friend of both the Chinese nation and the Japanese nation.

It seems to me that sometimes Western politicians, Western governments, tend to give advice to the Japanese or to the Chinese, to others in this part of the world, without having profound historical and cultural understanding of the Asian nations and of their historically developed civilizations and of their set of basic values.

I sometimes see the same phenomenon when Westerners, in vain, try to advise Russians without ever having read Dostoevski or Tolstoi, and it seems to me that it is as well to no avail if Westerners try to teach China or Japan without having caught the spirit of the Confucian philosophy and its impact on everyday life – for instance, the phenomenon of respect for leadership by a wise old man, for instance Deng Xiaoping in China or my friend Takeo Fukuda here in this country.

Now, being asked to talk about China in the twenty-first century – quite a subject – allow me first to try to give an overview of the present situation of the world after the demise of Soviet imperialism and then to approach the Chinese future, progressing stepwise from West to East. But I would say right from the beginning, in my view China is to play a much greater role in the twenty-first century than ever in the twentieth century or in the nineteenth century.

The breakdown of the Soviet Empire and of Soviet imperialism in approaching the end of the present century has changed the world: it has created optimism; it has created hopes; but also it has unveiled quite a number of regional and local conflicts that had been hidden hitherto.

One might interpret the demise of the Soviet Union – and some people do interpret it that way – as a victory of capitalism. Some interpret this demise as a victory of capitalism and democracy.

I myself would rather prefer to say that it was brought about by two main factors: first, by the domestic exhaustion and the inner decay of the bureaucratic system of Soviet governments and then by the sudden attempt to change almost everything at once and overnight; secondly, it was brought about by the quest for self-determination and freedom of the hitherto subdued peoples in the hitherto Soviet-dominated eastern half of Europe and also in Central Asia.

Next, to the great changes in Europe – for instance, the reunification of the German nation – changes that have been brought about by the collapse of the Soviet Empire. Very great changes, of course, are also happening in almost all of Asia as a consequence of the demise of the Soviet Union.

For instance, take the Middle East. Peace and agreements between Mr Rabin and Mr Arafat would never have taken place if the old Soviet Empire had still maintained its power to interfere. On the other hand, I would assume that the term "Middle East" may be getting some additional substance in the future. Countries like Kazakhstan, Turkmenistan, Uzbekistan, Tajikistan, Kirghizia, also Afghanistan, and even Azerbaijan – such countries may, in the future, be included if people in the world talk of the "Middle East" as distinguished from the "Near East" and from the "Far East."

Well, whatever the terminology in the future, certainly we are going to see competing influences in that part of Asia, that part which hitherto has been called "Central Asia." Russia will seek to regain its influence, so will Turkey, so will Iran, so will Pakistan, and so will China.

Great changes, of course, have been brought about in "East Asia" and the "Far East," as we Europeans call it. China has won a much freer hand in international politics than ever since the late fifties, since the clash between Moscow and Beijing – a much freer hand than ever in this century or in the nineteenth century.

India, on the other hand, has become indirectly weakened. So has North Korea, so has Viet Nam; but Viet Nam will quickly adjust to the new situation, which is an adjustment that is much more difficult for the large country of India with more than 800 million people.

The rise of China, to some degree, is also due to the alleviation of the nightmare of Soviet invasion. I very well recall the talks with Mao Zedong or with Deng Xiaoping 20 years ago when there was severe tension between the People's Republic, on the one side, and the Soviet Union, on the other. This has been alleviated now, and this does play some role in the rise of China.

But much more so, I think, is the rise of China due to Deng Xiaoping's economic reforms, of which the Vice-President talked about a quarter of an hour ago and which I personally have been admiring from the beginnings onward, the late seventies onwards. I have admired them particularly because of the wise gradual approach, of this stepwise approach.

An English friend of mine called Popper would have called it "piecemeal social engineering," to quote a phrase from Karl Popper.

On the other hand, one will not have to forget that Russia will remain one of the strongest military powers in Asia, and in the world, and also quite a power in the Pacific Ocean, despite Russia's present economic and political weaknesses and uncertainties. By the way, these uncertainties may take a long time to be settled. They may take a quarter of a century or even longer than a quarter.

It seems to me that these changes in Asia have not really changed the position of Japan. Certainly, the position of Japan has not been changed, basically.

But something has intrigued me all the time in the last 20 years

13

(and I have been a frequent visitor to this country for 35 years now), which did again come to the conscience of the Japanese public when – almost for the first time ever – last year the Hosokawa Government hinted at Japanese aggression onto other people's soils in Asia and also of crimes that usually go hand-in-hand with war and with occupation.

I think the decades-long denial of these historical facts of the twentieth century was not to the advantage of the leverage and freedom of Japanese foreign policies, and I think as well that my Japanese friends ought to be aware all the time of this fact and also of the fact that Japan's military posture is not necessarily welcome in the rest of the Asia-Pacific region.

If you look from the outside onto China, onto Russia, onto Japan, Viet Nam, North Korea, South Korea, the Association of South-East Asian Nations (ASEAN) group, it seems to me that my friend Lee Kuan Yew of Singapore was right when he said, a couple of years ago, that the least distrusted great power in this part of the world is the United States. But, to my view, the United States is ambiguous in her attitudes both *vis-à-vis* China and *vis-à-vis* Japan.

Now, ladies and gentlemen, forecasting is a tricky business, particularly if it's being directed at a whole new century. Forecasting is a tricky business, particularly if it's being done by an economist like myself. Never believe economists if they forecast, because what seems to be inevitable today may never happen in the future and, instead, it may be the unexpected that really does happen.

With this cautioning experience about economics, about economists' forecasts, let me try to voice a few thoughts, not about the whole twenty-first century but, let me say, about the future in the next 20 or 25 years or so.

It seems to me that, early in the twenty-first century, China will overtake the volume of Japan's GNP (gross national product). China will possibly as well, a little later on, overtake the GNP of the United States of America, and a little later on then the volume of the Chinese economy as a whole will be greater than the volume of the American and the Japanese economies combined, but this prophecy, of course, is in regard to the absolute figures of the Chinese GNP. It does not pertain by far to the GNP or the national income per capita, or the average real income in these three countries.

As the Vice-President has said, China still is a developing country – the largest developing country in the world, the largest country in the world altogether – and, as regards real income per capita, China will, for a long time to come, lag behind the income per capita in Japan, or in America, or within the European Union, for that matter.

But it is necessary to understand – for the Americans, for the Europeans, for the Japanese, for all of us – that China will be the biggest economy of all – the greatest market, the greatest importer, the greatest exporter – including, by the way, two financial centres probably – Shanghai and also Hong Kong.

Of course, there are difficult conditions to be met by China in order to reach such status in the future. Or, in other words, there are a number of great *ifs*. For instance, all this will happen *if* China is capable of avoiding domestic turmoils. Domestic turmoils have often enough occurred over the millenniums of Chinese history, and domestic turmoils have occurred in China only two and, again, three decades ago. So it's a great *if* that the future status of China will be attained *if* China is able to avoid domestic turmoil.

And, secondly, this will happen only *if* China can muster the effective capabilities to bring about a sufficient transportation and communication infrastructure inside the country in order to let the inland provinces – the hinterland – participate in the upswing – in the economic upswing – of the coastal provinces and, thereby, allow the rural population to participate in the upswing of real income and real standard of living.

Thirdly, there is another *if*. All this will happen, I guess, only *if* the capital inflow from the outside into China can be maintained.

I am deeply impressed, I must say, by the capital import into China by overseas Chinese, which the Vice-President has mentioned, very impressive capital import, which I judge to be a very impressive signal of confidence of overseas Chinese in regard to the PRC's future political and economic stability. These overseas Chinese, of course, have a much closer and better insight into the developments in the People's Republic than do Western banking corporations or financial industrial corporations of Western governments.

There is another *if*. I think all this will happen only *if* China is able to reduce the burden of a too-great military machine and a too-great defence industry. The size of the military and the size of the defence industry was maybe really necessary as long as the Soviet threat did exist, but now they are not necessary in the same size and order of magnitude. Their size, by the way, presently is one of the reasons for the fact that right now Chinese weapons exports are rather high. You see the same phenomenon in Russia and also in my own country after unification.

15

One of the further *ifs* is an *if* in the short run, namely *if* the Chinese authorities at present and in the near future can successfully dampen inflation rates.

Well, I do not dare prophesy on China's future strategic role; nevertheless, in perhaps 30 years' time, by the year 2024, China will then number anything in the order of 1.4 billion people – 1,400 million people – or beyond, and this number alone will make China certainly be regarded as a superpower. I always have regarded China as a superpower.

Two people who were leaders of their countries, Richard Nixon and Leonid Brezhnev, understood this already 20 years ago and 25 years ago: they understood that China was a superpower; they had foresight.

On top of the military importance of China, of course, and on top of the enlargement of the population, of course, China will be a superpower also in her capacity as one of the greatest and leading trading nations of the world.

Now, if we look onto the neighbourhood of China – Viet Nam – right now over 60 million people, will, in the future, and the rather near future, have taken the economic course either of the four so-called "tigers" or of the People's Republic of China, or of a mix. The Vietnamese are imitating, and will successfully follow, these examples.

And as regards Korea, it seems to me that, in 20 or 25 years' time, Korea will be reunited, even if this poses an enormous economic burden on the South – much bigger on South Korea than on West Germany in the German case of unification, because the numbers, the relative numbers between South and North Korea, are closer than in the case of Germany between West Germany and former East Germany.

It seems to me that the South-East Asian countries – Indonesia, Malaysia, Thailand, of course Taiwan and Singapore, also the Philippines – will be economically much further developed at the beginning of the next century compared with today, but some of them will be severely hampered by their population explosion, which also is a problem – always has been a problem – in the People's Republic of China.

If I think of Japan, that most important neighbour of China, over the time stretch of 20 or 25–30 years, it seems to me that in 30 years' time Japan will have undergone a rather sweeping social and economic restructuring. Japan is, and will remain, a high-wage country and is going to be a welfare state, maybe a very modern welfare state; certainly, wage costs, welfare costs as well, will play a much greater role in the future of Japan than hitherto, and will influence Japan's competitiveness in the world's market to a higher degree than in the eighties or in the seventies of this century.

I think it's very likely that Japan will not take recourse to rearming herself to a higher degree than hitherto but, nevertheless, Japan will be one of the most influential states in the world. I regard Japan as one of four or five world powers owing to her position as being the No. 1 financial powerhouse in the world's economy, because of the enormous propensity to save and to invest foreign capital in the Japanese nation.

But also my predictions about the future of Japan, of course, do hinge on several conditions or several *ifs*. This development will happen only *if* Japan, in the meantime, does keep a low military profile, and it will be enhanced *if* Japan will admit Japanese aggressions and crimes in the thirties and in the forties of this century, and it seems a bit too early today to say whether my Japanese friends will fulfil this specific *if*.

And the important *if* in the end is whether the anti-Japanese feelings in the nations around Japan, including China, will calm down and will go away.

If all this happens, on the other hand, I will not exclude for the next century the possibility of the emergence of an ASEAN yen trading zone but this, of course, will also depend on the behaviour of the United States and its North American Free Trade Area between the USA and Canada and Mexico. It will also depend, in the main, on the behaviour and attitudes of China and, most importantly, as I said earlier, it will depend on Japan's own behaviour.

By the way, I sometimes seem to detect a certain Japanese cultural inferiority complex *vis-à-vis* China, a hidden inferiority complex. Maybe it's going to subside in the next century, and vice versa. I hope that also the Chinese animosities *vis-à-vis* Japan and the Chinese cultural superiority complex *vis-à-vis* Japan will subside. The latter seems more likely, by the way, to me than the former.

But, under any circumstances, the fact of the relation of the magnitude of populations – China being ten times larger than Japan, and continuing to be ten times larger in the next century as well – will play a role in the next century and will play a role in the conscience of people in both nations. It seems to me that close cooperation between private enterprises, financial institutions and so on, is very likely in the future, but given the enormous difference in rate of population, ten to one, it seems much less likely to me that we are going to see close political cooperation between the two governments in the future.

Now, as regards the United States of America which, of course, is also a Pacific and Asian power owing to her presence here and owing to her ability to project power, I think also in 20 or 30 years' time the United States of America will remain a power militarily and politically in the Pacific.

On the other hand, the United States has to overcome great domestic problems in the next 10–20–30 years or so. But her trade with Asia in the next 20–30 years will greatly enlarge, particularly owing to the fact that the United States industries are producing more or less the same manufactured goods and investment goods that we Europeans are producing.

We Europeans, of course, like the Americans, are going to meet competition from low-wage countries – as in almost all of Asia – and also even low-wage countries such as Poland, or the Czech Republic, or Hungary. They can offer the same goods in the future that are offered today by West European countries or by America, but at much cheaper prices because of cheaper wages. For these reasons, quite a few branches of industry, quite a few corporations in the United States, will turn to the Asian markets and are already turning to this part of the world.

Politically speaking, I would expect that the United States will try to play a balancing role in East Asia, but such a balancing role of the Americans would necessitate a much better American understanding of Asia – for instance a much better understanding of the millenniums of the development of Chinese culture, Chinese history, better understanding of Chinese history, including the Opium War in the nineteenth century, or including the enforced colonial concessions on Chinese soil which the Vice-President has mentioned earlier on, or including the Japanese invasion in the twentieth century.

A balancing role of the United States would also require American respect for China being a world power.

If I personally was an American it would seem advisable to my American nation to abstain from giving China high-handed lessons on democracy or on human rights. After all, the Chinese have a history of 4,000–5,000 years of cultural evolution during which they have developed their own basic values – their set of values – whereas democracy and the abolition of slavery, let me say in ancient Greece,

18

or ancient Rome, or in Western Europe, or even in the United States, is, obviously, somewhat younger – much younger.

In that context, I would like to put a footnote here. It seems to be noteworthy that it is rather strange if Britain, after generations of colonial rule over Hong Kong, in the very last minute tries to establish a British type of democracy in that city.

America ought to understand this. The slower and, therefore, the steadier China's political modernization, the greater will be the probability that China is capable of avoiding disasters as we see them in Russia, or in the Ukraine, or in other successor republics of the Soviet Union after Gorbachev.

If I was an American, playing around with the possible denial of most-favoured nation status to China does not seem wise to me. Instead, China ought to become a member of the General Agreement on Tariffs and Trade – of the GATT – and one should also invite her to become a member of the Group of Seven, then the Group of Eight or, better to say, Group of Nine, because she should be invited alongside with Russia, who also will remain a world power.

America must ask herself whether she really does have a national interest in an ideological conflict with China, or whether she really does have any interest in trade conflicts with China or with Japan. One will have to understand in Washington, DC, that in the case of an American–Chinese struggle hardly any other major country – hardly any country at all in South-East Asia – will engage itself on the American side because all the countries know that China is big and that China is rather close by.

I quoted a friend of mine minutes ago about the United States being the least suspected power in this part of the world at present. Maybe this is true, but I would add now that the United States ought to be careful not to lose that qualification unintentionally. If she wants to maintain her capacity to play the role of a balancing strategic force in this part of the world, then she must avoid those thinkable conflicts with China, also with Japan, which from time to time she seems to be playing with.

The West as a whole, not just America, will have to give a few second thoughts to the recently invented scheme of so-called "Partnership for Peace," which has been offered by the United States and by NATO not only to Poland and the other European countries that have been liberated from Soviet oppression, but also to Russia, even to the umpteen successor republics, including the Central Asian republics of the former Soviet Union. These are countries immediately west of Chinese borders, and if the so-called "Partnership for Peace" centred around NATO includes Kazakhstan and so on in the future, it will be understood in China as being directed against Asia and as being directed against China.

By the way, the Poles and the Hungarians will still feel left in a security vacuum, but this is in parenthesis.

If I look on to the twenty-first century, it seems to me that there will be four, possibly five, major players in the world: two major forces, major powers, in Asia – China and Japan; a major power, of course, in the West – the United States of America; a major power – Russia (despite her weaknesses); and possibly, or (as a European I would say – as a German I would say) hopefully, the European Union; and not a trilateral configuration, as some Americans have envisaged, between America, Japan, and Europe. Four major players, hopefully five – but in the case of Europe, of course, it would be based on economic strength and international experience.

But in the case of Europe there also are, at least, three big *ifs*, namely, *if* we Europeans can arrive at one common foreign policy, *if* we can arrive at one security policy and, in the shorter run, *if* we can arrive at one currency. Right now we have 11 members; we'll have 13 fairly soon once Austria and Finland join.

I am one of the two persons who, 20 years ago, had and proposed the idea of annual Summits of Seven. Nowadays – and I have hinted this already – it seems appropriate that our successors in the seven governments should invite China to participate fully in these summits and should also invite Russia. China belongs to the League of the World Powers and, therefore, and to the benefit of all of us, China should participate in all important world organizations, as she does in the United Nations and the Security Council, also in the so-called "lonely" Economic Summits or in the GATT.

Well, if one does assume the rather unfortunate development that these five most powerful, most important entities on the globe will not, rather soon, learn to respect each other – respect each other as being players in the same league and as partners in the joint venture of managing the fate of mankind – then there will not be any such management of the fate of mankind. There still do exist grave global problems that do deserve and necessitate even joint management of the major players.

The Vice-President has hinted at grave regional problems in many parts of the world. He has hinted at the Bosnias, the Somalias, and one could name a number of places which need some cooperation between the major players if one hopes to prevent any spillovers from these local or regional conflicts into the world.

There are other kinds of problems, for instance the absolute necessity to reduce and dampen the global population explosion. When this, our century, started out in the year 1900, we were 1,600 million people – 1.6 billion – and in the year 2000 we will have surpassed 6 billion people. Mankind has quadrupled in just one century. If this goes on in the twenty-first century, we will see a further deep degradation of the global environment. We will see armed conflicts, and we are going to see mass migrations, and all this will be to the detriment of almost any country. What is necessary is the education of girls all over the world – of young women; necessary is family planning and necessary also are contraceptives, whatever the Holy See says about that matter.

There is, I mentioned already, the global decay of the environment. If we cannot avoid global warming, then, again, mass migrations and wars will become inevitable.

In the end, I would like to mention the necessity that all of us have to educate ourselves, educate our own youngsters, educate peoples and nations toward cultural tolerance. It seems necessary that we so-called "Christians" should try hard to understand Islam, Hinduism, Buddhism, Confucianism; and I think (for instance there will be one billion Muslims living at the beginning of the twenty-first century) that Islam should try hard to understand the so-called "Christian" societies, and so on.

I think the recent book by an American author, Samuel Huntington, on *The Clash of Civilizations* perceives this problem in the wrong way. We must not perceive the differences of civilizations and cultures as a "clash," with the implicit Western arrogance of believing how Western attitudes and values and behaviour are the only civilized ones; we must perceive them as a necessity for tolerance. If we Westerners would try hard to understand the Asian civilizations and at least if we pay respect to them – pay respect to China, respect to Confucianism, to Buddhism, to Islam – we would help the world.

And, by the way, on the Chinese side, if I may appeal to you, Mr Vice-President, if you would consider the example of Nelson Mandela in South Africa, who had been detained in prison for 20 years or so, why don't you consider his appeal to his own Black countrymen in southern Africa – namely, that one has to overcome the memories and the hatreds of the past – and Nelson Mandela even insisted *vis-à-vis* his own Black countrymen: "Forget the past!"

21

Maybe it is not necessary to go that far and forget the past, but it seems advisable to overcome the hatreds of the past, and this is the task of the intellectuals and the educators on all sides – to teach us tolerance and teach us the avoidance of cultural antagonisms.

Now, in the end, ladies and gentlemen, I must admit that the job of prophesying is a seductive one – a mischievous job – and altogether rather risky. Therefore, I would like to, in the end, stress once again that what I've said is my personal view and not that of any other person or authority – my personal view – and I beg your pardon, beg your tolerance, beg your understanding if, in any case, I may have unintentionally stepped on somebody's feet.

Thank you very much.

Session I
Economy

1

History, politics, and the sources of economic growth: China and the East Asian way of growth

Dwight H. Perkins

The theory of economic growth

When economic growth was confined to northern Europe and North America, as was the case through most of the nineteenth century, explanations of why growth occurred often referred to complex cultural elements, the Protestant ethic for example, or special features of pre-modern history, the prior accumulation of capital, or Europe's imperial conquests. When Japan entered into the era of modern economic growth, some sought to explain how Japanese culture had much in common with Europe, primogeniture in inheritance and much else. When other East Asian countries began to grow rapidly in the 1950s, of course, there were many analysts who attributed East Asia's and China's lack of growth to Confucianism.

Economists were never very comfortable with these historical and cultural explanations. They preferred to stick close to the familiar world of the production function, relying in recent decades mainly on analysis of the aggregate production function. The primary debate among economists has centred on the issue of whether economic growth is best explained by the accumulation of capital or by growth in productivity through the search for better ways to organize production and the discovery of new products. This controversy can be seen in the very different approaches to the subject by Adam Smith and David Ricardo (or Karl Marx). After the innovation of the Solow growth model, productivity as an explanation held centre stage among professional economists, although not on Wall Street. Today the debate is alive and well in the large and growing literature of the "new growth economics" that analyses the underlying sources of the growth in productivity of the traditional factors of production – capital and labour. Arrayed against the new growth economists are the neoclassical econometricians who, through careful analysis of the data, show how capital accumulation still can be made to account for much of the observed growth, at least in North America and East Asia.

For all of the controversy, there is not much doubt as to at least some of the elements that lead to modern economic growth. The controversy is over which of these is more important than the others. All agree that capital matters. A nation that invests less than 10 per cent of its gross national product (GNP), as was the case in China before 1949, will not enjoy sustained rises in per capita income. Human capital, in the form of education and ex-perience, is also important, although there are wide differences in opinion about how important. Some analysts stress the importance of particular kinds of capital – government infrastructure invest-ments or machinery, for example – and few would dispute that these are important.

If one departs from the world of the aggregate production function and enters the world of the policy analyst, capital accumulation tends to be taken for granted (although this was not always the case), and stress is put on policies that will raise the productivity of capital and labour. An economic system open to the outside world is seen to be central to economic growth. And a system that relies heavily on market forces rather than direct bureaucratic intervention is also perceived to be important. There is considerable debate over how pure the market system needs to be or how open the economy, but the failures of the Soviet-type economic system are too fresh for there to be many respectable advocates of a development strategy that stresses autarky and a centralized command system. Only a handful of economists, whether of the production function or policy analyst variety, have much to say about how politics and the political system affect economic growth.

China: Does history matter?

If one confines analysis to the above list of explanations of growth, there is a clear answer for why China did not enjoy sustained increases in per capita national product in the century prior to 1949, although there may have been a modest rise from the 1910s through the early 1930s. The failure to grow was due mainly to the lack of sufficient capital formation. One does not have to be a capital fundamentalist to agree that a nation that invests around 5 per cent of GNP, year after year, can do little more than maintain its capital stock. If there is population growth of any magnitude, per capita income will probably fall, not rise. And the few estimates we have of China's rate of capital formation in the pre-1949 period are generally around 5 per cent of GNP. Infrastructure investment by the state was virtually non-existent. The central government, whose total revenues came to less than 3 per cent of GNP in the nineteenth century and rose only modestly thereafter, simply didn't have the money. The early Meiji government in Japan, in contrast, had revenues equivalent to 12 per cent of GNP.

For many of the other sources of growth on the economist's list, China was in a strong position – at least when compared with most other developing countries in the nineteenth century. There are no really reliable figures, but the best guess of scholars is that roughly half of all Chinese males were literate in the nineteenth century – much the same as in late Tokugawa Japan – and at least tens of thousands had had 15 or 20 years of formal education, albeit in the Confucian classics. Chinese by the many thousands also acquired experience running the offices of government, and far more were involved in long-distance commerce. Foreign traders in China in the nineteenth century, for all of their gunboats and extra-territorial privileges, never played a direct role in China's internal commerce and they gradually saw their role in the international trade of China erode as well. Again, China in this respect was more like Japan than it was like so many colonies of the European powers, where government offices and commerce were largely staffed with Europeans (or with imported minorities such as Chinese in South-East Asia or South Asians in East Africa).

China in the nineteenth century, like most of the developing world, was also an open economy dominated by market forces. The openness was forced on China by European-dictated treaties, as was also the case in Japan, but it was still openness. The treaty-set 5 per cent *ad valorem* tariff (and freely convertible currency) may have been politically humiliating, but also made it impossible for China to pursue excessive import substitution, multiple exchange rates, and all of the other debilitating distortions so common in the developing world in the 1950s and 1960s. And some import substitution did occur despite the low tariffs. China's domestic cotton textile manufacturers – roughly half Japanese-owned, to be sure – largely eliminated imports from China's domestic market, not through protection but because they could produce goods of comparable quality at a lower cost.

If we stick with the economist's list of sources of growth, China's failure to enter into the era of modern economic growth at the same time as Japan is a puzzle. Capital formation was low in China, to be sure, but why was it so low? The weak government tax base is a partial explanation, but why didn't the government raise taxes in order to finance infrastructure? China was not governed by a colonial power with no incentive to promote development. China's government had all the incentive in the world to raise revenues and promote development, to safeguard its own sovereignty if for no other reason. But the Chinese government would not, or could not, do so. Nor did a dynamic private sector, freed of the necessity to pay high taxes, make up for this lack by raising its level of investment.

There is no great mystery as to why neither government nor the private sector failed to respond to the challenges facing China during both the nineteenth century and the first half of the twentieth. Partly, it was a policy failure. Many of China's political leaders, including several emperors and much of the Confucian bureaucracy, failed to understand the nature of the challenge. Their belief in the inherent superiority of their system and its capacity to prevail over the systems of the "barbarians" was so strong that they thought that all that was needed was to clean up their system, not to change it. The last effort of this kind was the Tongzhi Restoration of the 1870s. A decade or so later, China was easily defeated in war by Japan (1895), defeated again by the Imperial Powers as a result of the Boxer Rebellion (1900), and the dynasty collapsed (1911).

It took China nearly four decades to restore unity and acquire a government with the will and the means to promote economic development. Yuan Shikai's effort to set up a new dynasty ended in 1916; the country then split up into warring groups of local leaders (warlords) until 1928; the Japanese seized the north-east in 1931 and fought an all-out war with China from 1937 to 1945. When Chinese weren't fighting the Japanese, they were fighting their own Civil War, which did not end until 1949.

The core problem for China's development was the issue of governance. Modern economic growth requires a government that can provide the needed infrastructure for development, including stable and supportive policy and a stable legal environment for private (or public) investors. It took China about four decades (if one dates the start of its efforts from 1911), or over a century (if one starts from the first Opium War defeat in the 1840s), to make the changes in the political system that the external challenge required. In certain respects (to be discussed shortly) this political transformation was not completed until 1978 and may not yet be completely secure.

The contrast with Japan could not be more stark. Commodore Perry's Black Ships arrived in 1853, and the Tokugawa system fell in 1868. The Meiji system that replaced it faced up to the Western challenge immediately and, despite making fundamental changes in Japanese society, faced only one major rebellion (the Satsuma Rebellion), which was quickly suppressed. This short essay is not the place to explain in depth the difference in response between China and Japan. The point simply is that one system was able to achieve a fundamental transformation that provided the political framework for sustained economic growth and to do so quickly; the other system required a century to accomplish the same kind of transformation.

The problem of systems of governance that are both harmful to growth and difficult to change is not unique to pre-1949 China. The political systems of most African nations today are incapable of sustaining a development effort, and yet no one seems to know how to change these political systems so that they can acquire this capacity. Most international aid agencies are constrained from even studying how political change in a developmental direction might be effected. The same thing can be said about several countries in Central and South America, not to mention Haiti. No doubt at some point these systems will change and sustained development will occur, but will it be in 10 years or 50? A better understanding of why China and Japan's political systems responded so differently to the development challenge might be a start on obtaining a clearer view of the more general problem. I doubt that the kind of quantitative analysis being undertaken by a number of political economists, however, will provide the answer. These efforts usually count up the number of coups, riots, and other such events that are seen as measures of the degree of "political stability." But neither are these events a very reliable measure of stability nor is stability all that is involved. China's political system prior to 1911, except for the Taiping Rebellion period, was remarkably stable. South Korea, in contrast, between 1960 and 1987 experienced two successful coups, an assassination, and numerous riots of sizeable proportions, and yet, for investors, South Korea provided a stable and supportive environment.

What changed in 1949?

Soon after the Communist Party took over the government of China in 1949, economic growth, substantially more rapid than the rise in population, commenced. What is it that the Communists introduced that made the difference? In the 1950s many attributed their initial economic success to their introduction of a Soviet-type economic system complete with central planning, collectivized agriculture, and the virtual elimination of market forces. We now know that China was virtually the only low-income developing country capable of making this system work at all, although North Korea may have succeeded for a time. Cuba, Viet Nam, Albania, and less complete efforts as in Tanzania, were unqualified economic failures. China, it would appear, grew in spite of the economic system it adopted, not because of it. China's experience running a large bureaucratic system over the centuries, plus its educated people, were part of the reason the system worked for a time. The discipline and early internal cohesion of the Chinese Communist Party also had a lot to do with why the myriads of bureaucratic interventions didn't degenerate rapidly into corruption and other misallocations of resources for non-development ends.

The change that made the most clear-cut contribution to growth during the first decade of Communist Party rule was the rise in the rate of capital formation. From a level of around 5 per cent of GNP, the rate rose quickly to around 20 per cent, and then kept on rising in subsequent decades until it passed 30 per cent, where it has remained ever since. The GNP growth rate rose in tandem, reaching, according to official figures, an average rate of nearly 9 per cent a year during the first Five-Year Plan (1953–1957) and an even higher rate during the initial years of the Great Leap Forward (1958–1959). Official figures, because of distorted prices that exaggerated the contribution of industrial output to GNP increases, overstate the true growth rate, but the fact that growth accelerated to at least 4 per cent a year in per capita terms (6 per cent overall) is not in question.

Did capital formation cause this acceleration pretty much by itself? Certainly, it is hard to imagine the drive to build a heavy industry sector based on steel and machinery in the absence of a large amount of investment, including Soviet financial aid. It is also hard to imagine this heavy industry development in the absence of Soviet technical support. China did not have anywhere near enough engineers and managers to carry out this drive on its own. When these Soviet engineers and technicians were withdrawn in 1960, the system they were supporting nearly collapsed. It took years before the Chinese had trained enough of their own personnel to keep the heavy industrial sector running near capacity and growing. Technical assistance of this sort is rarely included in growth-accounting exercises. Including these engineers in the stock of human capital in China and then measuring their contribution in the usual way (by assuming that their wages measure their marginal product) understates their contribution by many orders of magnitude. Physical capital and technical support, in this instance at least, were joint inputs, neither of which was worth much without the other. If China had built its 1950s development effort on light industry and agriculture it might not have needed this Soviet technical support, but China chose heavy industry instead.

Some of the growth in the 1950s also represented recovery from 12 years of continuous warfare. It takes a lot less investment, in most cases, to repair a power line, reopen an irrigation system, or put a roof on a factory than it does to build the electric power grid, the irrigation system, and the factory in the first place. The Chinese date recovery from the devastation of war as being completed in 1952, but it is likely there were elements of recovery in the growth rate of the next several years. In the formal growth-accounting framework these recovery elements would show up as part of the residual, and there is a substantial residual in the few growth-accounting estimates that exist for this period. There were also major investments in human capital at all levels in the 1950s, but these investments could not have paid off until later. Most of the people receiving formal education as a result of the expansion of the education system were still in school in the late 1950s and not contributing directly to GNP at all.

The other major change in the 1950s that contributed to growth was the onset of a period of relative political stability. The country was unified and war on Chinese territory had ended. One uses the word "relative" stability because there was Chinese participation in the Korean War, which was in part also an excuse for suppressing potential domestic opposition (the "three and five anti" campaigns); there were the collectivization and socialization campaigns of 1955–1956, the purges following the "hundred flowers campaign" in 1957 and, finally, the Great Leap Forward that included the setting up of the commune system.

That many Chinese today look back on the 1950s as a period of stability is testimony to how far China still had to go before the nation had really created a governance system capable of supporting sustained economic growth. The Communist Party was in control, but the unity of the party itself was built on a shared ideology (Marxism–Leninism), credibility for effectiveness from having won the Civil War, and the leadership of a small cadre of people, particularly Mao Zedong.

If Mao Zedong had been interested in (and knowledgeable about) economic and technical matters, he might have led a sustained growth effort much like Park Chung Hee in South Korea. Certainly, Mao and the top party leadership had the power to overcome any interest group opposed to the structural changes required for growth. But if Mao had been more like Park Chung Hee, it is highly unlikely that he would have led a peasant guerilla movement capable of overthrowing the Kuomintang government. Revolutionary leaders seldom make good technocrats: the skills required are fundamentally different.

What Mao did instead was attempt to bring about a fundamentally different kind of Chinese society, one different from any other society in the world, a society that would in some sense truly realize the Communist dream. His technique was the mass mobilization strategy based on his guerilla warfare experience. For nearly twenty years, from 1958 (or 1955/56) until his death in 1976, Mao and a dwindling group of high-level supporters turned the nation upside down in an attempt to realize his messianic vision. No one was safe from the often unpredictable currents of the Great Leap and the Cultural Revolution, least of all investors in industry or long-term technical planners. The extraordinary thing is that, despite the destruction and death that was so prevalent in this period, the economy actually grew at a rate a bit above 4 per cent a year. High rates of investment continued, even though systematic discussion of how to use that investment efficiently was frequently impossible. Human capital fared less well, as schools were often closed and students spent much of their time on politics when they were open. Individually, many students struggled to learn on their own, often against vigorous criticism, and a surprising number succeeded, but it was not the same as having quality formal schools.

The problem caused by the two decades of putting politics first was not simply a problem of instability – strikes that disrupted production or outright fighting between students and workers. Even when one group was in relatively firm control and the streets and factories were outwardly calm, the atmosphere was not conducive to systematic investment strategies of any kind. The most damaging to economic growth were the extreme anti-foreign attitudes that prevailed. Organized harassment of the foreign diplomatic community was the least of the problems, although the published incidents did no good for China's international reputation. The biggest problem was the anti-foreignism extended to all aspects of modern technology. Any economic planner, among the few remaining in office in the 1966–1976 period, who had the temerity to suggest that importing foreign technology was a good idea, was likely to be subjected to vigorous criticism or worse. Home-grown Chinese technology was better, many argued. Those who disagreed kept their opinions to themselves.

Anti-foreignism was combined with a generalized attack on intellectuals, a term that included virtually everyone with more than a high-school education. Sending China's youth – and even many of its educated adults – to the countryside for a few years was not an altogether bad idea: China's élite did learn a lot about how their fellow countrymen lived, and many learned a lot about themselves. But the way it was done was vindictive and prolonged. For 12 years, China's formal education system was effectively closed down. If one counts the highly politicized school atmosphere of the earlier 1958–1961 Great Leap Forward, Chinese schools were either totally unable to function or were barely functioning for two decades between 1958 and the year 1978, when university entrance exams were reintroduced and teachers were finally allowed to give instruction in something other than politics. Those who were educated in an earlier period, when schools did function reasonably well, were seldom allowed to put that education to national use. Leaders of medicine mopped floors and senior engineers were locked in their offices, sometimes for years, and were let out only to be struggled against.

Mao, Jiang Qing, and their allies did not invent these anti-foreign and anti-intellectual attitudes. They exploited, for their own ends, values that existed in Chinese society well back into history, much as

33

the Empress Cixi used the Boxers in 1900. Again, the contrast with the Meiji Japanese leadership is stark. Anti-foreignism certainly existed in Japan, and one can even find traces of it today, as one can in many (or perhaps most) societies. But the Meiji leaders recognized quickly that the West had more of value to offer than a few advanced weapons and that they had better learn quickly what that was. Mao, in contrast, saw some value in Western nuclear weapons, but in little else the West had to offer, other than some Leninist ideas about politics.

Given the attitudes that dominated the Chinese leadership after the first spurt of economic growth in the 1950s, it should come as no surprise that growth slowed markedly in the 1958–1978 decades. Total factor productivity growth was negative throughout the period. The data we have available to measure productivity in this period are crude, but the conclusion that productivity growth was negative is not in serious doubt. Growth, however, did not come to an end: as already pointed out, average GNP growth, measured in a way that removes the worst relative price distortions, was about 4.5 per cent a year over the whole period. Only during the extreme disruption in the aftermath of the Great Leap Forward (1959–1961) and the height of the Cultural Revolution (1967–1969) were there years of negative growth, but recovery, at least after 1967–1969, was quick. What kept growth positive despite the nature of economic policies and the economic system? The answer has to be the continued high rate of capital formation, that averaged around 30 per cent of GNP throughout the two decades. Enterprise profits and taxes kept generating large revenues for the central government, and the government kept investing these revenues in industry, mainly heavy industry and related infrastructure. Agriculture mainly had to help itself, with mass labour mobilization for rural construction being the favoured method, but these efforts generated only 2 per cent a year growth in agricultural production. Such plans as existed, whether in industry or agriculture, involved doing little more than continuing forward the patterns of investment established in the past. Poor investment choices, weak project design, and few positive incentives for either workers or management probably account for most of the negative productivity performance.

What changed in 1978?

In December 1978, the Chinese Communist Party held the Third Plenary Session of the Eleventh Party Congress. The plenum began a process of fundamental systems reform and policy change that, so far, has led to 16 years of rapid uninterrupted growth, averaging around 9 per cent per year, or 7.5–8 per cent per capita. What changed, that made this performance possible?

One thing that did not happen was a rise in the rate of capital formation as a share of GNP. Between 1978 and 1982 the rate actually fell quite sharply and did not fully recover to the 1978–1979 level until the high growth years 1992 and 1993. Human capital does not play much of a role, either, during the first years of the post-1978 economic boom, although the situation after 1985 is a very different matter. Between 1978 and 1984, however, the reopened schools had not had time to turn out a new cadre of trained personnel, and few students had returned from abroad.

There are two primary components to the early rapid growth experience after 1978, and both represent an increase in productivity, although that was not all that was involved. The clearest case is agriculture: between 1978 and 1984 the rate of primary sector development accelerated to 7.3 per cent per year, even though agriculture continued to receive only a minuscule share of state investment (under – usually well under – 10 per cent). The reason for this acceleration is well known. Rural markets were freed up, so that much of what was produced could be sold directly to consumers at market prices typically much higher than those that prevailed when almost everything had to be sold to the state. At the same time the production teams were broken up, and by 1983 farming was once again being done on a household basis. Farmers were thus free to respond to the new market incentives.

The other early change was in the foreign trade sector. Changes in this sector had actually begun before 1979. Almost as soon as Mao Zedong had died and the Gang of Four had been purged, the policies that discouraged foreign trade were reversed. In 1977 and 1978, for example, there was a huge rush by state enterprises to purchase all the foreign imports they could get their hands on – only to discover that China lacked the foreign exchange to pay for such large purchases. Instead, China had first to push exports, and so an East-Asian-style export drive began in earnest after 1978.

No one as yet has attempted to measure the contribution of the expansion of foreign trade (and foreign capital inflows) to China's economic growth, but it has to have been considerable. For 18 years, from 1960 to 1978, Chinese investment had to make do with machinery and equipment manufactured by Chinese domestic firms using equipment imported from the Soviet Union and Eastern Europe in the 1950s, much of which was probably somewhat obsolete even when it was new. After 1978, China was increasingly able to import the most up-to-date capital equipment produced in Japan, the United States, and Europe. The increase in the quality of capital formation probably more than offset the reduction in the rate of increase in the quantity of capital.

But much more was going on than just the import of high-quality capital equipment. The increasing availability of foreign exchange made it possible to break bottlenecks of key intermediate inputs such as steel. The pressure to export more and more manufactures led Chinese industrial enterprises in these sectors rapidly to upgrade quality and style and to lower cost. These improvements spread quickly to the manufacture of items for domestic, as well as for foreign, consumption.

These improvements in quality carried over to the Chinese education system. Soviet and East European training in the 1950s provided China with a good technical base that was expanded and brought up to date after 1978 by the import of all kinds of technical information and by sending many tens of thousands of Chinese abroad for advanced training. Those who received marketable degrees from the United States often did not return, but tens of thousands of others did. Politics did not entirely disappear from the Chinese domestic curriculum, but few students paid much attention to it. Without all of these newly trained people and all of the vast amounts of imported information, the imported capital equipment would have made much less of a difference.

In the context of modern growth-accounting techniques, the above-described changes would show up in the residual. In principle, many or most of these inputs could be measured, but we do not have the necessary price and quantity data for most of these inputs, nor do we have an agreed-upon methodology for how improvements in education and knowledge interact with better capital equipment.

We know even less about how to measure the impact of the other major institutional change that began to take place from 1984 on. It was in that year that China began the process of introducing market forces into the urban and industrial sectors. There has been much criticism of the partial nature of these reforms, particularly as they applied to large state-owned enterprises, many of which operated in the red in the 1990s. But several efforts to measure the sources of growth in these enterprises indicate that the market reforms have led to significant increases in productivity in the state sector.

The major contribution of market reforms, however, was not to the large state-owned sector. It was the small- and medium-scale enterprises owned collectively or privately that benefited the most. New Township and Village Enterprises by the tens of thousands sprang up. Many older firms expanded into new niches ignored by the state system. Others competed directly with state firms, often forcing these state firms, in the commercial sector at least, to transform or go out of business. Substantially more than half of the growth in industrial production over the entire 16-year reform period has been accounted for by the development of industrial firms outside the state sector. There was new and rising investment in non-state enterprises, but nothing like the large sums being spent on the state sector and on infrastructure. The development of township, village, and other non-state industries is not primarily a story about capital formation: it is the story of a major change in institutions and a related shift in resources (some capital, intermediate inputs, and people) from low- to high-productivity uses. The small-scale sector could produce far more output per unit of input than could the large-scale sector, even when the latter was increasingly operating within a market environment.

Despite the decline in the rate of capital formation as a share of GNP, and the beginning of a decline in the growth rate of the labour force, Chinese GNP growth increased from a rate of 4.5 per cent a year prior to 1979 to a rate averaging 9 per cent from 1979 on. Over a 16-year period, Chinese GNP rose fourfold. Per capita GNP rose three times, to perhaps US$2,000 per year in purchasing power parity terms, although we have no reliable measures of the purchasing power parity of the Chinese yuan. This rise in income was brought about by a series of fundamental changes in the Chinese economic system and in the economic policies of the government. We have yet to sort out the contribution of each change but we may never be able to do so because, in a very basic sense, all of the changes interacted with each other so that the whole was more than the sum of its parts. Decollectivization, opening to the outside world, and the freeing up of markets at all levels each contributed to making the other more productive.

The future

But will the high growth unleashed by reform continue? Will the reforms themselves continue or will they be rolled back? There is the economist-level answer to these questions, which relies mainly on an analysis of the aggregate production function. And there is politics and the underlying forces that shape the nature of the political system.

If one assumes that China will successfully complete the process of creating a market system and that the political system will continue to provide a supportive environment for investors, then what can one say about the prospects for Chinese economic growth over the next several decades? What we know about this subject comes entirely from the experience over time of those nations that have succeeded in achieving industrialized status. Those nations are in Western Europe, North America, and East Asia (Japan, Taiwan, and South Korea – not counting Hong Kong and Singapore, which are more cities than nations).

Economic growth in Western Europe and North America began in the nineteenth century and has continued steadily for a century and a half with only occasional interruptions. Only in catch-up periods, such as after World War II in Europe, have nations sustained growth rates of 5 or 6 per cent for any length of time; rates of 3 or 4 per cent (2 per cent per capita) have been the norm. Some nations have been ahead of others in per capita income and technology, but relative positions have changed over time, and all of these nations have basically been on the frontier of modern economic growth. None has been able, across the board, basically to follow the path laid down by the leading countries, although individual sectors have certainly played "follow-my-leader."

For reasons not well researched or understood by economists, it is easier to follow along a well-trod path in the field of economic development than it is to be a pioneer. Presumably, part of the reason is that pioneers often take wrong turns, whereas followers can avoid many of these mistakes. For a variety of reasons, many tied in one way or another to politics, most developing countries have not been able to take full advantage of being a follower. But several nations in East Asia have done so, and it is these nations that provide us with what we know about the full potential of a follower country. South Korea and Taiwan are the best examples, but Japan also fits because it started growth later and from a much lower per capita income than Western Europe and because it fell well behind Europe again as a result of World War II.

What the East Asian experience tells us is that it is possible to grow for a time at rates of 9 and 10 per cent a year. In Japan, growth rates of this magnitude lasted for roughly 20 years. In South Korea and Taiwan, which started from a lower base, rapid growth has gone on for over three decades. But high growth does not go on for ever. Japan's growth rate fell sharply in the 1970's to only slightly above the levels achieved by other industrialized nations, and Japan's long-term growth rate may have taken another step down recently. Capital formation remained high, so that is not the reason. Oil price increases were the immediate cause of the 1970s decline, but they masked more fundamental explanations that were still there when oil prices came back down. The decline in the rate of growth in Taiwan and South Korea has been less marked, presumably because neither has really caught up (except in a few sectors), but a long-term growth of 10 per cent a year is no longer the norm.

China, starting from an even lower per capita base than either South Korea or Japan, has maintained 8 or 9 per cent growth for 16 years and well above 10 per cent for the last 3 years. How much longer will its follower status allow China to grow at this rate? If China's per capita income is US$2,000 today, it would be something over 20 years before China reached US$10,000 per capita, where Taiwan and South Korea are today, and another decade or so before the US$20,000 level of Europe and North America was reached. From a purely economic view, therefore, it would appear possible for China to continue high growth for another three decades.

If China does continue high growth for anything like this length of time, there will have to be considerable adjustment in the rest of the world. Total Chinese GNP by the year 2025 would pass US$20,000 billion, and China's energy consumption might be as much as 8,000 billion kW·h. Grain consumption – including grain fed to animals, fish, and chickens – could reach 800 or 900 million tons a year (it is 450 million tons today). China could become a formidable importer of both energy resources and grain, not to mention other resources. Some will argue that the large imports involved will not be made available by the rest of the world and that resource shortages alone will force China to slow down. But I feel that this is unlikely. Prices for grain and oil may rise in real terms but, if China continues to expand its foreign exchange earnings at anything like the rates of the past, the cost of even 200 or 300 million tons of grain imports will not be prohibitive for China.

The more difficult question to answer for China is whether the political system will remain supportive of modern economic growth for a period of three decades. A return to a Maoist world can probably be dismissed. That vision depended on having a population whose attitudes could be moulded because they knew next to nothing about what was going on in the outside world. The Chinese people today know a great deal about the world around them, and no one is likely to be in a position to make them unlearn it.

But Chinese xenophobia (and a belief by many that the outside world has little to teach them, outside of a few technology areas) is not totally dead. More important, China has not yet developed a system of government that is likely to be sustainable in the modern world. A system based on rule by one paramount leader, together with a party held together by a common ideology, is not going to be sufficient in the future. The paramount leader is mortal, and few people in China any longer believe in the ideology. Collective leadership of an authoritarian system might be stable for a time if the members of the collective really trusted each other, but there is enough factionalism in Chinese history to suggest that that level of trust is not very likely. On the other side, the forces that could provide the foundations of a democratic society are weak. A middle class is rising in the cities, but there is only limited pluralism in Chinese society and no tolerated opposition organizations or even individuals.

China, therefore, has not yet solved the problem it has been struggling with since the 1840s. The Confucian bureaucratic system maintained stability for centuries at a time, for more than a millennium. The Communist bureaucratic system has lasted for a bit over four decades and may not last for more than another one to three decades.

From the point of view of economic growth, does it matter whether China has found a viable political system for the long term? If failure means that China will again descend into chaos and civil war, the obvious answer is yes, it does matter for economic growth. But that level of instability does not appear very likely. If failure means that authoritarian leaders at the top change from time to time, through coups or other irregular methods, growth may not be much affected, even if central government policies change significantly when one leader replaces another. One of the virtues of a market system is that most economic decisions are made on a highly decentralized basis. The government does have to invest in infrastructure and support a system of commercial law, but it is hard to imagine a future leader of

China who would oppose investment in infrastructure, however that leader came to power. It is easier to imagine a Chinese leader who would give little support to the legal system, even the commercial components thereof. Still, the overall prospect is that China's political problems over the coming decades will not be sufficiently disruptive to derail rapid economic growth.

Comments

Zou Yilin

Professor Perkins has given an enlightening report. It is from one who is well acquainted with both the past and the present of China. He poses an important issue that should be considered by the Chinese leadership and Chinese economists. None the less, it seems to me that his conclusions are somewhat pessimistic, understandably out of his deep concern for the future of China, which I think should be appreciated by every Chinese scholar.

Here I would like to present my personal opinions on Professor Perkins' report. If I am erroneous, I would like to listen to your comments.

Professor Perkins rightly points out that "in the century prior to 1949 the failure of China to enter into sustained modern economic growth was largely the result of the inability of the Qing and early Republican political systems to provide a supportive environment for either private or public investment," but if we take the point further, we would find that a closed small peasantry connected with a most stable self-sufficient small peasant economy in China's long history did not, and could not, provide a strong social force for an open, democratic political system. In other words, a political system in correspondence with a modern economy can only be visible when the small peasant economy has been reformed from its roots.

As Professor Perkins says, some (but not all) of the conditions were improved as a result of the change of government in 1949, but we still have to notice that on the one hand, the huge Chinese peasantry, which accounted for over 80 per cent of the whole population, was still living in a natural economy and did not have the least idea of what advantage a modern economy would bring about; on the other hand, because the Chinese people, as well as the Chinese leadership, were vigilant and averse to everything Western as a result of the invasions and devastations of China by Western countries in the century prior to 1949, they were reluctant to adopt an economic system of Western style and thus slowed down the economic growth significantly.

To the Chinese, the historical reforms of 1978 are the second revolution since 1949. It is true that the reforms started from the economic sphere, but that itself meant a major political reform, since it was the ruling party that took the initiative. It also meant the decentralization of the ruling party's power in at least the economic sphere. From this point it was also the first step toward further political reform.

But why did not the reforms in China start with solving "the problem of creating a political system capable of supporting sustained economic development" rather than with economic problems? The reasons lie in the history and the present situation in the country. China is a country with a vast population and covering a vast area. Her natural resources (per capita) are relatively poor, and there are great regional disparities. Moreover, most of the rural areas are both poor and backward culturally. For the people, the most important thing was to have enough to feed upon and to keep warm. They would support the reform policy only if they were benefited by it. The second reason is that China has always been under authoritarian rule in its long history, and in the early period of the PRC, a certain centralization of power was indispensable, owing to the particular difficulties created by the political atmosphere both within and without. The experience of several decades has proven that such centralization hindered the development of a modern economy. However, it was difficult for most people, including officials indoctrinated with the ideology of the past, to realize this point. The resistance to further political reform would only disappear when they benefited from the economic reforms and when they realized that the old political system would hinder further economic reform and thus reduce their benefits. The history of several millenniums has shown that productivity and the economy would only be improved under a stable social and political environment, whether in a unified empire or in separate states, and whether under the rule of a relatively advanced race or under that of a backward race. Such is the situation in the periods of Beiwei (the North Wei), Wudai (the Five Dynasties), Wuyue, the Former and Later Shu, Liao, Jin, the Southern Song, Yuan, and Qing. It seems to me, therefore, that the most feasible way of political reformation is not to start the reform from the top but to continue economic reforms and to let the people realize the weakness of the old political system. Then further political reform from both the top and the bottom would be the natural result. As a matter of fact, the separation of the party and civil administration, that of administration and the management of businesses, of ownership and management, carried out or being carried out, and the introduction of a civil service system, are themselves further political reforms necessitated by economic reforms.

One result of the decentralization of power is regionalism. In Chinese history this is a recurrent phenomenon due to regional disparities, and Chinese politicians from the Qin and Han periods onwards have been tackling the problem consistently. The problem can only be resolved when the centre and the localities have a common interest. History has shown that the existence of regional disparities is disadvantageous to both the centre and the localities. Under the present situation, a strong central authority capable of mediating the interests of local provinces is indispensable, since the provinces sometimes find themselves at odds with each other as far as economic interests are concerned. The problem is already conspicuous in the disparities between the East and the West, and the Chinese government is contriving to solve the problem. In the long run, the development, both in the economic sphere and in the political sphere, can only be gradual, which fits the so-called "piecemeal model" proposed by Western scholars.

China certainly needs to learn from the so-called "East Asian model" in its economic development, but she cannot simply copy from Taiwan, Hong Kong, Singapore, or South Korea. China has a vast internal market which has yet to be cultivated. This is also where China can attract foreign investment and imports. In the future development there will be many difficulties to be overcome. Professor Perkins' report will certainly be helpful to overcome these difficulties, and we are grateful to him for this.

Comments

Yutaka Hara

I agree with Professor Perkins's analysis and evaluation, especially his description and appraisal of the historic background of the economic development in China up to the present. It is clear from statistical materials and my own observations that China is currently striving to achieve sustained economic growth based on its reform efforts since 1978, although the nation faces various issues.

However, I am not as optimistic as Professor Perkins about the future growth and development of the Chinese economy, based on my examination of the various issues that China faces. In particular, I am concerned that if Chinese government policies take the wrong course in the mid-term, namely the next five years, it is possible that an economic crisis will invite political instability and social mayhem.

I would like to point out various issues in this regard from three angles – system, gap, and scale.

The first issue is East Asian-type industrial policies and the Chinese economic system. Needless to say, each country's specific characteristics are reflected in their industrial policies for economic development (centred on economic reform). The industrial policies of the East Asian newly industrializing economies (NIEs) and Japan share a more or less common pattern, including measures actively to introduce foreign capital and technology, export-oriented industrialization policy, and market-opening measures (liberalization). Some of the industrial policies that China has taken are similar to the model offered by South Korea and have been successful in terms of promoting growth for the time being. However, policies do not function strictly according to a pattern. What will act as the driving force behind future economic growth? Will it be, for example, ideology, desire to raise the standard of living, competitive order, or another incentive? Will the current ad hoc mixed economic system function effectively? State-owned enterprises represent the public sector, and over half of these corporations are said to be operating in the red. How state enterprises (including joint ventures), some of which are managed by the central government and others of which are managed by local governments, will be handled is a major issue.

The second issue is how to secure a balance among the various sectors and among the regions. I would like to take the example of the problem of creating a balance between agriculture and industry.

The gap between agriculture and industry in terms of growth and income is expanding rapidly. With the breakup of communes, the introduction of a Household Responsibility System, and the liberalization of the agricultural market, farmer income rose dramatically in the 1970s. However, in the 1980s, with market-opening policies, including the establishment of the special economic zones, affixing prices to land, and the promotion of non-state enterprises (*xiangzhenqiye* or Township and Village Enterprises), the income of commerce and industry workers in cities, their surrounding areas, or coastal areas sky-rocketed, quickly surpassing the income of farmers.

Under the Park Chung Hee administration, South Korea adopted a policy of promoting both agriculture and industry. By absorbing excess labour in the industrial sector, lowering the relative price of capital goods, and lowering fertilizer prices, both farmer incomes and farm productivity were raised. This expanded the domestic market and created a positive relationship between agriculture and industry.

Even if the gaps between agriculture and industry in China were a long-term growth strategy along the lines of so-called unbalanced growth, they are now resulting in the so-called *mangliu*, or massive influx of farmers to urban areas, and hyperinflation. This phenomenon gives rise to the concern that it will lead to social unrest and, in turn, economic upheaval, which cannot be contained simply by political control.

The third issue is that China's economic growth has a major impact on Asia and the world, as well as repercussions in China itself. This issue should be considered on the 10-year range; however, if economic growth continues in China at the current high pace, there is a possibility that the impact will be accelerated and felt earlier, since the Chinese economy is enormous.

Exports are the leading sector of China's economic growth, and two-thirds of exports are to Asia. In the area of light industrial products, China is already becoming a strong rival for other Asian countries. China will soon import large volumes of oil, and this will influence international prices. It is also possible that China may become unable to maintain self-sufficiency in grain. Since these issues would have an impact throughout the world, there is concern that China may be caught in its own trap as a result of its expansion in scale (including its increase in population and in pollution) and its high economic growth.

2

China's "open door" and internal development in perspective of the twenty-first century

Shigeru Ishikawa

Introduction

China is regarded as having thus far achieved remarkable success in carrying out the economic system reform as well as the policy to promote rapid economic growth, both of which started in the late 1970s. The success is attributed to various factors, but the dynamism triggered by its policies, especially those component policies aimed at an "open door" to the world, has played a decisive role.

The question now is what will happen to this dynamism during the remainder of this century and the early twenty-first century. Another question is how the domestic system reform (in particular, the reform of the large and medium-sized state enterprises), as well as the domestic market-based growth policies, will evolve and interact with the possible changes in externally generated dynamism. The objective of this chapter is to address these questions.

In my research, I have followed four steps. First, as an overall framework for analysis, I have prepared a model of the economy composed of five sectors – state enterprises, non-state enterprises, agriculture, foreign trade, and foreign economy. Apart from the foreign economy sector, the four domestic sectors are assigned tasks of systemic reform and growth of differing difficulty.

Second, studies are made on the performances of systemic reform and growth and their determining factors, using the above model of reform and growth and separating analysis into both internal and external aspects.

Third, on the basis of several signs of changes that appeared in the early 1990s, explorations are made about three alternative scenarios for external and internal economic development for the remainder of the century and somewhat beyond that.

Fourth, I have offered observations on one of these scenarios, which, side by side with efforts to increase coastal-region-based exports, emphasizes development of an interior market based on domestic demand.

Owing to space limitations, I have limited myself in the following pages to presenting only a few main points of analysis and the conclusions to which they lead.

Analytical framework: A five-sector model

My five-sector model of reform and development adapts and expands the three-sector model (state enterprises, private enterprises, and agriculture) of the domestic economy constructed by Jeffrey Sachs and Wing Thye Woo of Harvard University, in such a way as to be applicable commonly to both China and Russia.[1] Sachs is a well-known supporter of a "shock therapy" strategy for stabilization and systemic reform in those former centralized planned economies trying to effect a transition to a market economy. This model seems to have been constructed bearing in mind the sharp contrast exhibited so far between Russia on the one hand (where the strategy of rapid transition enforced since 1992 has brought about a critical impasse for economic reform and for growth and stability) and China on the other (where a gradualist transition strategy since the late 1970s has brought about a slow but steady system reform and remarkably rapid economic growth, though some uncertainty remains concerning its stability). The aim of the model is accordingly directed at identification thereby of the differences in the economic structure of two economies, such that the explanation can be offered as to why Russia had to adopt a "shock therapy" strategy instead of China's gradualism. As the approach of starting the analysis of "transition strategy" from the level of economic structure is also my own approach, and because of the great reference value, for this chapter, of the contrast between China and Russia, I have decided to begin my presentation of the five-sector model by describing Sachs three-sector model and presenting the contrast between China and Russia in that framework.

One of the features of Sachs' and Wing's model is its attempt to describe the possible changes in national output due to the movement of labour among the sectors with different levels of labour productivity. In other words, in the economy assumed in the model, the marginal productivity of labour is largest in the non-state private enterprise sector, followed in descending order by the state enterprises and the agricultural sectors. Benefiting from wage subsidies that are funded from the taxes paid by the non-state sector and agriculture, however, workers in state enterprises get much higher wages than workers in other sectors. From the productivity point of view, if workers moved from state to non-state enterprises, the output of the economy as a whole could be expected to rise simply as a result, but the large subsidies give workers in state enterprises no incentive to seek such mobility; hence, no national output growth occurs thereby.

Next, the difference in economic structure between the two countries is shown in table 2.1 in terms of the different distribution of the workforce among the three sectors. It is apparent from this table that, in Russia, modernization and industrialization of the economy are far more advanced: state enterprises pervade almost all production sectors of the economy, and unorganized agriculture is a very minor part. In China, agriculture is an overwhelmingly large segment of the economy, and state enterprises occupy a very small part. Given these structural differences in addition to the three sectors' institutional characteristics, the effects in Russia would be very different from those in China. Under conditions prevailing in Russia, the difficulties of state enterprise reform (in particular, of making major cuts in salary subsidies) had the direct effect of seriously slowing the whole economy. In China, reform of state enterprises was equally difficult, but the still immense scale of the agricultural and rural sector meant that, when controls over agriculture were relaxed, a flood of workers into non-state private enterprises (*xiangzhenqiye*, or "Township and Village Enterprises") was unleashed, which together with *sanziqiye* (foreign-capital-related enterprises) entering the non-state enterprise sector, expanded exports and led to China's rapid growth in GDP.[2]

This three-sector model and the analyses on the basis of it would certainly be suitable for observing the economic difficulties that occurred in Russia prior to the 1992 reform; indeed, they explain the situations that required the adoption of "shock therapy strategy" for all-out privatization of the Russian state enterprises. But a few

Table 2.1 **Comparison of economic structure and income levels between China and Russia**

	China		Russia	
	1978	1991	1985	1991
1. Share of workforce employed by different sectors classified by type of ownership (total employment = 100 per cent)				
State enterprises	18.6	18.3	93.1	86.1
Collective agriculture farms	72.1	63.9	6.0	5.3
Urban collectives	5.1	6.2	na[1]	na
Rural collectively owned enterprises (Township and Village Industrial Enterprises)	4.3	10.0	na	na
Private sector and other categories	0.0	1.6	0.9	8.6
2. Size of workforce employed in agriculture and industry (total employment = 100 per cent)				
Agriculture, forestry and fisheries	70.7	60.6	20.2[2]	
Mining and manufacturing	15.2	17.0	25.9[2]	
3. Per capita GDP in US$ according to the Purchasing Power Parity Method 2	na	1,680 $(370)^{3,4}$	na	6,930 $(3,320)^{3,4}$

Sources: (Sector 1) Table 4 in Sachs and Woo (1994). The original data on China are from the same source as the next item. Russian data are from the IMF. (Sector 2) Data on China are from the Chinese National Statistics Bureau's *Chinese Statistical Yearbook 1992*. Data on Russia are from the IMF, World Bank, OECD, and EBCD's *A Study of the Soviet Economy, Vol. 2*, 1991, p. 196. (Sector 3) World Bank, *World Development Report, 1993*, pp. 296–297.

The following must be borne in mind when interpreting Chinese statistics in the first sector. The percentage of the workforce employed by state enterprises is based on the size of workforce employed by the units owned by the whole people, and includes employees of the government and state undertakings in addition to those of state enterprises. State enterprises alone accounted for 12.9 per cent of the Chinese workforce (in 1991). According to the note attached to Sachs and Woo's table, the non-industrial components of the Township and Village Enterprises for China are counted in collective agriculture. For Russia, post-1985 collectives are counted in "Private sector and other categories": State enterprises include leased state enterprises as well as (pre-1985) consumer cooperatives.

Notes:
1. na, not available
2. 1988 data.
3. World Bank, *op. cit.*
4. Figures in parentheses are those of per capita GDP estimated on the basis of domestic price system but converted to US dollar values using the official exchange rate.

substantive components must be added to this framework before we can explain, by this model, China's success up to the present. First, in order to effect a transfer of labour from agriculture to non-state Township and Village Enterprises, it is insufficient merely that the agricultural sector is initially very large and the control over rural economy is liberalized; a "breakthrough" must, in addition, be made in the increase in agricultural productivity. (The term "break-through" was used as a recent example for denoting an epoch-making increase in the grain yield that was realized as a result of seed inno-vations, known as the "Green Revolution." In China, the increased productivity from this Green Revolution was further enhanced by the institutional changes in the people's communes and the use of producers' prices for grain to strengthen producers' incentives for increasing production.) Without this breakthrough, transfer of labour out of agriculture was not possible, nor did the "structural changes" emerge, in the form of "rural industrialization." This is due to the fact that the productivity breakthrough is necessary, not only for creating demand for rural industrialization but also for bringing about supply-side conditions for it in raising funds for "primary accumulation" for rural industrialization.[3]

Secondly, one must not ignore the fact that serious, though not easy to accomplish, efforts are being made to reform such institutions as wage subsidies (in China, employer-provided social security is all-inclusive) and the so-called "soft budget constraints"[4] that impede improvements in profitability and productivity of state enterprises. In order to make the model more generally applicable, it is necessary to entertain the possibility that these reforms will succeed.

Furthermore, I have added the two external sectors (foreign trade and foreign economy) in an attempt to see how exogenous economic changes emerging in the foreign economy sector are perceived and captured by the activities of the foreign trade sector, and how these changes are synchronized with structural changes in the domestic sectors and bring about additional strength for growth. Enterprises in the foreign trade sector, depending on their efficiency to realize this synchronization, are also subject to the same reforms as state enterprises.

Performances of domestic reform and "open door" policy

In terms of the relationships among the three domestic sectors, the rapid economic growth that emerged in China in the period of economic reform was made possible mainly by rural industrialization – namely, a widespread rise of Township and Village Enterprises in the non-state enterprise sector that was generated by the institutional and productivity breakthrough in the agricultural sector.

The rural industrialization followed these steps: (a) an increase in land and labour productivity in agricultural production, which brought about, on the one hand, (b) higher per capita rural incomes, which expanded effective demand for potential output of rural industry, and, on the other hand, (c) provision of funds for "primary accumulation," production and marketing of "surplus" food, and increased release of "surplus" labour for off-farm employment; thus (d), both supply-side and demand-side conditions for the industrialization of local, rural areas, were created. Moreover (e), once capable human power and sufficient amounts of capital for establishing and maintaining local enterprises are supplied from within the local governments and farm family groups, rural industrialization is to take place. As there are variations in the strength of the productivity breakthrough among regions, steadiness in following these sequential steps varies significantly among regions. These causal relations between the agricultural productivity increase and the rise in rural industrialization, which is manifested in association with the regional differentials in development, are reflected comprehensively in figure 2.1. In this figure, the agricultural sector of each individual province throughout China is plotted in the domain surrounded by two axes: these are (1) the magnitude of output per unit of labour force in the rural sector and (2) the rate of rural industrialization in different provinces, measured in terms of the proportion of total labour force of the rural sector that is working in the Township and Village Enterprises. The resulting regression line (line 1) clearly shows a pattern similar to that of Colin Clark's law (figure 2.1).[5] (As is well known, Colin Clark's law is an empirical law indicating that there is a tendency of the ratio of primary industry output in total gross national product [GNP] to decrease, and the ratios of both secondary and tertiary industry output to increase, side by side with the economic progress measured in terms of the size of per capita GNP. The above-mentioned rate of rural industrialization is equivalent to the sum of the proportions of the secondary and tertiary industry output, respectively, in total output of the rural sector.) Line 1 of figure 2.1 also shows approximately the path of the time series changes in the same ratio in each province.

There is a view that the widespread rise in Township and Village

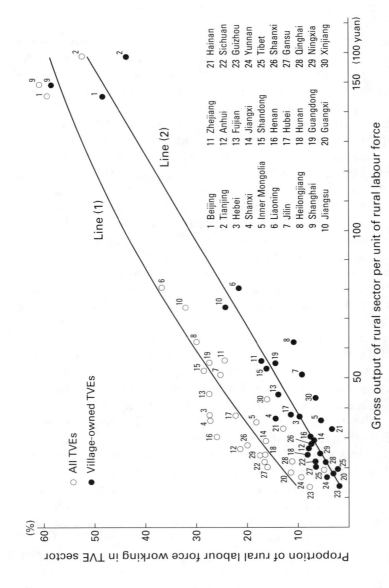

Fig. 2.1 **The relationship between gross output of the rural sector per unit of rural labour force (X1) and the proportion of rural labour force working in the Township and Village Enterprise (TVE) sector (Y1) or that in the *xiang* (or village)-owned enterprises in the TVE sector (Y2): line 1 = the relations between X1 and Y1; line 2 = the relations between X1 and Y2 (Source: *Chinese Agricultural Yearbook 1991*)**

Enterprises was a peculiarly Chinese event that is difficult to explain by economic principles. But this is not pertinent. While a case in which the agricultural breakthrough came first and rural industrialization followed is probably rare in the history of industrialization, the advent of Township and Village Enterprises itself is easily explicable as outlined above, according to economic principles. That the impact of the agricultural breakthrough is confined to rural (and does not affect general) industrialization is due to the market economy under-development, which impedes the spread of its effects to other sectors. The underdevelopment of transportation and communications infrastructures, and especially the underdeveloped economic systems obstructing inter-local distribution of goods, are related to it.[6] The persistence of restrictions on population movements from rural areas also acts as a factor.

Poor performances in total factor productivities and enterprise finance in the state industrial enterprise sector are well known. The rate of growth in their output is, on the whole, not bad. However, as shown in table 2.2, it is lagging behind the rate of growth in the collective industrial enterprise sector, especially that of the Township and Village (industrial) Enterprises, thus giving rise to the dualistic growth sectors in the domestic economy. Underneath these dualistic growth sectors are found two distinct types of development toward the developed market economy: one is represented by the state enterprise sector, where market-oriented reform is difficult to carry out, as the 40-year enforcement of a planned economy brought about an organizational structure and behaviour patterns of the basic economic agents that are entirely different from those of their market economy counterparts. The other is the underdeveloped market economy of the non-state sector, where the planned economy has had relatively little effect on the organizational contents themselves of the economic agents, simply imposing external constraints upon their external activities through regulation of distribution and prices. Therefore, with the easing of these regulations, China's former underdeveloped market economy, together with the component economic units, came back to life. These factors created an intersectoral dualism of output growth during the 1980s. Thus, a "higher growth sector" is the sector characterized by the second type of developing market economy, and a "slower growth sector" by the first type.

The same dualistic growth as observed among the three domestic sectors is seen in the foreign trade sector also. The characteristically "slower growth" sector includes a small number of gigantic central

Table 2.2 **Dualistic structure of economic growth in China**

	Annual growth			
	1978–1984		1984–1992	
	Weight[1]	rate (%)	Weight[2]	rate (%)
1. Rate of growth in output[5]				
Gross domestic product	100.0	7.5	100.0	9.1
Total agricultural output	35.1	6.5	46.4	6.6
Total industrial output	118.1	8.1	109.4	16.1
State industries	91.7	6.0	75.6	9.2
Township and Village	10.7	17.6	17.9	28.5
Enterprises (rural industries)	na[6]	na	16.7	28.5
Total value of production of the rural sector	na	na	72.8	14.2
Township and Village Enterprises	13.7	16.9	24.6	25.3
2. Rate of growth in expenditures[5]	100.0		100.0	
Consumption[3]	63.5	8.3	68.5	8.8
Investment[3]	36.5	4.5	31.5	6.5
Capital construction investment (completed amount)	16.8	2.6	13.0	7.4
Exports[4]	5.6	8.7	10.2	13.0
Imports[4]	6.3	7.7	10.9	11.6

Source: *Chinese Statistical Yearbook 1993*, excepting those noted below.

1. "Weight" referring to output in this column means output as a percentage of 1978 GDP; for expenditures, it means the percentage of "total available national income" (consumption plus investments) in 1978.
2. "Weight" referring to output in this column means output as a percentage of 1984 GDP; for expenditures, it means the percentage of "total available national income" in 1984.
3. While in Sector 1, GDP figures are obtained by the SNA (UN System of National Accounting), these figures are based on the former Soviet Union's MPS (Material Product System). China's national income measured by the MPS was 83.9 per cent of SNA-based GDP in 1978, 81.1 per cent in 1984, and 82.6 per cent in 1992. Both consumption and investment by this MPS are probably likewise smaller than consumption and investment measured using the SNA.
4. Imports and exports are indicated in terms of overseas dollar prices. These figures were converted to real prices using the American GNP deflator calculated by the IMF (where the 1978 baseline is 100, the 1984 deflator is 149.3 and the 1992 deflator 182.0).
5. The growth rate was estimated by the following procedure:
   (a) The real inflation-adjusted annual series data needed to calculate the growth rate are not given in *Chinese Statistical Yearbook 1993* for the variables in this table. With regard to GDP, industrial and agricultural output, and consumption, however, it is possible to estimate deflators indirectly from published statistics, and to calculate thereby the growth rate.
   (b) A GDP deflator was used to estimate "total value of production of rural sector" and output of Township and Village Enterprises.
   (c) Investments were derived by estimating the domestic investment deflator. The same deflator was used to derive real value of capital construction investment.
6. na, not available.

Table 2.3 **Guangdong Province's export trade: The structure by types of trading and by product categories of commodities from 1980 to 1992**

	Percentage of total			Annual growth rate (%)	
	1980	1985	1992	1980–1985	1985–1992
By region					
Exports to Hong Kong and Macao	51.3	73.4	85.7	14.0	38.8
By types of trade					
Exports by trade outlet	95.9	83.0	49.8	3.1	20.8
Specialized foreign trade corporation	95.9	70.3	26.9	−0.3	13.2
Regional market entry-seeking corporation	0.0	12.6	22.9	0.0	41.5
Processing of brought-in raw materials and assembly	3.8	9.2	5.4	27.1	20.4
Compensation trade	0.3	0.3	0.5	5.4	61.9
Foreign investment-related enterprises (*sanziqiye*)	0.0	7.5	44.2	0.0	67.4
By category of product					
Farm produce	30.2	27.1	14.4	3.8	7.4
Processed farm produce	9.4	7.3	8.1	1.0	19.3
Light industry goods and textiles	30.8	32.7	57.6	7.4	27.4
Heavy industrial goods	25.5	15.8	19.9	−3.3	67.1
Total	2,194.7	2,952.7	18,439.5	6.1	29.9
(Absolute amount in million US$)	100.0	100.0	100.0		

Source: *Guangdong Statistical Yearbook 1993.*

state general import–export trading companies and a growing number of large- and medium-sized state industrial enterprises with authorization for engaging in foreign trade. They are internally linked to the slower-growth state-owned producing enterprises. The higher growth sector consists of *sanziqiye* (foreign capital-related enterprises), principally linked domestically to Township and Village Enterprises and urban collective industries in the forms of processing of brought-in materials, joint ventures, partnerships, and so on, and newly established smaller regional state trading companies.[7] (Available statistics do not show the dualistic growth structure of the foreign trade sector in a straightforward manner. Tables 2.3 and 2.4 indicate only partial figures.) The central state general import–export trading companies are in the slower-growth sector because, despite legislative progress toward liberalizing foreign trade,[8] it is still man-

Table 2.4 **Contribution of Township and Village Enterprises to total exports**

Year	(1)	(2)	(3)	(4)	(5)
1988	140.7	26.9	19.1	2.94	10.9
1992	281.3	119.2	42.4	19.73	16.6

Source: *Chinese Township and Village Enterprise Yearbook 1993*, pp. 272–274.
(1) Total value of purchases by all Chinese public corporations engaged in foreign trade (billion yuan)
(2) Total value of supplies by Township and Village Enterprises (billion yuan)
(3) Item 2 divided by item 1 (per cent)
(4) Amount of processing fee earned from processing of brought-in materials, etc. (in billion yuan)
(5) Item 4 divided by item 2 (per cent)

datory for the enterprises in question to engage in exporting and importing the minimum necessary for the operation of the whole Chinese economy, in exchange for which they are granted the "privilege" of "soft" budget constraints; for this reason, they have no incentive (nor institutional conditions) to increase profits and for that purpose to increase exports with comparative advantage. On the other hand, the foreign capital-related enterprises (*sanziqiye*) and the newly established smaller trading companies qualify as agents in the rapid-growth sector because they arose during the period of reforms and, being unconstrained by planned-economy structures, they are able easily to ride the wave of trade liberalization. Moreover, most have commercial ties with trading companies in Hong Kong or Taiwan.

Enterprises in the higher-growth group engaged in the foreign trade sector were quick to detect the dynamic changes occurring in the foreign sector (especially in the United States and Japan, the newly industrializing economies [NIEs], and the Association of South-East Asian Nations [ASEAN]) and to transmit the information about these changes to the domestic growth sector. The most remarkable development in this area was the synchronization of the evolution of Township and Village Enterprises with changes in the Special Economic and Free-Economy Zones in Guangdong Province, in which such enterprises had sprouted after 1985 as wages soared in Hong Kong and manufacturers making labour- and skill-intensive goods (principally apparel, home appliances, and electronic components) began to seek their production bases overseas.[9] Total amounts of exports from Guangdong Province, in which labour-intensive goods dominated, increased from US$3 billion in 1985 to US$8.2

billion in 1992. (The amount of labour-intensive goods exported solely by foreign enterprises in Guangdong Province rose from US$200 million in 1985 to US$8.2 billion in 1992.) At the time, the United States, Japan, and other markets in which these goods were sold were still able to absorb surplus without much difficulty. This, too, has been a primary characteristic of the "foreign economy sector" up to the present day.

Scenarios for the twenty-first century

In thinking about scenarios for the twenty-first century, a few new developments and changes should be noted that are appearing in the latest phases of China's economic reform.

First is the realization of the possibility that "there is no longer much room left" for China to expand further her foreign markets for labour-intensive industrial goods, which hitherto had fuelled China's export growth. The Chinese government itself is beginning to take this possibility into account.[10]

Second, the rapid economic growth achieved by Township and Village Enterprises since 1984 was supported on the supply side by the existing surplus labour in the rural regions, as well as by the massive use of energy, raw materials, transport capacity, and capital funds. But the use of these inputs aggravated supply bottlenecks facing the state enterprises by "crowding out" their potentially available inputs. This "crowding out" effect was especially serious in the field of capital construction investment by the government and in the provision of working funds from state banks and credit cooperatives. In addition, ample use of these inputs and funds has lowered the management efficiency of the Township and Village Enterprises. It is officially considered necessary in the coming years to reduce the growth rate of Township and Village Enterprises to an extent commensurate with the growth rate of state enterprises.[11]

Third, foreign direct investment in Chinese industry in the form of *sanziqiye* has been concentrated in the general processing and labour-intensive branches; the greater part of this investment has come from overseas Chinese merchants and smaller-scale industrialists in Hong Kong, Taiwan, Macao, and other foreign countries, with the result that the enterprises have been small scale.[12] However, this has changed recently: the Chinese government's policy now is to initiate negotiations with Japanese, US, and European multinationals and their affiliates regarding large-scale investments in capital- and technology-intensive industries and sectors. The recent announcement of a new policy regarding passenger cars and subsequent negotiations with major Japanese and US automobile manufacturers typify this change.[13] Once joint ventures with foreign capital begin to adopt this form, striking increases in efficiency are likely to be seen in this key area of manufacturing industry.

Fourth, until recently, the conventional view of the Chinese economy was that state enterprises' technological and financial performances have not improved, despite reform efforts, and that this failure to improve was the greatest obstacle to the advancement of economic policy as a whole; this view has recently begun to be questioned by some World Bank and American economists' studies at the microeconomic level of Chinese state enterprises. Results indicate fairly widespread cases of increase in the total factor productivity of state enterprises; the apparent recent fall in profitability is interpreted in these studies as evidence that competition is beginning to permeate relations among state enterprises and between state enterprises and non-state enterprises.[14] It is hoped in China that this will lead to a more active state enterprise sector.

Alternative scenarios for development on the eve of the twenty-first century can be drawn by placing different emphases on different aspects of these changes. Presently, at least three scenarios proposed are worthy of note. The first is drawn in connection with the Chinese government's Ten-Year Plan (1991–2000). An export strategy based on coastal region development is still the mainstay of growth in this scenario, but the principal engine of export industry will be shifted from labour-intensive goods by small-scale factories to the manufacture of machinery and electronic devices by large and medium-sized state-run enterprises. The main exports are expected to be shifted increasingly to automobiles and auto parts, petrochemicals, complete sets of industrial plants, ships, and high-technology machine tools. Side by side, production and possibly exports in labour-intensive and low-technology industries will be moved to the interior provinces.[15]

The second scenario is that of the World Bank. It questions the feasibility of turning heavy industry into China's main export industry and states that efforts should be made to make China's labour-intensive products more export competitive. That there is no longer room in the world market to absorb another large expansion of exports of these products is a conclusion based on the assumption that the technology and quality in these products will remain unchanged; China's share of export markets, however, can be increased if technology and quality are significantly improved. This scenario also stresses the importance of diplomacy in trade policy.[16]

The third scenario urges China to seek a further source of growth in domestic (inland) market expansion, while making parallel efforts to promote exports. This is the view of, among others, Lawrence Lau at Stanford University. Lau says that China, with its huge under-developed frontiers, should harness the dynamism of internal demand, rather than exports, because to continue to seek enormous dynamism from exports is vain in a world that no longer has any markets left to absorb them. In projections for 1993–2000 made by Lau jointly with the Chinese Social Sciences Academy's Institute for Quantitative Economics Research, export and import dependence on GDP will converge in the long run at the traditional 10 per cent level and generate an average GDP growth rate of 8 per cent per annum.[17]

Feasibility of inland market development strategies

I am not prepared to talk here about the criteria for comparing these three alternative scenarios nor about the final choices based thereon. I will address only the feasibility of the third scenario, which thus far has hardly been discussed.

First, I will take up that interior region referred to as "Western China" and examine its economic characteristics. "Western China" consists of 11 provinces: these are Inner Mongolia, Guangxi, Sichuan, Guizhou, Yunnan, Xizang (Tibet), Shaanxi, Qinghai, Ningxia, Gansu, and Xinjiang. These areas are almost identical in extent to the Western Region in the regionalization of the Eastern, Central, and Western regions used in the seventh Five-Year Plan (1981–1985). Western China attracts attention because it was the central zone for the building of defence and supporting industries called "Third-Front Construction," promoted during the period of the third and fourth Five-Year Plans (1965–1975) in preparation for the possible outbreak of war with the Soviet Union. Sichuan, Shaanxi, Guizhou, Gansu, Ningxia, and Inner Mongolia were particularly affected by this. During this period, about one-half of the total national amount of state capital construction expenditure was allocated to the "Third Front" construction. Elsewhere in Western China and in most provinces of Central China, low per capita GNP, together with lagging economic infrastructures, are seriously adverse economic characteristics of each province. But in the "Third-Front Construction" provinces, in addition to the above characteristics of a generally underdeveloped economy, a large sector of state enterprises in the defence industry – conventional weapons manufacturing, aviation, aerospace, electronics, shipbuilding, and nuclear armaments – and the support industries thereof, still constitute the strategic centre of the provincial economies, although they are presently facing the extremely difficult task of converting production to the direction of catering for civilian needs. In these economies, agriculture is clearly lagging and hence development of the Township and Village Enterprises is as yet rudimentary. The result is that each provincial economy constitutes a distinctive dualistic structure. (See figure 2.1, in which provinces in Western China are all scattered in the domain near the most southwestern section of two regression lines). Meanwhile, the very nature of the defence industry means that its large enterprises are directly under the jurisdiction of the central government and unrelated to the provincial governments, a fact that further enhances the isolation of the large state enterprises from local economies as an enclave.[18]

Three provinces – Guangdong, Jiangsu, and Liaoning – typify the characteristics of the economic structure of the coastal regions, though there are considerable differences even between them. In Guangdong and Jiangsu, state enterprises are relatively unimportant, whereas rural industrialization (the emergence of Township and Village Enterprises), propelled by the development of agriculture, has primed rapid growth of the economy as a whole. In Guangdong, growth of the Township and Village Enterprises has been reinforced by links with *sanziqiye* foreign enterprises; in Jiangsu, their growth has been strengthened by integration of their production with that of the state enterprises or by creating so-called inter-firm cooperation networks within the province and with Shanghai. In short, Guangdong's development was directed outward, Jiangsu's toward domestic markets. Liaoning's situation is different: it is the centre of a northeastern region, destined for heavy industry construction since the start of the planned economy era, where state enterprises are preponderant. Rural industrialization has made progress, together with the development of agriculture, but the contribution of rural industrialization to the region's industrial development as a whole has been relatively small (table 2.5).

For the study of interregional differences in the stages of agricul-

Table 2.5 **Comparison of employment structure and per capita income data among selected typical provinces in Western and Eastern China in 1989**

Data	Province					
	Western			Eastern		
	Shaanxi	Guizhou	Yunnan	Guangdong	Jiangsu	Liaoning
Percentage of total workforce						
Total public sector	19.9	6.7	12.9	16.9	14.9	35.0
Non-state enterprises	16.9	15.1	7.2	30.1	36.2	31.0
(Rural non-state enterprises)	(11.3)	(6.6)	(4.2)	(20.6)	(25.9)	(8.6)
Agriculture	63.2	78.2	79.9	53.0	48.9	34.0
Per capital national income[a] (yuan)	859	631	774	1,729	1,630	1,977

Sources: General Affairs Department, National Statistics Bureau, *Historical Statistical Data on China's Provinces, Autonomous Districts, and Directly Administered Cities, 1949–1989, Zhongguo tongji chubanshe* (China Statistics Publishing Company) 1990; *Chinese Statistical Yearbook 1991.*

a. Please refer to note 3 under table 2.2 regarding national income.

tural development and their impact on the farm economy, a typological county-by-county survey conducted by the Institute for Agricultural Development Research of the Chinese Academy of Social Sciences on peasants' working hours and incomes is an important data source. Table 2.6, summarizing some of the results, clearly shows the correlations among the changes occurring: progress in agriculture (as measured by annual cash income per labour force unit) on the one hand and diversification of peasant labour allocation, peasants' secondary employment trends, hours worked per day per labour force unit, and so on, on the other.[19]

Observation of such information and data suggests that, assuming that the interior, west-bound market development is a feasible strategy orientation, it is advisable first, as sequential steps for designing the developmental strategy of each interior province, to devise measures for developing the agricultural, rural, and farm economy, and then to establish and implement an industrial policy on the basis of careful studies on the initial industrial structure of that province, as well as some other related model provinces. The question is whether all this is really feasible. As sources of total investment in the agricultural sector, state investments that take place through various channels are found still to dominate (table 2.7). Moreover, the critical importance of "collective investments" at the local level of rural cooperatives for repair, maintenance, and expansion of basic infrastructure for agriculture has been recognized anew, and the once-abandoned policy of organizing individual farm households for providing public services of a collective good nature has recently come to be re-examined. In sum, the Chinese policy makers seem to have a large latitude in choosing the strategy of developing interior markets, with the use of powers both for allocation of public investment and for designing policies of rural organization and agricultural production. Yet an equally important step toward making these strategies feasible is to remove the potential local government powers to enforce economic blockade that separate province from province and county from county – potential powers that are still very strong today.

If a target model for the interior market development is to be chosen from among the coastal provinces, Jiangsu is a better model than either Guangdong or Liaoning. Moreover, when public investment funds are used as an instrument of the interior market-development strategy, the "dualistic" structure, which is a hangover from the past "Third-Front Construction," must not be allowed to be strengthened thereby.

Table 2.6 Comparison of annual incomes and hours worked in peasant households in five "typical counties" in China from 1988 to 1989: results of a survey by the Institute for Agricultural Development Research of the Chinese Social Sciences Academy

	Average daily working hours per year per labour unit[a]	Percentage of total annual working hours actually worked[b]	Percentage of total annual working hours used in different industries					Fixed assets of peasants' households		
			Agriculture	Industry	Other industries	Labour exports	Other	Value in yuan per labour unit	Percentage used in farming and transportation	Others (%)
Jiangsu, Wu County	9.5	118.7	18.1	52.4	12.0	0.8	16.7	4,061	4.2	95.4[c]
Hebei, Guan County	5.1	59.3	63.9	4.1	17.8	6.3	7.9	759	84.1	4.8
Hubei, Zhenxiang County	6.4	79.4	51.4	4.3	22.5	2.1	19.7	702	95.0	1.0
Guangxi, Guiping County	9.0	114.2	66.2	1.0	6.4	7.5	18.9	1,506	23.3	76.5
Guizhou, Wangmo County	5.8	72.4	87.8	0.7	0.8	—	12.3	626	94.9	1.2

65

Table 2.6 **(cont.)**

	Annual cash income per labour unit (yuan)	Percentage of cash income from different sources			Income per hour worked (yuan)	Percentage of peasants engaged solely in farming and holding side-jobs				
		Income from collective operating	Sale of farm produce grown on private family plots	Other household income		Engaged in farming only	Quasi-specialized in farming[d]	Often engaged in farming[e]	Engaged in farming as a side-line	Not engaged in farming
Jiangsu, Wu County	3,152	51.1	23.6	25.3	1.11	2	1	31	65	1
Hebei, Guan County	1,775	5.3	40.9	53.8	1.15	4	43	27	25	1
Hubei, Zhenxiang County	1,462	10.0	52.1	37.9	0.73	–	26	48	26	–
Guangxi, Guiping County	1,055	0.7	75.9	23.4	0.39	–	–	–	1	–
Guizhou, Wangmo County	600	0.5	70.0	29.5	0.34	4	75	20	1	–

Source: Yu Dechang (1991)

a. These figures are derived assuming that every working unit of the sample peasant households works 300 days/year.

b. Normal annual hours worked per labour unit were calculated by multiplication of 300 days by 8 hours and were compared with actual hours worked.

c. This figure is high in Wu County because of intensive investment in housing construction.

d. This is the category of peasant households who spend at least 70 per cent of their total working hours in agricultural production.

e. This is the category of peasant households who spend from 50 to 70 per cent of their total working hours in agricultural production.

This survey by the Institute for Agricultural Development Research was conducted in the following steps. Five "typical counties" are selected from among all the counties in China. Villages of different types and sizes are selected by random sampling from each of these counties and a total of 100 households in these villages are surveyed. The five counties in question have the following characteristics:

Jiangsu, Wu County: With a well developed rural economy, Wu County represents the possible direction rural development is taking in China. Located in the Huadong district in the suburbs of Jiansu City, the economic centre of gravity of its rapidly growing rural economy is shifting toward the secondary and tertiary sectors.

Hebei, Guan County: A prime example of a northern Chinese rural district, located on the Huabei Plain near Beijing, Guan County's rural economy is relatively well developed and its economic growth is beginning to accelerate.

Hubei, Zhenxiang County: Remote from large Chinese cities in the hilly Zhongnan district, but with relatively good access to transportation, Zhenxiang has a rural economy whose development is presently middle-level, combining all the features of the greater part of China's rural areas.

Guangxi, Guiping County: Guiping has all the characteristics of a typical rural district in Southern China. Located in the Huanan district under conditions very similar to Zhenxiang County's, it is distant from any large Chinese cities yet relatively accessible and is part of a regional economy whose development is middle-ranking.

Guizhou, Wangmo County: An autonomously governed county located in the extremely inaccessible mountainous south-west, inhabited by two minorities, the Buyi and the Miao, Wangmo has a rural economy that is still at an underdeveloped, semi-closed state of development.

Table 2.7 **Investment of agricultural funds in the agricultural sector, by source of investment**

Investment source	1982 (million yuan)	(%)	1986 (million yuan)	(%)	1989 (million yuan)	(%)
Total agricultural funds invested	49,529	100.0	103,916	100.0	172,836	100.0
By the government	33,294	67.2	75,457	72.6	115,439	66.8
Investment in fixed capital			4,326	4.1	6,216	3.5
Working funds			91,131	68.5	109,217	63.2
By collectives	6,635	13.4	2,677	2.6	11,441	6.6
Investment in fixed capital	na[a]		1,987	1.9	4,381	2.5
Working funds	na		690	0.7	7,060	4.1
By peasant households	9,600	19.4	25,782	24.8	45,962	26.6
Investment in agricultural fixed capital	2,400	4.8	4,338	4.2	5,624	3.3
Working funds	7,200	14.5	21,444	20.6	40,338	23.3

Source: Li Sheng, Wang Lejun, "*Nongye touzi zhuti zhiyi*" (Query into Agricultural Investment), Agriculture Ministry Policy Reform Legislation Department. In: *Zhongguonongcun: Zhengce yanjiu beiwanglu 3* (Rural China Countryside: Memorandum of Policy Research No. 3), Gaige Chubanshe (Reform Publishing Co.), 1992.

a. na, not available.

These statistics are based on data collected by Li and Wang in *1979–1988 Zhongguo Nongcun Jinrong Tongji* (Chinese Rural Economic Statistics 1979–1988), *Fenjinde Sishinian* (Advancing Forty Years), and Township and Village Enterprises statistics from the Ministry of Agriculture, with supplementary data from the *Chinese Statistical Yearbook*. The concept of investment of "agricultural funds," as the term is used here, is not the one used in national income: it includes recurrent funds.

Postscript

The intention of this chapter was to make clear, at least broadly, the following points. (1) That the high rate of growth of China's economy that was achieved under the reform and open-door policy was brought about, as the main cause, by the operation of the domestic growth mechanism in which major dynamism arose from the productivity "breakthrough" in agriculture and brought about widespread rural industrialization (in the form of Township and Village Enterprises) and, in some areas, even triggered small-scale urban industrialization. (2) The high rate of growth thus generated internally was further accelerated externally by the synchronization and interconnection of this rural industrialization with the tendency of labour-intensive export industries in neighbouring East Asian areas to shift their production base toward coastal China in search of lower-wage manual labour. The chapter then discussed a new situation, emerging in the early 1990s, that is likely to obstruct the continuation of the high rate of growth due to the above two causes, and then attempted to draw up three alternative scenarios that may preclude such an obstruction.

The new situation in the 1990s denotes first, domestically, the way that Township and Village Enterprises are facing investible resource constraints and second, externally, the emergence of export constraints that the labour-intensive manufacturing products are likely to encounter. Next, the three alternative scenarios are (a) continuation of the current growth strategy on the basis of the efforts to increase productivities of the labour-intensive manufacturing exports, (b) switching the priority of the export strategy from the labour-intensive manufacturing exports to the more capital- and technology-intensive manufacturing exports, and (c) while the effort at export promotion is continued, changing the priority of the growth strategy to the development of domestic interior markets.

In this chapter, the discussion has not yet reached the stage in which the merits and demerits of the three alternative scenarios can effectively be compared. A comparison of the first two scenarios requires far more study, not only of the static but also of the dynamic comparative advantages, taking into consideration the possible direction of changes in industrial structure. As for the scenario for developing domestic interior markets, we have first to investigate, in terms of an economic mechanism, how the economies of interior provinces operate, and how further economic development can be triggered. These are, however, tasks we have to tackle in the future.

Notes and references

1. Sachs, Jeffrey, and Wing Thye Woo. 1994. "Reform in China and Russia." *Economic Policy*, Spring.
2. This article argues that it was necessary for Russia to go ahead with all-out privatization in 1992, because it proved impossible to carry out thorough wage subsidy cuts simply on the basis of the state enterprise reform within the framework of perestroika. Here I discuss neither this question nor the question of how skilfully monetary management was carried out in the reforms of 1992.
3. Ishikawa, Shigeru. 1993. "*Chugoku no okina ikoki*" (China's transition period). *Aoyama Kokusai Seikei Ronshu* 28: October.
4. The terminology "soft budget constraint" was devised by the Hungarian economist Janos Kornai, denoting the peculiar practice in the socialist economy in which the state enterprises, even if incurring financial loss, are exempt from financial sanctions or bankruptcy, with support coming from budget subsidies or state bank credits.
5. Line 2 is the regression line for the case where managers and capital were initially supplied by the local *xiang* or village governments. Line 1 is the regression line for this case and the case where managers and capital were initially supplied by individual farm households or their groups, combined. The relationship in regression line 1 is almost explained away by the regression line 2. This paper does not address the implications of this fact. See Ishikawa, Shigeru. "*Kaihatsukeizaigaku no Kihonmondai*" (Basic Issues of Development Economics), Iwanami Shoten, 1970, p. 249.
6. On the concept of underdevelopment of the market economy, see op. cit., ch. 7.
7. These small trading companies are noted by the World Bank for their greater dynamism (World Bank, "China: Foreign Trade Reform: Meeting the Challenge of the 1990s," 18 June 1993, pp. 113–114). However, a precise demarcation for distinguishing them from large state trading companies in the low-growth sector is not provided in this report.
8. As indicators of the progress in foreign trade liberalization, the following are reported. (1) The number of broad product groups under mandatory planning of imports was reduced to as few as 11 for 1992, accounting for only 18 per cent of total imports. For exports, mandatory planning was totally abolished in 1991. (2) The controls through "canalization," meaning that foreign trade is permitted only when commodities are channelled through designated state export–import companies, are reduced to 14 product groups, 20 per cent in imports (1993) and 15 per cent in exports (1992). (3) There are also controls by licensing. In 1993 they cover 53 product groups, 38 per cent for imports and 48 per cent for exports (IMF sources). In assessing the overall degree of foreign trade liberalization in China, we have to be careful about the fact that the steps for liberalization are taken separately and almost independently in the field of (a) control over companies and other units engaged in foreign trade, (b) control over export and import of goods and services, (c) control over foreign exchange transactions and, (d) overall planning of foreign trade. Those activities that are liberalized in either of these fields are not necessarily liberalized in some other fields.
9. With regard to "synchronization" of changes in Guandong Province and those in Hong Kong, see Nobuo Maruyama, ed., *Kanan Keizaiken* (South China Economic Zone), Institute of Developing Economies, 1992 and JETRO, *Kanan Keizaiken* (South China Economic Zone), Tokyo, 1992.
10. State Planning Commission, Institute of National Planning, 1992. *Zhongguo Yanhai Kaifang Diqu jiushi niandai jinji fazhan zhanlue janjiu* (Studies on Economic Development Strategy of the Coastal Open-door Area in China in the 1990s). China Planning Publishing Co., pp. 52–53.
11. Li Bingkun. 1991. "*Xianzhen qiye de yunhang de honguan diaokong jizhi* (Mechanism of Macroeconomic Control over the Township and Village Enterprise Activities)." In: Ministry of Agriculture, Centre for Economic Policy Research: *Zhonguo Nongcun: Zhengce Janjiu Beiwanglu*, 2 (Rural China: Memorandum on Policy Research, 2), Reform Pub-

lication Co. One reservation: there are many reports in official newspapers and articles on examples of undue government intervention into the management of the Township and Village Enterprises, such as, among others, taxation at discretionally determined tax rates and ad hoc allotment of various administrative expenses imposed by the local governments upon the Township and Village Enterprises, and compulsory charges of dues and expenses made by the local party and self-governing bodies (*tanpai*) upon them.

12. Jian, Huang. 1994. "*Wo guo waishang touzi qiye de shizhong fenxi*" (Empirical Analysis of Foreign Direct Investments in Our Country). *Guanli Shijie*, No. 1.
13. Mori, Yasuaki. 1994. "*Chugoku no kokka sangyo seisaku-nisennen eno shojun*" (National industrial policy of China – With Focus on Year 2000). *Nittchu Keikyo Journal* (September).
14. Gelb, Alan, Gary Jefferson, and Inderjit Singh. 1993."Can Communist Economies Transform Incrementally?" The World Bank (October) (mimeo). Jefferson, G., and Thomas Rawski. 1994. "Enterprise Reform in Chinese Industry," *Journal of Economic Perspectives* 8 (2) (Spring).
15. State Planning Commission, Institute of National Planning (see note 10, *op. cit.*).
16. The World Bank, *op. cit.*, pp. 158–166.
17. Lau, Lawrence. 1993. "The Chinese Economy in the Twenty-First Century." Asia/Pacific Research Center, Stanford University (November) (mimeo).
18. State Council, Center for Development Research. 1991. *Jiushi Niandai Zhongquo Xibudiqu Jingji Fazhan Zhanglue* (Economic Development Strategy of China's Western Region during the 1990s). South China Publication Co., April 1991.
19. Yu Dechang. 1991. *Nonghu Jingji Hangwei Ji Laodong Xijian Liyung Diaocha Zuliaoji* (Collection of Research Materials on Economic Activities and Labor Hour Utilization of Farm Households). China Statistical Publication Co.

Comments

Wu Jinglian

Reading Professor Ishikawa's chapter with great interest, I perceived that it is obviously another of his contributions to modern China studies. In this chapter, he analysed the sources of the sustained economy growth in China since the beginning of the economic reform in 1979 with his "five-sector model", and pointed out that the main contributors to the rapid growth have been both the foreign-investment-related sector and rural industry (consisting of Township and Village Enterprises, the TVEs). Their prosperity to a large extent depended on exports in the 1990s because there would no longer be enough market to absorb them. According to this analysis, Professor Ishikawa suggested that China should put the emphasis on "cultivating domestic markets while doing its best to increase exports" beyond "shifting exports from labour-intensive products toward machinery and electronics" put forward by the Chinese government's Ten-Year Plan (1991–2000) and "improving the competitiveness of export products," as suggested by the World Bank.

While cultivating the domestic market and promoting competitiveness of exports are not mutually exclusive, given the existing situation in China (a large country with an underdeveloped domestic market and a very high level of dependence on foreign trade) and the world market (hyper-competition and a rising trend of protectionism), the author's giving priority to the cultivation of domestic markets shows that he is a genuine China expert with insight.

It is worth pointing out that, if we read this chapter with the author's other works on China's development, such as *Medium-Term and Long-Term Prospects of the Chinese Economy* published in 1983 and "The Economic Reform and the Cultivation of the Market Economy" presented at the Sino-Japanese Academic Forum in 1993, we will be able to understand the profound significance of this chapter.

As for the opinions set out in this chapter, I'd like to make the following comments and supplements.

First, it seems that Professor Ishikawa agreed with Jeffrey Sachs' explanation of why "gradual reform" should be successful in China (given the economic structure of China in which agriculture plays a leading role while the state-owned sector has only a small part, thus differentiating it from that of Central and East European countries) and sees his own "five-sector model" as an adoption and compensation of Sachs's "tri-sector model." In my opinion, since China's most successful reform has been rural reform accomplished within two years, it would not be correct to say in general that China adopted a "gradualism strategy" in its economic reform. In fact, the "gradual" method only existed in the state sector, and the state sector's reform was not successful. The reason why the reform has succeeded is that China adopted a strategy of "reforming the economy out of the planned economic system first." This strategy brought about both enormous progress and serious problems, such as inflation, corruption, and an increasingly widened income gap between regions and different social groups (see Wu Jinglian, *The Road Leading to the Market Economy*, 1992, pp. 116–126). Jeffery Sachs' explanation of the "temporary success of China's reform" is not so much a realistic analysis but a sort of defensive answer to why his "shock therapy" approach has not been verified in China's reform. In being applied to China, his tri-sector model has neglected a very important factor in China's 15-year development – that is, the Government's policy of encouraging the expansion of the non-state sector and opening-up to the outside world. These policies brought about the solid foundation for economic development and social support in the transitional period. Professor Ishikawa's model differs fundamentally from Sachs' model. In his five-sector model, Professor Ishikawa attached great importance to rural enterprises and added two foreign-related sectors, thus conducive to understanding the secret of China's hyper-growth in 15 reforming years.

Second, it can be concluded from the above analysis that the challenges China encountered in the 1990s are mainly caused by the lengthy protraction of the above-mentioned strategy of "reforming out of the system" and the protracted delay of the reform in the state sector. I feel that when we discuss this problem it is very helpful to adopt the "anti-Fel'dman model" (*Medium-term and Long-term Prospects for the Chinese Economy*) and the concept of the "poorly developed market" ("Economic Reform and the Cultivation of the Market Economy") put forward in 1983 and 1993 by Professor Ishikawa. Because of the delay in the reform of the state sector, it is rather difficult to solve the problems resulting from the "poorly developed market" while the various negative results of the Fel'dman Model, such as that of the "lopsided development of heavy industry," are still troubling China's economy, thus constituting the foundation for the present economic problems, including the difficulties of enterprises.

Third, the problems faced by China's agriculture and rural economy are also related to the delay of reform in the state sector. The main reason for the problems with China's agriculture and rural areas is the slowdown and reversal of the "A. Lewis process." In his "Economic Reform and the Cultivation of the Market Economy," Professor Ishikawa points out that the Chinese economy has reached the "Lewis turning-point," but if some problems "are not properly dealt with, the danger still exists that the economy may reverse from the turning-point it has just reached." This conclusion reflects the author's deep insight into the Chinese economy. In reality, the low levels of productivity and of investment efficiency have not allowed the state-sector and rural enterprises to create adequate job opportunities for the surplus agricultural labour. The number of agricultural people who shift to non-agricultural industries has dropped from about 13 million annually between 1983 and 1988 to about 4.5 million annually between 1989 and 1993. The increase in the stock of surplus agricultural labour is the source of a series of economic and social problems in China.

Finally, to put all the questions discussed above in a nutshell, just as Professor Ishikawa states in his "Economic Reform and the Cultivation of the Market Economy," the key problem is how to put an end to the situation of a "poorly developed market" and speed up the cultivation of a market economy. The key to doing so lies in accelerating reforms in the state sector, including state-owned enterprises, state-owned banks, and the fiscal and taxation system. In accordance with the "Decision on Certain Questions Concerning the Establishment of a Socialist Market Economy" adopted at the Third Plenary Session of the Fourteenth Central Committee of the Chinese Communist Party in 1993, in order to build up primarily a market economy before 2000, the following aspects of reform have been implemented since the beginning of this year: (1) reform of the fiscal and taxation system; (2) reform of the banking system; (3) reform of the foreign exchange administration system; (4) introduction of a new enterprise system in state enterprise. Whether the Chinese economy can avoid the "great fluctuations" of "the fifth model for economic development," described by Professor Ishikawa in *Medium-term and Long-term Prospects for the Chinese Economy*, and develop smoothly for a long time, depends on the progress of these reforms.

Comments

John Wong

Professor Ishikawa is Japan's foremost China expert and he has made many significant contributions to modern Chinese economic studies. With his half-a-century experience of "China-watching," he is, without doubt, in a good position to offer us insight into the long-term development of China. I certainly consider it a great honour to be asked to discuss his paper.

For any prognosis of the future course of the Chinese economy, one can dissect the growth process into three phases. In the short run, from now to perhaps the end of this decade, the Chinese leadership will be preoccupied with the post-Deng political transition, on the one hand, and trying to complete the unfinished business of economic reform (especially the state-owned enterprises or SOEs) on the other. One major economic target for China to achieve during this period is to develop an effective macroeconomic management tool. So there will be some trade-off of high growth for stability, e.g. slowing the financial sector reform in order not to create too much unemployment. A less dynamic leadership would not like to make too many hard decisions on reforms.

In the medium term, perhaps after the year 2000, growth will be sustained by exploiting the sectoral or regional productivity differences, i.e. the processes of transferring labour from agriculture to manufacturing and from the state sector to the non-state sector, and of spreading development from the coastal region to the interior.

In the long run, growth is conditioned by such well-known determinants as population growth, technological progress, and ecological balance. Given China's already large population, *vis-à-vis* the uncertainty of its future technological progress, one can easily become pessimistic about the long-term prospects of China's economic growth. Does China have enough land and enough water to sustain the continuous improvement of the standard of living for its people? Can China develop a reasonable degree of material affluence without upsetting its basic ecological balance?

First, in discussing the linkage between China's open-door policy and domestic economic development, Professor Ishikawa has rightly focused on the crucial role to be played by agriculture, one of the most "original" sources of China's economic growth in recent years. The past 10 years in China has indeed witnessed the tremendous expansion of Township and Village Enterprises, or TVEs, which was made possible by the continuous growth of agricultural productivity since the early economic reform. The growth of agricultural productivity itself was made possible by the institutional changes associated with the successful agricultural reform in the early 1980s and remarkable technological progress, the basis of which was laid in the 1970s.

Thus, in October 1993, the former Minister of Agriculture He Kang was awarded the World Food Prize for having led a "successful agricultural revolution that had made China self-sufficient in basic foods." In recent years, grain production in China has indeed continued to increase, despite shrinking cultivated acreage and the annual recurrence of natural disasters. This came about because of China's success in intensifying the use of such modern secondary inputs as chemical fertilizers and in the aggressive dissemination of its improved varieties. According to an American expert, the Chinese breakthrough in developing hybrid rice represents "a scientific achievement of world importance," with China being the only country to produce hybrid rice commercially on a large scale.[1]

So far, so good. But can Chinese agriculture continue to sustain its long-term technological progress in agriculture? By the year 2000, China needs to produce more than 500 million tons of grain in order to feed its growing population.

In recent years, Chinese agriculture has been playing a diminishing economic role in the face of rapid industrialization progress. Agriculture's share in China's GDP, in constant prices, declined sharply from 33.8 per cent in 1978 to only 20.6 per cent in 1992. As in other densely populated East Asian economies, the agricultural sector in China has also been rapidly losing its comparative advantage in international trade to labour-intensive manufactures. But this does not mean that agriculture won't pose problems for a country the size of China.[2]

Not surprisingly, agriculture is recently back in the political limelight again. Prompted by rising peasant discontent and the worsening rural–urban income gap, Jiang Zemin and Li Peng in recent months have kept urging officials not to neglect agricultural problems. However, the Chinese government has done precious little to address the long-term need of boosting agricultural productivity. The state investment in rural infrastructure has continued to fall behind, and the agricultural research system and extension services are breaking down. As a result of the spread of materialism, there are fewer and fewer dedicated "barefoot" agricultural scientists; they are now increasingly unhappy because they are paid only a pittance. There are, indeed, worrisome trends in Chinese agriculture, which may well be the first sector to sound the alarm bell, probably sooner than we expect.[3]

Second, thanks to the open-door policy, external demand based on the expansion of the labour-intensive manufactured exports has constituted an increasingly important source of China's economic growth. China's trade–GNP ratio increased from 10 per cent in 1978 to 36 per cent in 1993. I agree with Professor Ishikawa that China's future export growth will still depend primarily on labour-intensive manufactures. But the Chinese economy will never reach the level of export dependency of the newly industrializing economies (NIEs), because the existing world trade system just would not be able to absorb such a colossal flood of labour-intensive goods from China.[4]

This means that domestic demand will remain a more important source of China's long-term economic growth. China can continue to achieve high growth by harnessing the "dynamism of internal demand," or what Professor Ishikawa calls "extending the development frontier to the west (or the interior)." Unlike the small NIEs, China has the whole continent to develop, and it will certainly take many decades to exhaust its total development potential. China is big enough to start its own "domestic flying geese pattern of growth."

However, for economic growth to spread from the coastal region to the interior, China needs to overcome the enormous infrastructural constraint and many other institutional barriers. Faster economic growth in its interior will further strain the existing tenuous central–local relationship. China eventually needs an effective federal constitution to define the proper division of authority between the centre and the localities.

Suffice it to say that China will, no doubt, continue with its high economic growth over the short and medium term. It has taken the NIEs about two decades after their industrial take-off to become "middle-income" economies. It will take China longer to achieve this status because of its vast size and complex problems.

Further, economic growth in China will continue to be full of ups and downs. It will also be accompanied by far-reaching institutional and social changes. The economic and social consequences of China's long-term growth, both for China and the world, cannot be grasped with confidence at this time. History has no experience of such a gigantic economic entity industrializing itself at such high speed.

Notes

1. Wiens, Thomas B. 1982. "Technological Change." In: Randolph Barker *et al.*, eds. *The Chinese Agricultural Economy*. Boulder: Westview Press, p. 116.
2. As the editorial of the *People's Daily* has bluntly put it, "Ours is a big country of 1.1 billion people. If our grain production falters, no other country is able to help us". ("The Whole Party Should Always Pay Serious Attention to Agriculture and Rural Work", 19 October 1993).
3. Lester Brown has recently warned that China is fast losing its capacity to feed itself. By 2030 China could have a grain shortfall of 216 million tons, which would exceed the world's entire grain surplus of 200 million tons in 1993. ("China's Demands Are Seen Straining Food Supplies", *Asian Wall Street Journal*, 25 August 1994).
4. In 1992 China's export–GNP ratio was 16.8 per cent compared with 9.2 per cent for Japan and 25.8 per cent for South Korea. But the Chinese ratio is exaggerated because Chinese GNP is underestimated. So the Chinese economy is still not highly dependent on exports.

3

China's economic reform: Successes, challenges, and prospects for the twenty-first century

Liu Guoguang

The development and experience of China's reform

From its foundation in 1949, the People's Republic of China adopted, for a long time, a highly centrally planned economic system. The third Plenary Session of the Eleventh Central Committee of the Communist Party of China (CPC) held in December 1978 initiated the policy of reform and opening up. After 15 years of market-oriented reform, fundamental changes have taken place in China's economic system. There are six such changes:

1. With public ownership as the dominant element, a heterogeneous structure of state ownership, collective ownership, individual ownership, a private economy, and a foreign-funded economy has emerged. The rapid development of the non-state-owned economic sector, causing its share of output to expand, has made China's economic growth more dynamic.

2. The operation mechanism of state-owned enterprises is gradually changing with the implementation of various forms of reform, including decentralization, the contract responsibility system, and the share-holding system.

3. The role of the market is more and more prominent. At present, controls have been relaxed over the prices of more than 80 per

cent of the means of production, more than 85 per cent of agri-cultural sideline products, and more than 95 per cent of industrial consumer goods.

4. The state's control of the macroeconomy has begun to shift from direct control through administrative order to indirect adjustment through economic and legal means.

5. The household contract responsibility system in the rural economy has been further consolidated and improved. The booming town-ship enterprises are playing an active role in absorbing rural surplus labour and promoting the integration of rural and urban areas.

6. International economic and technological exchanges are widely carried out and a new structure of all-round opening to the outside world is taking shape.

The achievements of the reform and opening-up policy have ushered China's economy into a phase of rapid development. China's eco-nomic growth rate for the past decade is one of the highest ever achieved, not only elsewhere in the world, but also in the booming Asian economy. Compared with those countries that used to adopt traditional socialist planned economies, China's economic reform is quite successful. In explaining the success of China, we must empha-size the following aspects of China's experience:

1. In carrying out the policy of reform and opening up, China has endeavoured to absorb and make full use of the achievements of a modern market economy. However, this does not mean an abso-lute duplication of other people's economic systems. China insists on a way with Chinese characteristics. For example, the adoption of the household contract responsibility system, the development of township enterprises and the trial run of the share-holding sys-tem in rural reform are all the creations of Chinese peasants in the tide of market economy reform. And, in the reform of its owner-ship structure, China has neither rushed to overall privatization nor has it curbed the development of the private economic sector. In fact, China is actively promoting the integration of public own-ership and the market economy by boosting the development of the non-publicly-owned economic sector, on the one hand, and restructuring the form of public ownership, on the other hand.

2. China has carried out an active, yet gradual, reform programme instead of a "pre-packaged reform" or "shock therapy." China is a large country with an enormous population. Its economy still lags behind those of the developed countries. Levels of economic

development differ from area to area. Therefore, the adoption of an active and gradual reform programme has helped China accumulate useful experience through practice.

3. China is integrating domestic reform and the open-door policy. There are tens of millions of Chinese in Hong Kong, Taiwan, Macao, and overseas who have been of great help to China's reform by contributing the capital and experience they have accumulated in a market economy environment.

4. China has properly handled the relationship between political reform and economic reform. Since 1978, China has shifted the focus of its government to economic construction and economic reform. At the same time, China has carried out a stable and gradual political reform, targeted at providing a stable social and political environment for economic reform and economic development. It has been proven that this way is effective and fruitful.

The basic structure and outlook of China's reform in the new phase

During the Fourteenth National Congress of the CPC, held in 1992, it was announced that the goal of China's economic reform is to establish a socialist market economy system. This marks the beginning of a new phase in China's economic reform.

There are several different opinions about this new phase, among China's economists:

1. One opinion is that the reform has entered a phase of "storming the fortifications." According to this opinion, China's reform before the end of 1991 was basically a kind of "battle at the periphery." Many problems remain unsolved after more than ten years of reform. For example, the separation of direct government administration and enterprise management has not been fulfilled in the full sense; state-owned enterprises have not become independent agents in the market; markets, particularly financial markets, are not sufficiently developed and standardized. The state's macroeconomic control is still carried out by means of instructional plan and administrative order, rather than through indirect instruments. Therefore, according to this viewpoint, the target of reform in the new phase should be to solve all these remaining issues quickly and to allow the market to play the fundamental role in resources allocation by replacing the plan.

2. A second opinion is that reform has entered a phase of unification

of two different systems. According to this opinion, China's reform has created a structure in which two different systems coexist in China's economy, i.e. the old plan system and the new market system. This structure is the natural result of a gradual reform programme and was conducive, for a certain period, to the reform process. However, this structure has also caused various conflicts and does not conform to the long-term development of China's economy. Therefore, reform in the new phase involves unifying the two different systems, which actually means expanding the new market system while reducing the old plan system.

3. Still another opinion is that reform has shifted from "outside the traditional system" to "inside the system." According to this opinion, reform of the past decade was a kind of reform outside the traditional plan economic system. Therefore, the major part of the old system, especially the state-owned enterprises, are still left untouched. The reform in the new stage is to expand reform to the old system itself, including state-owned enterprises, so as to ensure a complete take-over by the new system.

Therefore, while there are differences of emphasis, all three opinions agree that the new phase of reform is of great significance. In the new phase, the scale of reform will be unprecedentedly large. It will be much more difficult to proceed to this next stage of reform, as the establishment of a new system involves changing the way of people's thinking, as well as readjusting the existing structure of vested interests.

The "CPC Resolution on Certain Issues regarding the Establishment of a Socialist Market Economic System", passed in the Third Plenary Session of the Fourteenth Central Committee of the CPC in 1993, outlined the basic structure of the socialist market economic system. According to this structure, reform in the new phase will be carried out in the following fields:

1. Straightening out the relationship between ownership and management of enterprises and establishing modern enterprises systems. During the past 15 years, the reform of state-owned enterprises was carried out through the partial decentralization of profit and management decision-making authority. Though enterprises gained some autonomy through reform, the traditional system that fails to separate the functions of government and enterprises largely survives. As a result, the efficiency of state-owned enterprises remains low. In the future, the basic mode will be to convert large- and medium-scale state-owned enterprises into modern

legal entities with the stock company as the major form. Small state-owned enterprises may be contracted, leased, or sold to collectives or individuals. We must treat all enterprises with different kinds of ownership equally and create an environment of fair play.

2. Fostering and developing the market system. During the past 15 years, reform has focused on the development of a commodity market that includes both consumer goods and the means of production. The market for key factors of production remains undeveloped. In the future, in addition to improving the commodity market further, we shall pay special attention to fostering the market for key factors of production, which includes capital, labour, and land. The major task of price reform in the coming phase is further to lift restrictions on the prices for competitive commodities and services, to accelerate the unification of the dual price system for means of production, and to relax control over prices for key factors of production.

3. Setting up an effective macroeconomic control system. The government's control of economy will shift from direct administrative intervention to indirect macrocontrol. The government will guide the development of the economy by means of monetary and fiscal policies and a long-term plan to ensure the equilibrium and structural balance of the state's economy.

Reform of the system of macroeconomic control requires reform of the fiscal tax system, the financial system, and the investment system. As for reforming the fiscal tax system, the first step is to convert the present contract fiscal responsibility system of local governments into a system of tax sharing between the local and central authorities, so as to enhance the capacity of the central government to maintain macroeconomic control by increasing its share in the total national income. It is also necessary gradually to unify the income tax of Chinese and foreign-funded enterprises and individual income tax, and to implement a turnover tax system with value-added tax as the major component.

Reform of the financial system consists of three parts: (1) to convert the present People's Bank of China into a central bank in sense; (2) to establish a policy bank and gradually to convert the present specialized banks into real commercial banks, so as to separate policy lending and commercial lending; (3) to reform the management system of interest rates and exchange rates and to relax control over these rates. An administered floating exchange rate system, based on the market, will be established in place of the official fixed rate so as to transform the Chinese Renminbi (yuan) gradually into a convertible currency.

The above-mentioned issues are the core for establishing a socialist market economic system. In addition to these, the reform of labour compensation, the establishment of a social security system, further reform of the rural economic system and the system of foreign trade and investment, and reinforcement of the legal system are all important components of establishing a socialist market economy. Plans and implementing methods for the above-mentioned reforms are being drafted at present and are being put into practice from the start of 1994.

The further reform of China's economic system can be divided into two phases: (1) From 1994 to 2000, a preliminary socialist market economy will be established. This will conform to the second step of China's economic modernization strategy – that is, by the end of the year 2000, China's GNP will be four times that of 1980 and Chinese people will be leading a relatively comfortable life. (2) From 2000 to 2020, the system will be further improved and perfected so as to accelerate the fulfilment of the third step of that strategy: that is, by the middle of the next century, China's per capita GNP will reach the same level as that of a moderately developed country and the people will lead a well-off life. By the year 2050, China's modernization will be basically achieved.

Before 1949, the market economy in China was underdeveloped. And during the 30 years after the founding of the PRC, China has adopted a planned economic system. Therefore, even though a market economy system is beginning to take shape through reform, its foundation remains thin. The development level of most of the economy remains low. Therefore, the market economy system established during the last two decades of this century can be termed only a partially developed market economy system. Experts predict that, in the twenty-first century, China will establish a modern socialist market economic system with these features: (1) different forms of ownership will be further interwoven into a so-called "blended economy" that will represent a large share of the national economy; (2) the market system, especially the market for key factors of production, will be further perfected and the financial market will play an essential role; (3) the system of macroeconomic control, emphasizing indirect means, will be more effective; (4) in income distribution, performance will be given priority, while the principle of fairness will be observed and the social security system will be further improved; (5) the economic legal system will be improved so that law and regulation will guide the market economy; (6) the domestic market will be integrated with the international market and international practice will be broadly observed; (7) political reform will be further implemented.

China is a large country. Its economic development varies greatly in different areas. It is the same case with reform. In economically developed areas, such as South China and the coastal areas, it is very likely that, by the year 2010 or 2020, their economic development will reach that of a moderately developed country. In these areas, reform has been carried out in advance and it is likely that, by the year 2010, the new economic system will have been established. The emerging model of reform in these areas will serve as an example to other undeveloped areas in their process of furthering reform.

The problems and possible resolutions of reform

We are very optimistic about the prospect of China's economic reform in the twenty-first century. Both the domestic and the international situation have provided a favourable environment for China's economic development. Now is the time to press forward with reform. However, China's reform is never plain sailing. In the transition period from one system to another, a lot of conflicts turn up. These, together with contradictions in the process of economic development, have created quite a few problems for China in its reform process. Most important among these problems are the following:

1. Repeated bouts of inflation. For a long time, the phenomenon of "eating from the big pot" and the soft budget constraint and their influence have not been completely shaken off. The phenomenon of blind pursuit of output value and expansion of investment scale still exists. All these have caused the repeated occurrence of economic overheating and inflation, which eventually results in periodic economic fluctuation impeding the reform process.

2. The lagging reform of state-owned enterprises. This is not only because of defects in the traditional system but also because those enterprises are shouldering a heavy burden which includes:

   (a) Employment: state-owned enterprises are responsible for the job arrangements of too many people; especially in those old enterprises, there are a large number of retired workers who cannot be simply dismissed or ignored;

(b) Debt: enterprises used to turn over most of their income to the state. The source of current capital was basically bank loans and the investment in capital construction and technical updating and transformation for the past decade relied mainly on bank loans. As a result, the debt has increased greatly;

(c) Welfare: enterprises are responsible for providing various types of welfare to employees, ranging from housing and medical care to the education and employment of the children of employees;

(d) Taxation: enterprises bear an increasingly heavy burden of tax and fees, as there occurs this phenomenon of "arbitrary charges and indiscriminate levies."

3. Pressures for employment creation. The rich labour force resource of China is undoubtedly an advantage. Nevertheless, it has also brought about the problem of unemployment. Since the 1970s, the township enterprises and other non-agricultural industries have absorbed more than 100 million of the surplus rural labour force; however, presently there is still a surplus of 170 million in the rural labour force. This varies from area to area. As a result, the phenomenon of "rural labour force rush" occurs. Surplus labour flows from undeveloped areas to developed areas: these have grown from 1–2 million at the turn of this decade to more than 5 million recently. Besides, the reform of state-owned enterprises, the restructuring of industries, and the transformation of government functions have all created a large surplus labour force, which, if handled incorrectly, will affect the stability of society.

4. Growing differences in levels of economic development in different areas, and expanding income gaps. Since the implementation of the reform and opening-up policy, the economic growth rate of south-east coastal areas has always been faster than that of the western and northern areas. As a result, the differential of economic development level and residents' income between the two areas has become more and more prominent. Meanwhile, the income differential between rural and urban areas is also becoming more and more obvious. There are also some people who become extremely rich through illegal business operations instead of arduous work. This has brought about certain social conflicts and will affect the reform process if not treated properly.

5. Emerging social problems. The social environment of the PRC used to be healthy and favourable. Since carrying out the policy of reform and opening up, some ugly phenomena have begun to

show up, including pornography, drug dealing, violence, corruption, and abuse of power for personal gain.

6. The continuing slow pace of efforts to streamline government organization. Among the various reform resolutions, transforming government functions and streamlining government organization is a key issue. However, as it involves the redistribution of power and changing personnel, reform is carried out with great difficulty and is slower than hoped for. These conditions have curbed the fulfilment of other aspects of reform.

To ensure China's reform moving smoothly into the twenty-first century, we must resolve the above-mentioned problems facing China's economic reform. These problems are now being widely discussed in Chinese economic circles. Generally, suggestions to solve these problems include the following:

1. We shall provide a favourable macroeconomic environment for China's reform. The smooth economic development of China needs a sustainable moderate rate of economic growth. Development of the economy and implementation of reform will be hindered if economic growth is either too fast or too slow and if the economy fluctuates greatly. During the transition period, from now to the end of this century when a socialist market economy will take shape, we shall control annual economic growth at a rate of 8–9 per cent through control of the scale of investment and other macroeconomic measures in order to moderate periodic economic fluctuations – in particular, to prevent and curb the occurrence of economic overheating and serious inflation.

2. We shall ease the burden of state-owned enterprises and accelerate reform of the enterprises system. Only after being relieved of the burden can state-owned enterprises transform their operating mechanism. As for employment, enterprises can solve this problem by perfecting the social security system and reforming the labour employment system. Part of the surplus can be absorbed by newly established enterprises and tertiary industry. As for debt, the problem can be resolved by converting debt to shares and writing off bad and old debt. As for welfare, we should single various welfare items out from enterprise and turn over these functions to tertiary industry. As for taxation, we can carry out tax reform and levy taxes on enterprises of different ownership types on the basis of fairness. As for those enterprises that have suffered a long-term loss and are not able to recover on their own, we can

encourage bankruptcy and mergers. Of course we shall make proper arrangements for the re-employment of their workers.

3. We shall create various opportunities for the transfer of surplus rural labour. We shall actively develop township enterprises and establish more towns in rural areas. In addition, we shall further develop labour-intensive industry while promoting the capital- and technology-intensive industries. It is also very necessary further to reform the old household registration system separating urban and rural areas, so as to promote the movement of labour to different areas. The transfer of rural labour to non-agricultural industries, and the employment restructuring of other industries and enterprises, demand that the quality of the labour force be enhanced. It is necessary, therefore, to enhance the rural education system and to establish an effective job-training system.

4. To narrow the gap in economic development level between different areas, the inland areas should no longer simply rely on financial assistance. Instead, they should accelerate the development of agriculture, transportation, the exploitation of natural resources, and processing. They should make full use of their rich resources of land, minerals, and labour. Meanwhile, the state should focus on constructing infrastructure, such as railways and communication facilities that will connect coastal and inland regions, the South-East and the Middle West. The state should also work actively on combining capital, technology, and professionals from the coastal areas with the resources of inland areas. The state should draft more flexible policies for foreign investment in inland areas, so as to speed up the exploitation of resources and economic development of these inland areas.

5. In reforming income distribution, we shall further observe the principle of giving priority to performance while also promoting fairness. We shall eliminate unfair income distribution that results from price differentials of the dual-track system, such as differential interest and exchange rates. Meanwhile, we shall carry out the income tax system and gradually eliminate the unreasonable income gap. Eventually we shall achieve broad-based wealth for most of the people.

6. We shall reinforce the education and legal systems in order to minimize unhealthy social phenomena. It should be noted that, in a certain sense, these phenomena are inevitable while we proceed with reform, and what we need to do is to fight them unremittingly

with effective means. China is now paying great attention to ethical, as well as material, progress. On one hand, we shall improve the education and enhance the moral sense of the common people, especially the young people. On the other hand, we shall strengthen the legal system by drafting even more strict laws and regulations. One key issue here is that government officials should be law abiding and be alert to corruption, so as to provide a fine example to the people.

7. Finally, we shall make more effort to transform government function and streamline government organizations. Issues related to restructuring power should be resolved through the further implementation of political reform and administrative reform. Issues related to the re-employment of surplus personnel should be solved through assigning them to various economic and cultural entities, as well as retraining them.

As you can see, China's economy, the Chinese people, and the Chinese leadership have a long way to go before successfully making the full transition to a complete socialist market economy. If, however, the success of the past 15 years can be taken as a guide, we must all agree that the prospects for successfully completing the transition are very good.

Comments

Ryutaro Komiya

The Chinese economy has been growing markedly in the last 15 years under the policy of market-oriented reform and "open door" towards foreign trade, investment, and finance. Yet it has also been experiencing – and will be experiencing – considerable difficulties of various kinds. I am not definitely pessimistic about the prospect of the Chinese economy in the latter half of the 1990s and in the early part of the twenty-first century, but I cannot be optimistic either, since there seem to be many uncertainties.

In the last ten years China has experienced a surge of economic overheating and inflation several times, and has not found the way to sustain economic growth without inflation. In their respective high-growth periods, Germany and Japan achieved economic growth without inflation, and in more recent times Asian newly industrializing economies (NIEs), Malaysia, and Thailand have grown without inflation or with a much more moderate rate of inflation. Repeated overheating and inflation could lead not only to economic inefficiency and inequity but also to social and political instability.

China has not yet established a rational system of controlling the level of investment and allocating investment funds. One of the results is economic overheating and inflation, and another is pro-longed bottleneck situations in energy supply and transportation.

Also, environmental problems, especially air pollution, have become quite serious.

High economic growth has so far been taking place primarily in the "peripheral" areas such as agriculture and village and town industries. Reform of the key sectors of state-owned enterprises and infrastructure has long been talked about, but marked progress has not yet been observed. A large proportion of state-owned enterprises are said to be still running losses.

China's economic growth in the future depends crucially on foreign trade. If the current high growth rate is to be maintained, its import of oil will have to increase rapidly. Also, there must be foreign countries which import a rapidly increasing amount of Chinese products. Whether these are possible is still an unresolved question.

Another issue which I would like to raise is concerned with the so-called "socialist market economy." I still do not quite understand what it means. I read the recently published book *What Socialist Market Economy Is* edited by the Development Research Centre, the State Council, and the Chinese Academy of Social Science, of which Professor Liu is one of the co-editors. A large part of the book is explanation about the market economy at an elementary level, and it explains little about the "socialist" aspects of the "socialist market economy."

In the "ordinary" market economy, the total size and allocation of investment funds, outputs of various commodities and services, the level of exports and imports are all determined, in principle, by activities of private enterprises interacting with each other. If the "socialist" market economy is basically different from the "ordinary" market economy as well as from the socialist "planned" economy, I feel that the authors of the blueprint of the "socialist market economy" should explain how it is different from the other two. I would like to know how the government or any other public bodies participate and intervene, in the socialist market economy, in the process of allocation of investment funds, determination of the output and price levels of various commodities, the levels of exports and imports, and so on. Unless these points are clarified, one cannot evaluate the significance of the concept of a socialist market economy, or the usefulness of the socialist market economy itself.

Comments

Werner Kamppeter

European optics

Being a European, and one with little knowledge of China, the only thing I can possibly offer at this symposium is a European view of the changes going on in China in recent years. Here one might ask, first, what do Europeans, when we look at China, see, and through what glasses?

During the early Enlightenment, Leibniz, Voltaire, and others admired China for having, in their view, achieved a political system based completely on the principles of reason. Admiration turned into fascination when Chinese porcelain and other objects of art occupied the hearts and minds of the nobility. The rococo style was an offspring of this fascination. Yet, already with Herder the intellectual mood changed. The views of Hegel, and later of Marx, on China were aggressively negative and contemptuous. Still a few decades later – possibly as an outcome of social Darwinism or as a subconscious attempt to justify *ex post facto* the murderous European history in China – some Europeans even became xenophobic (the "Yellow Peril"), while others, possibly for the same reasons, adopted a glorifying, romantic view of China. Still others looked, and are looking, for consolation and for salvation from spiritual emptiness. Finally,

93

when the Cold War had brainwashed us into thorough hate of communists, we quite naturally believed that Peking systematically brainwashed the Chinese people.

In other words, Europeans always seem to project their intellectual fashions, dreams, fears, feelings of guilt, etc. onto China.

Against this background it may come as no surprise that the very remarkable advances of China since 1979 have generated a new wave of hopes and anxieties.

The hopes are again hopes of salvation, this time from economic stagnation. We are unable, or unwilling, to sort out our economic problems in Europe. Instead, we hope that Chinese and East Asian economic dynamism will give our economies another run, through increased exports and direct investment opportunities in China.

Yet, we are unsure whether these hopes could overcome our anxieties. In the first place, we fear that our markets will be flooded with cheap imports from China, thus provoking massive unemployment and reducing our wages down to Chinese levels. There's the new "Yellow Peril"!

In the second place, we fear that China could be successful in increasing considerably the incomes and the standard of living of the Chinese people, reaching eventually European levels. This is an absolutely frightful scenario for Europeans, because we firmly believe – and probably rightly so – that our poor Mother Earth could not support such a development in terms of her resources and of environmental damage. Again, we are projecting our feelings of guilt into China, because everybody knows quite well that we are appropriating an excessive and unsustainable share of world resources and the environment – yet, again, we are, just like others, unwilling to act responsibly.

European transformations

One might think that some aspects of European development experiences could shed some light on the recent process of transformation of Chinese economy, society, and polity. The Western European experience could be of particular importance because the Western European nations have managed to keep disparities in incomes, social security, and regional development within more or less acceptable limits, while productivity and incomes have grown to unprecedented levels. These countries have effectively become capitalist democracies with high levels of legitimacy.

I will return to the development experience of Western Europe in a moment. Let me draw your attention first to the transformation processes in Eastern Europe.[1]

One could say that economic reform in Eastern Europe has three dimensions:

1. Property has to be privatized.[2]
   - The purpose is to reduce production costs by freeing enterprises from all responsibilities except the one for the production of goods or services.
   - Consequences:
     - Enterprises stop being multi-functional, i.e. economic, social, and political units.
     - Labour becomes contractualized: the right to work, to permanence, and to a guaranteed real income disappear.
     - There are losers and winners: the unemployed and marginalized versus the new millionaires.

2. Prices have to be liberalized.
   - The purpose is to reduce transaction costs.
   - Consequences:
     - Price subsidies for goods of mass consumption are reduced. This affects workers and, in particular, people who lost jobs and income, as well as pensioners.
     - Relative prices change drastically; inflation is likely.

3. State budgets have to be stabilized.
   - The purpose is obvious.
   - Problems:
     - Fiscal income tends to decline during the transformation period.
     - (a) and (b) give rise to new types of costs, i.e. the economic and social costs of system transformation. They arise from:
       * the devaluation of large parts of physical and human capital
       * the need for infrastructural investment
       * the absorption of non-production costs borne before by enterprises, e.g. hospitals, schools, nursery homes, pensions for retired workers
       * the need to support the victims of transformation, in particular the ones thrown out of work.
   - Consequences of faltering social systems:
     - Social and political opposition to transformation increase:
       * Transformation cannot be as quick as might be desirable: future gains in productivity (and fiscal income) are sacri-

ficed for present social stabilization (for example by main-taining state enterprises through subsidies).
* Transformation itself can be questioned (by conservative forces and the affected social groups, sectors, or regions).
- The reappearance of old forms of social security, such as, for example, extended family systems, clans, secret societies, mafias.
- The weakening of law and order (in a situation where both already are under transformational stress) and the increase of theft, violence, extortion, black markets, illegal exports, corruption.

These phenomena are, or can be, a direct result of the faltering social security systems.[3] They (further) reduce fiscal incomes and the authority and the implementing capabilities of the state. Hence, success, sustainability, and legitimacy of transformation strategies decisively depend on the distribution of the economic benefits and of the social costs of transformation at the relevant levels.

This is easily said, but difficult to achieve. The relative stability and social harmony of the Western European countries was achieved through a long-lasting historical process: (1) the consolidation of the nation-state; (2) the constitutional guarantee of liberal rights, and the protection of private property were, by and large, established during the nineteenth century; (3) democratic participation, and (4) the guarantee of the material rights of citizens to minima of security and, correspondingly, the redistribution of income became established during the twentieth century.[4] The latter were achieved only after (often bitter) social conflicts, in which labour unions and social democratic parties played an essential role. The Cold War helped too, as the capitalist countries, in competition with the socialist ones, had to become a social success.

Nowadays, in most Western European countries one can distinguish clearly between politics and production, social security and enterprise, employers and employees, rural and urban, regional and national interests, etc. (in socialist countries such distinctions had no meaning). Equally, rules have been established and institutionalized to deal with conflicts within these pairs.

Could it be said that the institutionalization of such distinctions and means of conflict resolution would also have to be the aim of institutional transformation and innovation of the Chinese economy, society, and state? The answer seems to be yes, as Professor Liu mentioned several such distinctions in his presentation.

The next question is, then, whether this transformation could be achieved solely through political actors at the centre – avoiding the social and political conflicts and crises we went through in Western Europe, and which we can observe now in Eastern Europe. In a somewhat different way, this poses the question put forward by Professor Perkins in the morning about the sustainability of the present system of governance and, more importantly, of the political system.

One final comment might be made in the context of these observations on disparities. It emerges from an appreciation of European integration.

Within the European Community, one can observe enormous differences in productivity and incomes. Mechanisms have been established to reduce these differences, yet with limited success: unequal development has not been stopped. In order to reduce these differences in income and development potentials, much larger transfers from the rich to the poorer regions would be needed. For this, no consensus exists. Here is one of the reasons why a European supernation-state is unlikely to be formed. The European Community can hardly be more than a relatively loose confederation of nation-states.

As unequal development has been a persistent feature of economic development in China, one wonders whether the central government will be able to institute sufficient transfers from rich to poor regions in order to maintain the political, social, and monetary cohesion of the centralized Chinese nation-state. Could the importance of Beijing be reduced to the one of Brussels?

Notes

1. Offe, Claus. 1994. *Der tunnel am Ende des Lichts, Erkundungen der politischen Transformation im neuen Osten*, Frankfurt/New York: Campus Verlag, has been very useful for the following comments.
2. Privatization is compatible with mixed property regimes as described in Professor Liu's paper. What matters is who exerts control and for what purpose. All that is needed is that the purpose is profit maximization (or in other theories, cost minimization). Ownership and control can be separated (which is usually the case in stock companies).
3. Richard Rose speaks of the emergence of the "uncivil economy" in this context ("Towards a Civil Economy," *Journal of Democracy* 3(2): 13–26).
4. E.H. Carr calls this process the "socialization of the nation-state" (*Nationalism and After*, London: Macmillan, 1968 [orig. 1945]).

Session I summary

Ryutaro Komiya

In Session 1, under the common theme of "The Chinese Economy in the Twenty-first Century," three reports and a discussion session were presented. The contents of the reports and the discussion session were very varied. Therefore, in the following pages, the author, who was the chairperson, will choose a few especially interesting themes from among the many interesting themes and will point to some of the tasks left for the future. This will be put in place to allow for overall comments.

It is always difficult to forecast the future and point out any problems. It is even more difficult to forecast the future now that we are in a period of transition from the age represented by Deng Xiaoping to the next generation. Nevertheless, the effects of stability and progress in China on the stability and progress of the rest of the world are very large – especially (as has been pointed out in the keynote speech) when we have, on the one hand, the collapse of the Soviet Union and the renewal of ethnocentric trends that previously had been contained under the Cold War system and, on the other hand, moves toward creating new economic blocks, such as the North American Free Trade Association (NAFTA). Under such circumstances, the stability and progress of large countries like China will have great significance for the stability and progress of the rest of the world in the twenty-first century, especially for Asia. At such a turning point in history, China is engaged in a grandiose "experiment" of building a "socialist" market economy which is open to outside forces. We hope, from the bottom of our hearts, that this experiment succeeds. But this is the first attempt to build a "socialist" market economy, and it cannot be denied that there are many problems. The task of the Session is to spotlight the current problems of China, with a focus on economic aspects, and to forecast the future.

First of all, as for the reforms of the Chinese economy which were started at the end of the 1970s, evaluations were generally high, although various problem areas were pointed out.

As far as future forecasts are concerned, however, there are major differences of opinion, depending on who is giving the forecast. For example, Professor Perkins is of the following opinion: China has realized high levels of growth because it started at a very low income level. In order for China to reach the current level of Taiwan, it will be necessary for China to maintain a high growth rate for over 30 years. This, however, depends entirely upon whether the political system that has maintained and promoted current economic development can survive over the next 30 years. Although there are many unresolved problems in the political–social system of China, it does not appear likely that there will be such extensive instability as to prevent economic development. To this, Professor Hara has pointed out that it is not possible to be as optimistic as Professor Perkins in view of the following facts: there is a gap between agriculture and industry; there is a problem of migrating people to close the gap; and there are major effects on the world economy, such as problems of energy availability, associated with the progress of the Chinese economy given China's huge population. In spite of these problems, Professor Liu Guoguang, reflecting back on the past 15 years, said that if it is possible to think of experience as an example, all people will agree that the transition to a socialist market economy will be a success. Professor Komiya argues that, in view of the uncertainty of the political and economic conditions faced by China in the latter half of the 1990s and at the beginning of the twenty-first century, one should not be clearly pessimistic nor optimistic, but the transition will be full of ups and down in many ways.

As stated below, whether the economy will become independent, in terms of being able to evolve toward a market economy despite changes to the political leadership, is the point in question.

Another major theme of the Session is to clarify the differences, if there are any, between the growth patterns of the Chinese economy and the East Asian countries. Professor Perkins is of the opinion that what is important for growth is whether conditions exist that promote investment and whether economic growth is of the East Asian type. Concerning this point, Professor Hara points out that although China has not been committed to one policy pattern, the industrial policy adopted by China is closer to the Korean pattern, rather than the East Asian pattern, and it has had the effect of promoting growth to a certain extent. In his comments to Professor Liu, Professor Komiya supports a Klugman type of thinking that argues that the high economic growth in China is based on a process of effectively absorbing excess domestic labour into production activities, which is what happened in East Asian countries.

An interesting problem is proposed by Professor Ishikawa concerning the growth patterns. After developing a five-sector model by adding external trade and foreign countries to the Sachs Model, which consists of national corporations, private corporations, and agriculture, he makes the following assumptions. The liberalization of the agricultural sector, which makes up a large share of the economy owing to the drastic improvements in agricultural productivity, promoted industrialization in non-national corporations and the high growth rate of the 1980s. However, this led to industrialization only in the agricultural area, and it was never generalized. The reasons for the limited spread of industrialization are the underdeveloped market economy, the limits on the movement of the agricultural population, and an underdeveloped infrastructure. As a result, a dual structure of high-growth and low-growth sectors developed. This dual structure exerted influence on the export sectors, and there emerged a "rapid growth sector," consisting mainly of tri-capital corporations and regional-base corporations for which regulations are weak, and a "low-growth sector," consisting of the major national corporations. However, as far as the future is concerned, there is little room for labour-intensive types of industrial expansion, which have conventionally shouldered rapid growth. Also, the growth of national corporations has placed restrictions on regional corporations as the national corporations compete for funds and labour needed for expansion. On the other hand, in recent years, re-evaluations have been performed for the attainment of national corporations. Professor Ishikawa argues that, in view of the possibilities of a vast domestic market, it is desirable to have policies that place more importance on domestic markets, while at the same time making efforts toward exports.

Professor Wu points out that it is wrong to think of Chinese reform as one "development strategy" as a whole. He points out that, interestingly, if there is a strategy, it is only one of "administering the system." He also points out that the biggest problem is that there is still the danger of reversal, as seen in the stagnation of agricultural products, although the "turning point" that is part of Lewis' theory has been passed. He argues that, in order to avoid reversal, it is necessary to reform the national corporations, the banking system, the tax systems, and the financial systems.

Professor Wong categorizes the problems as short-term, mid-term, and long-term. The short-term problems are related to the stable transition of hegemony in the post-Deng Xiaoping age, and the development and improvement of policy measures for effectively managing demand. The major mid-term problems are associated with the transfer of labour from the agricultural sector to the manufacturing sector, from the national sector to the private sector, and from the coastal areas to the inland areas. The long-term problems are related to increases in population, technological progress, and the environmental problems that come with progress. He argues that the result of long-term speculation is pessimism. The opinion of Professor Wong is in accord with that of others in that his opinion places importance on agricultural production in relation to disclosure policy. He directs attention to reductions in agricultural production in China in recent years.

Professor Wong, however, questions the opinion that there will be increased importance placed on the export of labour-intensive industrial products, from the point of view that the products absorb the capabilities of overseas markets. The author is of the same opinion as Professor Wong when he states that, historically, we have never experienced the vast economy necessary to industrialize rapidly.

Professor Liu Guoguang was previously Vice-Director of the Chinese Academy of Social Sciences, to which he is an advisor, and he is currently a professor at Beijing University. Professor Liu has provided us with a comprehensive and excellent insight into what are the future problems and countermeasures to move China into the twenty-first century. Since 1978, China has adopted a reform and open policy, while making efforts to proceed gradually toward building a modern market economy. In 1992, China established a plan to construct the initial level of a socialist market economy by the year 2000, with the ultimate goal of realizing a "socialist market economy." The plan calls for increasing the 1980 per capita GNP fourfold.

101

As an action plan for realizing this agenda and overcoming the many problems anticipated, Professor Liu points to the need for the following: (1) to maintain an appropriate annual growth rate of 8–9 per cent while avoiding inflation; (2) to develop measures to alleviate the current and past burdens created by the national corporations; and (3) to create employment opportunities for absorbing excess labour in the local regions and to revise restrictions placed on the migration of agricultural population. In addition, Professor Liu points out that it is necessary to put into practice an income redistribution policy, to develop and improve the educational and judicial systems, and to prevent corruption and streamline administration. He points out that, in spite of the many problems, he is "optimistic about the prospects of economic reform in twenty-first century China." His views are very close to the official view of the Chinese government, but he accurately points to problem areas.

After admitting, in a straightforward manner, that among Westerners there are ambivalent feelings toward Chinese economic development and anxieties that Chinese economic development may adversely influence resource availability and the world environment, Mr Kamppeter points out that China can learn a lot from the Western European experience. There is a diversity of ethnic groups in Western European countries, and there is much variety in income and social security, depending on region. These experiences include the privatization of assets, the liberalization of prices, and the stability of national finances. Mr Kamppeter points out that it was only in the nineteenth century that freedom and private ownership of assets in Western Europe came to exist, and he questions whether the goals listed by Professor Liu can be achieved only by the actions of the central government without social and political conflict and danger.

Professor Komiya takes up the issue of "repeated inflation" pointed out by Professor Liu. Professor Komiya severely criticizes the idea that a system can rationally distribute investment funds for the economy as a whole, and he points to the lack of a real body of a "legal nation," because there is no balance in power between the central government and local government and a lack of autonomy to the central bank. Furthermore, Professor Komiya points to the fundamental problem in the concept of a "socialist" market economy, in that it is not clear what kind of economic system a socialist market economy is.

As for the so-called "mixed economic" system, there is no general consensus about to what extent interventions by the national government are permitted. There is quite a difference in the extent of government intervention in England under the Labour administration that held power after World War II and the Conservative, Thatcher, administration, although both are called mixed administrations. When a system exists where, on the one hand, there are freedoms in private ownership of assets and businesses, and selection of occupations, and, on the other hand, the government supplies public and semi-public assets and also appropriately redistributes income, whether we call this a mixed economic system or a socialist market economy may not be an important problem. What should be most avoided is the creation, by political turmoil, of chaos in the economy. Therefore, it seems that what is most needed by China is the securing of the reality of a "legal nation" and the establishment of a system where administration is not operated at will.

Session II
Management

4

On the adjustment of China's industrial structure: The lateral unification of automobile industries

Chen Qiaosheng

Introduction

Technology-intensive, capital-intensive, and labour-intensive are prominent characteristics of the automobile industry. Because the development of an automobile industry has a great influence on economic growth and social progress, and because the level of the automobile industry is always considered as a reflection of economic strength, developing an automobile industry has been a main goal of our government. In "The Automobile Industry Policy" promulgated in 1994, it was explicitly pointed out that we should continue to rationalize the structure of our automobile industry, increasing the production scale, improving production technology and product development capacity, and upgrading products to increase the industry's competitive capability in world markets and creating a sound foundation for it to develop into a principal industry in the national economy by the end of 2010.

Developing automobile industry into one of the national economy's leading industries has long been the dream of Chinese automobile makers, as well as of more than one generation of Chinese people. From the beginning of economic reform and opening to the world, DongFeng Motor Corporation (DFM, formerly the Second

Automobile Factory), in order to realize this dream, has been searching for an approach to get rid of the constraints of the planned economic system, form economic cooperation with other enterprises, rationalize industry organization, and, thereafter, accelerate the development of China's automobile industry. Even though the search has been full of obstacles, the past 15 years' experience has shown that (by means of lateral cooperation of enterprises) formation of an enterprise group is necessary for the creation of China's automobile industry. Looking forward to the twenty-first century, China's automobile industry can be, and ought to be, the principal industry in the national economy and also can become one of the top automobile makers in the world.

The evolution of industrial organization

Old China did not have her own automobile industry. In order to meet the social demand for automobiles as the national economy keeps on developing, the state government invested a centralized labour force and financial resources to establish the First Automobile Factory in Changchun in 1953, and achieved a 30,000-unit annual production capacity by the end of 1956. In 1969, the building of the Second Automobile Factory was started in Shiyan, Hubei province. By the end of 1978, the annual production capacity of this factory reached 30,000 units, including both military and civil use. During the special period of the "Great Leap" in 1958, every province and autonomous region started building so-called "small but all-inclusive" automobile factories on the basis of automobile repair plants. Later, these small factories were forced to shut down, or to be annexed, or to change over to other manufactures. However, during the period of the Great Cultural Revolution came the second tide of "automobile fever," and much more "small but all-inclusive" factories appeared. In 1980, the number of automobile factories was up to 56, but the overall annual production was merely 222,000 units.[1] The automobile industry was in a diffuse state of low-level repetitive production. After the beginning of economic reform and opening to the world, owing to the introduction of foreign funds the third tide of "automobile fever" occurred and the scattered, disordered, low-level automobile industry became more and more prominent. According to government statistics, in 1992 there were 131 automobile factories in all while the overall annual production was only 1,061,700 units, an average of 8,100 units per factory. In only 22 factories did annual production reach 10,000 units. Even the two largest makers, DFM and the First Automobile Factory, had an annual production of only 138,000 and 136,000 units, respectively. The number of factories with 5,000–10,000 units in annual production was 15 whereas there were 94 with less than 5,000 units. The average annual output of the 109 small factories was 2,165 units. The five top automobile makers manufactured 43.56 per cent of the total annual production. Let us have a look at the following comparisons. In 1991, China's average output per employee was only 1.35 units, whereas the highest recorded in Europe, USA, and Japan was 178 units; the average value of fixed capital per employee in China was 30.500 Chinese yuan (Renminbi; RMB), while in developed countries the average capital per employee amounted to US$0.2–0.4 million; the profit per employee was merely 5,200 Chinese yuan, much lower than the developed countries' US$15,000–30,000; our research and development investment was less than 1 per cent of total sales, and it was 3–6 per cent in developed countries. Up till now, only two enterprises – DFM and the First Automobile Factory – have the ability to develop new products by themselves; most factories have to rely on introducing old models from external sources and then making simple copies. Some just do nothing more than knock down (KD) assembly. The situation of no heavy vehicles, and a shortage of light models and cars, has never been changed.[2] The penalty incurred by this lagging automobile industry is the pouring in of imports. By the end of 1990, 1.74 million units had been imported, costing about US$5 billion. Over the last 3 years another 0.7 million units poured in, including those through smuggling.[3]

The poor state of the industry is directly linked with the backward management system. Under the control of the planned economy, which is characteristic of highly concentrated administration, like all other state-owned enterprises, automobile factories were divided into state and local enterprises, each subordinated to a superior governmental department. Government directly intervened in the management of enterprises. As the famous Japanese scholar, Ryutaro Komiya, pointed out in 1985, there is no (or nearly no) enterprise in China.[4] If it can be said that there was enterprise, then the whole nation itself was an enterprise. The automobile industry could be considered only as a department of a large company, or a branch directly subordinated to the central government, with dozens of small branches added and subordinated to the local governments. Automobile enterprises, no matter whether large or small, all acted as workshops belonging to these branches. In these circumstances, with planned raw material allocation in terms of administrative order, governmentally decided production programmes, integrated expenditure and revenue, and state monopoly of purchasing and marketing, the natural links between enterprises and the relations between enterprises and consumers were artificially severed. This kind of system caused manufacturers to rely more and more on the government and, in the end, resulted in low productivity, slow technological progress, and no activity at all. This kind of industrial structure no longer accommodated itself to the development of socialized production.

In order to promote the healthy growth of the national economy, several adjustments had been tried in the past decades. The right of administration had repeatedly been given back to the local government and then taken back by the central government. In August 1964, industrial trusts were also tried, the "China Automobile Company" being one of the nine experimental trusts. This approach was very effective in a very short period. However, because of a fundamental failure to get rid of the blockage in the administrative section of the planned economic system, the automobile industry was always in a strange state of being "dead when stripped of the management right and disordered when given it".

From the opening of the Third Plenary Session of the Central Committee of the Eleventh National Convention of the Chinese Communist Party (CCP), the traditional economic system started to change into the market economic system. The role of enterprise in the market was gradually taken into account. With the slow formation of an economic market, a number of enterprises that understood and learnt to use economic reform policies relatively earlier under the guidance of the government, began to organize economic cooperation in production technology and the internal markets. This gradually released them from their connection with the administrative sections in the planned economic system. Based on the division of socialized production and the situation of the economic market, various forms of lateral unification were founded. In July 1980 the State Council issued the "Temporary Regulation on Promoting Economic Unification." In this it was pointed out that (1) the inter-enterprise union (horizontal cooperation) is beneficial for making use of the advantages of each individual enterprise and to improve productivity and speed up the pace of economic construction; (2) this kind of unification can help to break down the barriers between local regions and that between different governmental departments by forming economic relations; (3) this kind of unification can help to restructure industry according to the cooperation of specialized production divisions; (4) this kind of unification is a good method for attracting funds and resources for urgent national construction from local regions and individual enterprises. It was also pointed out that the formation of various types of economic unification is essential to both the adjustment of the national economy and the furthering of economic reform, and it is an eventual trend towards progress of the national economy. Previously, the organization of automobile industrial unions had long been considered; however, the practice had been severely impeded by the outmoded economic system and outdated concepts. At this stage, challenged by the spirit of the new Regulation, an automobile industry union headed by DFM was rapidly organized and later played a leading role in promoting industrial unions in the whole country.

To encourage the healthy growth of lateral unification, the State Council issued another document, the "Stipulates on Promoting Lateral Economic Unification," in which the aims of (and the rules for) the formation of lateral economic unification were further explained, and related guidelines were proposed. It was also pointed out in this Stipulate that inter-enterprise unification is a key point in forming lateral economic union and, based on this kind of unification, it is possible gradually to form some new economic units and ultimately to develop them into enterprise groups. This is the first time that the term "Enterprise Group" appeared in a formal central government document, which can be considered as marking the birth of the new industrial organization. At about the same time, the Prime Minister announced that the Enterprise Group could be the embryo of China's new industrial structure.[5]

In October of the same year, the State Planning Commission permitted the formation of economic plans, particularly for the Dong-Feng Group (formerly the Second Automobile Company Group), the First Automobile Industry Group, and the Heavy Truck Group; this was called the "Separated List". Meanwhile, the function of the original superior body, the China Automobile Industrial Company, was changed and it was renamed the China Automobile Coalition. This was the first instance of an enterprise existing without superior governmental administration. Even though the "Separated List" was

111

only a mild reform, which still belonged to the category of a planned economy, it did act as a catalyst in promoting inter-enterprise unification and the transformation of government function.

At the end of 1987, the State Economy Commission and State Commission for Economic System Reform issued "Some Opinions on Organizing and Developing Enterprise Groups," in which the definition, organizing rules, and developing guidelines for Enterprise Groups were set out.

Developing enterprise groups had become an important task in (and the main approach for) our country's economic system reform. In "Suggestions for Drawing Up the Next Ten-Year Economic and Social Development Plan, and the Eighth Five-Year Plan," the Party's Central Commission advocated the following: making detailed strategies and policies to promote enterprise restructuring; unification; annexation; and mergers to build up a number of trans-regional and trans-sectoral competitive enterprise groups in a planned way. In 1991, the State Council decided to carry out a reform experiment in 55 selected large enterprise groups in the whole country. In 1993, eight enterprise groups among those 55, in which the three automobile enterprise groups were included, were further selected to experiment on management with consigned property rights.

Along with the state's economic reform, significant changes had taken place in our automobile industrial structure. First, from primitive inter-enterprise cooperation, and later annexation and mergers, enterprise unions were finally developed into enterprise groups. At present, there are more than ten groups in the automobile industry, including the DongFeng Group, the First Automobile Industry Group, the Heavy Truck Group, and the Nanjing Automobile Industry Group, and other groups affiliated to local governments. Secondly, direct government interference has been largely reduced. Except for military purchases, all administrative orders have been cancelled. Sales price is basically determined by the market. However, investments beyond certain limitations still need government permission. The third is the speeding up of international cooperation. All groups have founded their own international joint ventures and/ or cooperation. Meanwhile, manufacturing techniques, product quality, and management have all been significantly improved. However, the state of diffuse, disordered, low-quality and low-level productivity has not yet been fundamentally changed. This indicates that, at present, automobile industry groups are far from strong enough, and have not yet been able to shoulder the tasks of a principal industry. The course of development for enterprise groups is still full of obstacles.

The DongFeng Automobile Group (DFG)

DFM is the core enterprise of DFG. As an important project of "Third Frontier" engineering, the company was built up by concentrating the country's human and financial resources in the prevailing difficult economic and social conditions. A certain truck production scale was formed in 1978. With the responsibility of vigorously developing our country's automobile industry and the objective requirement of participating in social cooperative production, DFM began, in 1978, to explore how to unify automobile enterprises. In 1980, with the encouragement of central government, the concrete work of promoting union of the enterprises was started. The Dong-Feng Automobile Industry Union Company was ratified by the government in February 1981 and organized formally on 8 April of the same year. In this company, DFM played a core role; other local automobile factories belonging to various provinces (Hubei, Guangxi, Zhejiang, Guangdong, Guizhou, Yunnan, Sichuan, and Xinjiang) were also involved. This company was called the Erqi Group for short and was renamed the DongFeng Group in September 1992.[6] The progress of union can be divided roughly into three stages, as outlined below.

The years 1981 and 1982 marked the stage of product unification. DFM supplied the parts for the DongFeng 5 ton truck at low prices to six enterprises that had produced whole automobiles before union, and then the parts were assembled and sold at good prices locally. In this way, enterprises could get money to perform technological reconstruction. In other cases, DFM provided special car mainframes to some enterprises to make special and passenger cars. DFM also managed some enterprises to produce truck parts for assembly by DFM and maintenance in the market. At the same time, a number of car repair factories became maintenance plants.

The years 1983–1985 were the stage of unification for management as well as research and development. In 1982, the production capacity of DongFeng trucks by Erqi had reached 55,000 and was expected to reach 100,000. Production sites were also going to be expanded, from Shiyan to Xiangfan and Wuhan. Although enlarging the scale of cooperation had to be considered, stabilizing and reinforcing this cooperation was more important. To meet the above needs, it was necessary to establish a property relationship between the attached enterprises and the core Erqi. But at that time the enterprises were still subordinated to specific government departments and the social production system was blocked. The method of establishing the property relationship was simply a matter of administrative redistribution between government departments on the basis of the enterprise's agreement: that is, the enterprises belonging to the local governments of Kunning, Liuzhou, Hangzhou, Xinjiang, etc. were redistributed from local to central government, and then were entrusted to Erqi for united planning and management. This method was called the "6-to-1," that is, the combination of personnel, property, materials, provision, production, and sales. In addition, many enterprises gained a better contract relationship with Erqi.

After 1986, the stage of property union started. The essence of enterprise union is the property union. To reach property union, the old system must be destroyed. A number of economists, Ma Hong and others, went to Erqi to investigate and were in favour of this union and development. In order to push the enterprise union forward, they made four suggestions to central government: (1) to let Erqi become the country's experimental site for establishing enterprise groups; (2) to give up direct interference from administrative organizations, let the enterprise have more decision-making power for itself, and let Erqi have an individual plan in the state budget; (3) to permit Erqi to build an investment trust for itself (called a financial company later) so as to get financial support; (4) in order to simplify the administrative system and reduce its power, enterprises belonging to "6-to-1" should be managed by Erqi directly. All the four suggestions were accepted by central government and thereafter the formation of enterprise groups was stimulated, and a great change in the automobile industry occurred.[7] The enterprise had more power of self-management, the government function began to change, and a reform in the enterprise system was brought forward.

After that time, DFG made great efforts to implement its normalization. First, the original administrative "6-to-1" was combined with DFM in property. Some of the combined enterprises became branches of DFM, and some of the branches were divided further into DFM-owned or stock-controlled subordinate companies. Secondly, some management divisions of DFM became DFM-owned subordinate companies: for example, DongFeng Import and Export Company was established. Thirdly, DFM invested capital, assets, or industry property rights to build up DFM-controlled subordinate companies and some companies linked by DFM-owned stocks. For example, the DongFeng–Citroen Automobile Co. Ltd was established as a joint venture with Citroen Co. of France, and the Dong-Feng Automobile Industry Financial Co. was established with funds from all DFG member enterprises. Fourthly, from 1987, a reform in the enterprise system was initiated and a transformation to company form was realized. Fifthly, a stock system reform was performed. In DFG, the departments that have a close link with automobile production, including the divisions of technology development, equipment making, production, sales service systems, and stock-controlled subordinate companies, were to be formed into a limited company. The limited company would sell stock and put its stock on the overseas stock market by means of increasing capital and separating stock. As the stock controller of the limited company, the headquarters take charge of DFM's social service and management. Through these important reforms, the process of connecting DFM with the world economy will be accelerated and the goal of making the company an automobile group with influence in world markets will be achieved more quickly.

Fifteen years have passed from the lateral unification of enterprises to the formation of an automobile group with a certain scale. By June 1994, DFG included 79 stock-controlled subordinate companies, 143 stockholder enterprises, and 264 coordinated enterprises.[8] A multilevel organization with DFM as the core has already been formed (see figure 4.1). There are 230,000 heavy trucks in DAG's annual production, and the sales volume reaches nearly 20 billion Chinese yuan.[9]

DFM has made a remarkable achievement in promoting the lateral economic union of enterprises and has completed a series of undertakings that were difficult under the old system. A way to develop China's automobile industry by combining state ownership and market economy has been successfully discovered.

First, the vitality of the enterprise was enhanced. On the economic scale, DFM is in China's "top ten." The automobile factories of Liuzhou, Yunnan, and Hangzhou have also joined the 500 largest enterprises. Although over one-third of state enterprises are running at a loss, few of the state enterprises in DFG are in the same poor shape. Second, a system of speciality mass production was formed. In the initial stage of union, six types of inferior brand cars were abandoned. Among the series of DongFeng automobiles, every member

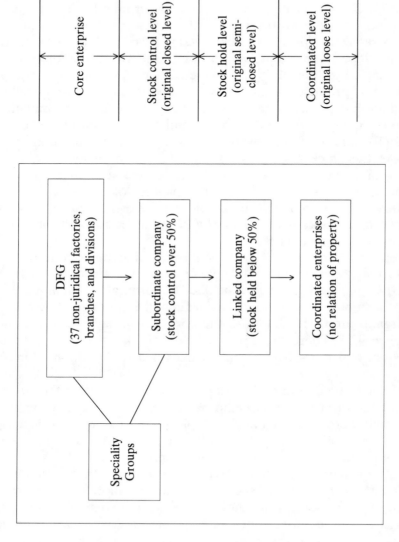

Core enterprise

Stock control level
(original closed level)

Stock hold level
(original semi-
closed level)

Coordinated level
(original loose level)

DFG
(37 non-juridical factories,
branches, and divisions)

Subordinate company
(stock control over 50%)

Linked company
(stock held below 50%)

Coordinated enterprises
(no relation of property)

Speciality
Groups

Fig. 4.1 **Structure of DFG**

enterprise in the group produces the most suitable, depending on their own speciality. The specification of production is developing from that of product to that of technology and even to multi-level cooperation. All of these actions lead therefore to local economic development. For example, the manufacturing industry in Shiyan city and Yunyang district, which are both located near DFG headquarters, is characterized by automobile production, over 90 per cent of which serves DFM. The development of correlated enterprises also benefits. Third, much improvement has been made in products and management. With DFM in the lead, DFG has become a greater force for the independent development of trucks. The current leading types of automobile are at a modern international level and both the 3 ton goods vehicle series and the 1.5 ton desert cross-country motor are also good quality. Through imports, absorption, and extension, the management level and enterprise quality of DFG have made overall progress. Fourth, reform in the enterprise system has been promoted. In the process of lateral union, a great many enterprises were gradually set free from the traditional planned economy system and formed an enterprise group in which the large enterprise plays the core role and is combined with other enterprises; thus, by way of the product, the market economy system was well built up. Fifth, because of the impact of enterprise unions against the traditional system, a series of suggestions has been proposed, such as the form and content of a union, "Separated List" groups, the establishment of group financial companies, systems reform from the current enterprise to company form, and the entrusting of groups to manage state property. All the above suggestions have accelerated the reform of the macroeconomy over a wide range.

The reason for the formation of the automobile industry union and its development

Our automobile industry imitated the economic management system of the Soviet Union after the foundation of the People's Republic of China in 1949. This imitation has played an active role in establishing the basis of replacing the economic law with an administrative approach, low efficiency in resource allocation, and being more and more unsuitable for social mass production. In the 1960s, it failed finally in organizing the Industrial Trust consisting of the primary automobile producers under government order. Some scholars think that this unsuccessful trust was one kind of enterprise union. A trust built on the basis of enterprise union in a market economy is essentially different from that built in a planned economy because, in the latter case, the enterprise is not independent and the union only means the re-arrangement of controls whereas resource allocation does not change. I think that it is important to realize this point.

First, the formation of an enterprise union is the result of social mass production based on the market economy. In the regime of a planned economy, social mass production is organized by the government as one kind of government behaviour. For example, DFM didn't take the problems of resources, coordination, and sales into account at all, even though its annual truck production reached 50,000 units, since the government organized more than 60 per cent of its accessories and raw materials. For example, when the company wanted to obtain tyres, the basic request went from the DongFeng Motor Corporation to the Automobile Industrial Company (Ministry of Machinery Industry), to the State Planning Commission (Ministry of Materials), the Ministry of Chemical Industry (Responsible Materials Company) and the DongFeng Tyre Factory; finally, the contract was signed between the last two units according to an order for materials distribution from the government. In this arrangement, the enterprise didn't consider the requirements of union. Only under the condition that market plays a basic role in allocating resources will a union, or enterprise group built up on this kind of union, match reality. The market economy is the soil for the birth and growth of enterprise groups. The reason why many "enterprise groups" organized only by the administration cannot be kept alive is simply attributable to the fact that the formation of these "groups" is in conflict with the objective economic law.

The reason why DFG could be formed under the condition of a poorly developed market is that weak local automobile producers lost the direct protection of the government when the state economy was in the second adjustment stage, and thereafter they had objectively to depend on a strong enterprise and a good product. This breach of the planned economy made such an enterprise union possible. Because this kind of union could avoid the bankruptcy of the automobile enterprises, it was supported by the government. Meanwhile, such kinds of union had also been promoted by the encouraging policy from the central government.

Secondly, internally the enterprise union is motivated by both the competitive pressure of the market and the development wishes of the enterprise. The enterprise union is actually a union of the market. During tough market competition the enterprise has to seek an approach that accomplishes the best benefit with the lowest consumption for the sake of its development; that is, it has to find the most beneficial position through entering a specific field in the social mass production system. Consequently, the enterprises surrounding the same market target naturally tend to form a union. During the transition from planned to market economy, this union starts from the enterprise products and then implements the unification of enterprise property. The sharper the market competition, the faster the formation of the union. Until now, DFG has experienced three periods of market depression, and the period of every depression is just the time when the government provides the worst direct protection to its enterprises, and is also the best time for the union's development and progress.

Thirdly, the union with one major enterprise as its core is a realistic choice. The current various enterprise groups in our country are basically a series of factories surrounding a large-scale enterprise. The automobile industrial group is an especially typical example. This results from both the poor development of the market and the characteristics of the automobile industry. The automobile industry must have an economical scale in order to avoid bankruptcy. For an automobile factory, the high quality of management, technology, and organization are the bases of running the enterprise, for which it must be equipped with (1) the ability of independent product development, (2) the ability to produce and develop manufacturing equipment, (3) the ability to collect and absorb capital, (4) the ability of marketing and after-sales service. These four abilities compose the four "wheels" of an automobile enterprise and no one ability can be neglected. A large-scale enterprise has generally been equipped with this advantage but it cannot do well in every detailed manufacturing field, whereas many medium/small-scale enterprises might have a specific advantage in some fields although they lack the overall advantages. Therefore, it is a most realistic choice that a large enterprise with its existing strong foundation absorbs a group of medium/small-scale enterprises to make a well-known product on an economical scale, on the principle of accomplishing speciality division of labour and making use of mutual advantages. The role of the member enterprises in DFG is coordinated according to this principle: some of them are engaged in making special-purpose cars, some in making cars for special uses and special transportation, some in making automobile accessories, some in making technical equipment, and some in sales promotion. In reality, dependence on a large enterprise is substantially dependent upon a well-known product by the large enterprise, i.e. the current and potential markets of the well-known product.

Fourthly, the lateral unification of enterprise property is essential, and the connection of the property between member enterprises is a basic characteristic of the enterprise group. The unification of property was an unavoidable issue in the first year of the formation of DFG. The first six automobile producers surrounding DFM to make up DFG had to disregard their previous products and turn to making the DongFeng brand automobile, replacing much old manufacturing equipment; thus, they were finally controlled by the core enterprise, the original DongFeng Motor Corporation. The greater the specialization of the prosperity, the more important the stable market relationship between the member enterprises. In order to avoid being "kicked out" by the core enterprise, the member enterprise asked for a "close" mutual relationship. On the other hand, as the core enterprise, DFM was afraid of interference from the government and any "defection" by the "brother" member enterprises once they grew strong enough; it, therefore, also hoped to stabilize this kind of market relationship. How could they come close to each other? According to the circumstances at that time, a government administrative method called "close union" was followed: this was in accordance with the wishes of the enterprises and the agreement of the local government; the central government then entrusted DFM with the responsibility for the management of these previous local enterprises. However, this union was obviously affected by the government and, thereafter, a method called the "Separated List" was proposed, to avoid multi-level interference from the government; furthermore, property unification among all enterprises within the group was achieved so that the relationship between the core and member enterprises was gradually changed from "brother-to-brother" to "mother-to-son." The unification of property can be guaranteed under the condition of the same substantial benefit among the members, though property might have different features in different enterprise unions. Up to now, the enterprises establishing the property connection are the ones that currently play an important role in the group development plan and occupy an important position in market distribution.

Major difficulties in the development of the enterprise group and the corresponding policy

After many years' practice in the lateral unification of enterprises in our country, the advantage of enterprise groups has been shown. As the main force of economy development, the enterprise group is an effectively organized form carrying out adjustment of industrial structure, a government supporter conducting a macroeconomic adjustment, and an organizational medium in building our socialist market economy. The vitalization of our Chinese automobile industry is determined by the growth state of the automobile enterprise group. Therefore, the automobile industry policy issued in 1994 proposes that the government should encourage the building up of trans-departmental and trans-regional enterprise groups in the forms of annexation, mergers, and stockholding, so as to combine with the right to manage state property to accelerate the current enterprise reform, and finally to set up a modern enterprise system; the government will primarily support two, three, or four large automobile enterprises to grow into an enterprise group with certain competitive abilities in the world market.

The enterprise group is the product of the market economy and its growth and maturity depend on the development of the market economy. On the other hand, the growth of the enterprise group greatly brings forward the maturity of the market economy. Over the last decade, enterprise mergers have been accelerating the impact, and the contrast between the new regime has become visible. The development of our enterprise group still needs to overcome various obstacles and some major difficulties, as follows.

Growth of the enterprise group requires the basic reform of the current state enterprise system

The enterprise is the real entity of the market and the essence of the enterprise system is the system of property rights. Making state enterprises active has been the core problem in the reform of our economy. However, this problem has not been resolved basically until now, although the government has released many powers and benefits to state enterprises. The reason is attributed to the unsolved problem of the property system of the existing state enterprises. The success in rural reform is attributed to the formation of many independent property entities. Why the stock company is vigorous can be explained by the fact that the property relationship is very clear – that is, the relationship between the owner, manager, and worker has been clarified. The innovations in the current state enterprises need to resolve a series of deep-rooted conflicts; some of the most important are outlined below.

First, it is necessary to resolve the "tribalism" of the state enterprise. Owing to the history and currently prevailing system of our country, all state enterprises have a common "sickness": the enterprises depend on the government and the workers and even their family members depend on the enterprise; the government directly operates the state enterprise, while the state enterprise replaces the function of the government to manage society, which means that the state enterprise has to conduct a whole process of management for its workers ranging from birth control to birth, sickness, and death. Modern enterprise becomes a primitive tribe and its manager then becomes the chief of that tribe. The imbalance of such a society leads to the degeneracy of the state enterprise and seeks a profitable target; however, it pays much more attention, on the other hand, to the "self-development" of its "small society." It is intended to occupy the market but puts more emphasis on its own tribe's stability. These dualist goals result in disordered behaviour of the enterprise. Consequently, the separation of enterprise function from social function is necessary.

Second, an incentive and constraint system of property rights must be built up. The enterprise is composed of the property and the workers using that property. The property is provided by the investors and thus the investors are the owners of their own property in the enterprise, whereas the manager and the workers participate in the enterprise operation with their physical and intellectual abilities. They are the owners of their own physical and intellectual abilities. In the tribal state enterprise, who owns the state capital is unclear and therefore the enterprise interest cannot be protected. The enterprise managers as government officials lack independence, while they are usually responsible for the "tribe" instead of the owners of the enterprise property. The managers' income should be in good agreement with their management and, moreover, should take up part of the enterprise. As the members of the "tribe," the workers in the state enterprise are also independent and lack competitive pressure; their incomes also do not reflect the principle of "to each according to his work." The existing policy that connects the total income with the economics of the enterprise mixes further the profits from the property and work, respectively, and therefore makes the already tangled relationship between property and profit more tangled. This is why adding the encouragement and constraints of property into the state enterprise will be the core problem in the reform of the property system. If the separation between the responsibilities of government and enterprise, the separation of the governmental function of macroeconomic management from the function of the property owner, the separation of the tax from the enterprise's profit, are regarded as the reform of the relationship between government and state enterprise, then the internal reform of state enterprise must insist on the principle of separating property earnings from work pay. Enterprises must also become an independent entity in the market competition. It can be visualized that, if not every cell is vigorous, a vigorous and active organism cannot survive.

The third innovation is to form a new enterprise leadership system, since a leadership system is the guarantee of the property system. In order to manage an enterprise, establishment of an enterprise leadership system should be given strict attention. It is more important to depend on the system and law than on the manager's ability, although the latter is also very important. The board of directors is an effective organization system, since this is a closed right and supervision system embodying the separation of policy decision from execution, and is useful for determining the policy in a democratic and scientific way. Owing to the lack of any system of property incentive and constraint, the current management responsibility system has great limitations and provides an opportunity for the development of manager's personal authority and mistakes in policy decision. The relationship between the stockholders' conference, the board of directors, and the supervisory committee (three new organizations) and the Communist Party commission, the worker delegation conference, and management committee of the enterprise (three old organizations) should be well considered during the establishment of the enterprise board. The party organization is political and should play a core role in the field of politics, whereas the enterprise is economic and should seek a profitable target. The supervisory role of the party organization in the enterprise management should be guaranteed through the organization system, such as through the participation of the party leader in the supervisory committee, and the exemplary role of the party is expected to be played by excellent party members. Mixing the different properties of political and economic organization must result in weakening the role of the party in the enterprise. Having the party

secretary as the enterprise manager has also mixed these two different organizations. The manager is employed by the owners and is the
representative of the owners, whereas the party secretary is elected
by the members of the party in the enterprise as their political leader.
It is unquestionable that the manager employed by the enterprise
ownership should become the party secretary if he obtains the support of the workers and their election. However, it will be unreasonable if we administratively appoint the party secretary to be the
chairman of the board. It is a very important topic to bring the initiative and the participation of the workers in the enterprise's democratic management into full play and to give full play to the worker's
union. Decisions regarding the enterprise concerned with the interest
of the workers, such as salary and welfare, should absorb opinions
from both the individual worker and the worker's union; therefore, it
is reasonable that some representatives of the workers should form
part of the supervisory committee of the enterprise. Also, it is reasonable to withdraw the management committee, since this committee more or less overlaps the stockholders' conference.

Growth of the enterprise group depends on macroeconomic reform

Although the enterprise has been expected to strengthen its own
power with the aid of strict management for many years, the great
burden makes such an endeavour almost impossible. There will be a
deficiency in macroeconomic reform relative to enterprise reform
whose progress is also slow. It can be seen from many socio-economic
phenomena that it is time for the government to change its function.
The centralization and decentralization of state power between central and local governments should be the problem of changing the
function of the central government, whereas this leads actually to
decentralization of the state property rights. Meanwhile, the market
actors should be the adjustment target of government, whereas in
reality the government is adjusting itself. Obviously, however, the
standardization of market and enterprise behaviours requires normalization of government behaviour and, consequently, solution of
the following problems is very important.

First, it is necessary to reform the current state property system. The
reason why, until now, enterprise could not be separated from government has been that government is not only the organization of
political power but also the representative of state property, and is

both the governmental department of economic management and the direct manager of state enterprise. And the reason why the government is involved with enterprise is substantially the mixing of government and enterprise property. Therefore, it is essential that our government should issue a law to separate political power from state property. The practice in the enterprise union has verified that the reform of the state property system is the key problem. Starting from this consideration, DFM asked for government permission to manage state property early in 1989, for the following reasons:

1. The enterprise union requires a unification of property. Because this property transition is essentially transition of ownership between different government departments, the rearrangement and adjustment of economic interests leads to great difficulties in performing this union. The "6-to-1" type "close union" is based on a government administration order, and once the government changes its order the union will not exist any more. For example, in 1988, although the Hanyang Special-Purpose Automobile Factory in Hubei Province obtained the agreement of local and central governments to be closely attached to the DongFeng Company, this attachment was easily broken again by the government within a year.

2. The behaviour of the "mother" company more or less determines the production of many "son" companies after the formation of an enterprise union. However, the mother company remains unable to make its own decisions and always has to obey the sluggish or even conflicting orders from the different "owners." In order to have independent enterprise behaviour, it is necessary to become the owner of independent management state entities within the predominant state ownership system; the market relationship will be unable to exist inside the state ownership system and, furthermore, the market economy system will not be able to be built up at all. In the old economic system, state enterprises actually meant different department-owned ones. The market disorder resulting from the connection of government with the ownership of state enterprise has objectively required the creation of a group of independent management entities for state enterprise.

The state property management entrusted to DFG indicates that the representative of state property permits DFM as a company managing state property to manage all the state properties, including that of DFM itself, and its close "son" companies, as well as that covered by their capital.

During the trial, the responsibility, rights, and interest were clarified in a trust certificate signed by the authority and awardee. As the authority, the representative government department of the state property standardizes the treatment of state property through the administrative legislation and state law, appoints the board of directors and supervisors, approves the regulations, monitors the operation of the group, and bears the risks of operating the group. The board of directors of DFM (legal organization), as the awardee, assumes the power of a legal entity and bears the responsibility of increasing the value of state property.

At present, this trial is being carried out and the following good outcomes are expected: (1) the formation of a "separation layer" between DFM and government will make possible the independent operation of the subordinate DFG; (2) DFM will be transformed to become an absolute state enterprise and then will control its subordinates as their stockholder; (3) the construction of the modern enterprise system will be accelerated – that is, the managed part of the current DFG will be reorganized as a stock company and the current DFM will become the stockholder of state property in this new stock company; (4) it will lay a systematic foundation for the optimal distribution of resources, the full play of the overall advantages of the Group, and the establishment of an enterprise group with strong competitive ability in the world market, with the aid of the adjustment of the current property relationship between government and enterprise.

Second, a set of measures in macro-coordinate economy reform should be fully undertaken. Since it is necessary for the activation of the state enterprise and the transformation of government function to have a systematic market economy environment, our government is doing its best to put forward reforms of the tax, price, finance, and investment systems and the establishment of a social welfare and insurance system. It is very difficult to carry out these reforms because of the necessary rearrangements of the benefits and power in society. Nevertheless, we must insist on the reform policy, no matter how strong the resistance. The aim of taking measures of tax division is to establish a reasonable income relationship between the central and local governments on the basis of the reasonable division of power belonging to the central and local governments at every level, and then to establish a finance and tax system that is helpful for fair enterprise competition and a stable increase in government income. However, in practice, the previous tax system is still being employed:

that is, the income taxes of central and local enterprises still belong to central and local governments, respectively. Such a tax system has serious results: (1) the state property is acknowledged objectively to belong to different classes of governmental organizations, while the classification of the managed stated property is treated as another problem, i.e. the old tax system still works; (2) the administrative relationship between state enterprise and different governmental organizations is solidified; (3) state enterprise is located in a situation of unfair market competition, since the local government can actually provide various privileges to its subordinate state enterprise, although the same tax system and interest rates are superficially required to be adopted; (4) the reasonable flow of capital and the establishment of social mass production are hindered. Local government cannot obtain income tax from central enterprises; thus, it will be difficult for the flow of capital of local state property to follow the industry policy issued by the central government; the regional closed-door policy will again be popular and the development of trans-regional enterprise groups will, consequently, be more difficult.

During overall-coordinate economic reform, it is also very important to encourage and support the establishment of various social medium organizations such as professional associations and societies, and to give full play to accountants and lawyers. During the establishment of the social insurance system, social self-help organizations such as the various social welfare foundations should receive adequate attention.

In the macro-coordinate reform, adjustment of the social consumption structure should be promoted. The aim of production is consumption, while consumption adjusts production. A multi-consumption structure will finally replace the present single public consumption; this is of special importance in the automobile industry.

One reform measure in the macro-coordinate reform is closely related to another. The success of all steps in reform depends on an effective productive factor market and the reasonable reaction of enterprises to the market. Therefore, the final force driving macro-economic reform will still be the enterprise, especially large- or medium-scale state enterprises.

The future of China's automobile industrial structure

The development of our automobile industry, from simple production cooperation to the formation of enterprise groups, took place in

127

a particular environment where the planned economic system was changing to the socialist market economic system. Inevitably, this kind of new industrial structure still has great limitations. There are many problems waiting to be explored and solved. However, it is certain that our industrial structure will be more and more rational with the speeding up of internationalizing the automobile market, encouragement by the state automobile industry policy, the improvement of laws and regulations, and the foundation of a social insurance system. Looking forward to the twenty-first century, three or four of China's automobile industry groups will become competitive enough to step into the world market and join the line of world top automobile manufacturers.

The following is the type of situation that China's automobile industry will face in the future:

1. Take-overs and mergers will become prominent and the concentration of both capital and production will be intensified. A number of enterprises weak in product development and financing will have to be absorbed into a few large industrial groups.

2. Enterprises will generally shift from manufacturing factory to company form, such as stock companies and limited companies. A small number of companies' stocks will be sold and bought on the stock exchange. Company property rights will be dispersed, which means there will be not only state stockholders but also social legal entity stockholders, as well as personal stockholders; there will be not only domestic stockholders but also overseas stockholders. The company that first goes to the world stock exchange market will, of course, be the first to accept the baptism of capital's internationalization.

3. Large companies will introduce the strategy of a diversified economy. Besides automobile manufacturing, the social service facilities originally existing in the enterprises will be developed into profitable branches, such as those engaged in real estate and the food industry. Some accessory-making divisions and other assistant departments, originally closed inside enterprises, will be opened to the whole society and grow into important forces in the diversified economy.

4. Industry will seek financial support. Accordingly, companies originally founded in large enterprises will seek further expansion to supply more financial services. The potential of our automobile industry will also be quite attractive to foreign funds. The direct combination of industry and finance is the inevitable trend.

5. The pace of management's internationalization will become faster and faster. On the basis of the vast domestic market, our automobile industry will seek cooperation or unification in a wide field, including product, capital, and industrial property rights.

The adjustment of the automobile industrial structure has happened in a particular environment in which the planned economic system is changing to the socialist market economic system. The adjustment itself is an important part in the reform. A major obstacle faced by economic reform, particularly enterprise reform, is the extensive redistribution of power and benefits. To implement the existing policies and regulations is even more difficult. We are sure that China's automobile industry will experience a new "leap".

Notes

1. *The Automobile Industry of China*, ed. by China's Automobile Technology Research Centre, 1989.
2. There are two explanations for these statistics. One is the time difference: the figures for China are for the year 1991, whereas the overseas counterparts are for 1988–1991. The second is that the standards for comparison are not completely consistent. For example, in China, about one-third of total employees are engaged in daily life services instead of production. In the "average value of fixed capital per employee," the "value" refers to the original value of fixed capital. Also, the data on "production concentration" were obtained from the statistics of individual enterprises, even though enterprises' groups have formed, which cannot tell any story. In the 22 auto-makers, three produced the same DongFeng brand products. Therefore, the annual production should be 165,000 units.
3. *Daily of Economy*, 8 July 1994, p. 1.
4. Jinglian, Wu. *The Economic Reform in Large-Medium-Size Enterprises – The Foundation of the Modern Enterprise System.*
5. *People's Daily*, 16 March 1986, p. 1.
6. "DongFeng Joint Operation Company of Automobile Industry" was not a real economic entity: it was a consultation organization. At that time, a "company" was somehow a governmental administrative department. Although this "Joint Operation Company" was organized under the State Commission of Mechanical Industry, it did not make any industrial and commercial registration.
7. Ma Hong, famous economist and general secretary of the State Council's Economic and Social Development Research Centre at that time, made a 6-day investigation at DFG at the end of 1986. The investigation report was submitted to the Prime Minister and then sent to the State Planning Commission, who headed the implementation of the suggestions in this report.
8. At that time it was stipulated, according to the regulation of enterprises' group, that an individual enterprise should submit a formal application and become a member of the group after being permitted. The group members mentioned here are counted according to the capital investment, including subsidiary companies of the stockholder companies. As for the enterprises engaged in production cooperation, only the directly linked ones are counted.
9. Refers to the accumulated productions and sales of both parent companies and their subsidiaries in 1993.

129

Comments

Fumiaki Fujino

Today, I have been greatly impressed by Mr Chen Qiaosheng's comprehensive and detailed remarks about the present status of, and future outlook for, China's automobile industry, which is currently drawing worldwide attention. Mr Chen is from the Research Institute of the DongFeng Motor Corporation.

The development of the automobile industry is extremely closely related, and crucial, to the overall development of national industries. At the same time, it is indispensable to the success of China's socialist market economy as the twenty-first century draws near.

There are upwards of 100 small-scale automobile factories throughout China. The Chinese government has launched a very ambitious policy to organize and merge these factories into three to four, or four to five, large corporate groups by the year 2010 in order to augment the domestic market share and enhance international competitiveness. I believe that, if corporations from all countries in the world, chiefly Europe, the United States, and Japan, extend cooperation, including financial and technical cooperation, China's domestic markets will further expand and the Chinese economy will be more integrated into the world economy. In response to demands for the enlargement of the Chinese automobile industry and an increase in local content, Japanese corporations, too, should not only extend cooperation in assembly but also aggressively provide business co-operation on the financial and technical fronts.

The gist of China's national industrial policy in the 1990s was determined and adopted by the State Council in March 1994, following the decision to adopt a socialist market economy line made at the plenary session of the Central Committee held in November 1993. The bedrock of this policy comprises, among other factors, the following: (1) reinforcement of agriculture and development of the rural economy; (2) drastic consolidation of key industries, and development of traffic systems, transportation, energy, oil, coal, and hydraulic power; (3) acceleration of the development of key industries and full-scale promotion of the national economy; (4) expansion of economic trade with foreign countries, promotion of exports, consolidation of the Export–Import Bank, and direct trade of large corporations; (5) development of high-tech industries; (6) promotion of tertiary industries.

With agriculture as a basis, the growth of the inland provinces will be spurred by promoting the sprawling rural economy. At the same time, infrastructure development will be stepped up to enlarge overseas trade, and high-tech and tertiary industries will be promoted. Giving priority to the development of key industries is a sound policy that looks to the future of China. The idea of firmly establishing macroeconomic control measures to realize this policy by steadily spearheading reform of the banking system, tax system, and enterprises merits much attention.

Among the fields of key industries, machine electronics, petrochemicals, automobile manufacture, and the construction industries will be developed with priority. These are all vital industries that give China its all-round strength. At the same time, the efficient development of a socialist market economy calls for the consolidation of merchandise distribution and the expansion and reinforcement of the telecommunications industry. For this purpose, it is essential to open the market to foreign capital with respect to these fields as well.

Moreover, in order to advance China uniformly in an efficient manner and reduce the disparity between coastal and inland provinces, policies will be arranged by taking advantage of the special characteristics of each region. For instance, policies aiming at an outward-looking economy are being implemented in the Eastern Coastal region, while policies aiming at using resources and expanding border trade are being pursued in the Central and Western regions.

In any event, the general principles of China's industrial policy for the twenty-first century are, in many ways, very similar to the policies adopted by the Japanese government during the post-war period. As relations between Japan and China grow in the future, the fields in which Japan can provide cooperation will also increase.

Comments

Tetsuo Minato

Mr Chen Qiaosheng has been involved in restructuring the automotive industry as a management specialist in the DongFeng Motor Group, one of the three major automobile-manufacturing groups in China. Drawing on this experience, he has given a detailed and accurate account of the industrial reorganization and managerial reform issues that China's automotive industry faces today and the process of overcoming them.

The automotive industry is a large industry based on economies of scale, and the automotive industry in China formerly had very low efficiency due to its small scale and highly vertically integrated system. To reform this production system, China has attempted lateral unification since the beginning of the 1980s, aiming to increase specialization and the division of labour among corporations. At first, they aimed for a loose coupling of state-owned enterprises in which the property rights and affiliation relations among the enterprises were not changed. Under this loosely coupled structure, however, coordinating conflicts of interests, including adjustments of products and price formation, was difficult.

Mr Chen has described in detail his 14 years with the DongFeng Group, including appealing to the government and changing the property rights and stockholding relations and affiliation ties to form a corporate group with strong unifying ties, as well as the results of these efforts.

Mr Chen has emphasized that the united control of property rights, including stockholding, is a key factor in the management of a corporate group. In fact, the number of cooperative corporations that are not involved in stockholding has remained unchanged at 264, while the number of subordinate companies (companies 50 per cent or more of whose stock is owned by the group) and linked companies (companies less than 50 per cent of whose stock is owned by the group) that are involved in stockholding has risen dramatically from 67 in 1992 to 222 in 1994. The formation of a corporate group through capital ownership strengthens the ability to control the members in the group. On the other hand, however, this is likely to result in weakening its organizational flexibility, through the creation of fixed business relations, and in dampening stimulation from competition. Increasing the proportion of subsidiaries in a group is likely to over-strengthen the initiative of the DongFeng Motor Corporation in the group's decision-making process and to weaken the sense of belonging to the group of cooperative corporations that are not involved in stockholding. It is difficult to reconcile the ensuring of control as a group and the ensuring of the autonomous managerial efforts of each corporation. How is the DongFeng Group managing this issue? Moreover, the automotive industry is formed through the cooperation of many parts-supplying companies. What kind of competitive incentive do you give to the parts suppliers in the DongFeng Motor Group and how do you evaluate their technological and managerial level? What is the business relationship with suppliers outside the group?

Massive funds and technological transfer are required for the industry to modernize rapidly. How will joint ventures with multinational enterprises be handled? What position will joint ventures be given in the corporate group?

In closing, there are bright prospects that leading Chinese automobile corporate groups will be among the world's top manufacturers by the year 2010 and will enter the world market. It is said that it is highly possible that annual automobile production in China will reach 3 million vehicles in the early stages of the twenty-first century; however, it will not be easy for the Chinese automobile industry to be highly competitive in the international market unless the weakness in the automobile parts industry is overcome.

5

Managerial reform of Chinese state-owned enterprises: A shift to joint stock corporation

Mitsuo Morimoto

Introduction: Awareness of problems

A fundamental challenge pertaining to the management of Chinese enterprises in the twenty-first century is how to adapt all state-owned enterprises to an open market economy and how to vitalize these enterprises.

Today, some state-owned enterprises have already perfectly succeeded in adapting to a market economy and are launching impressive operations. A typical form of this adaptation is "privatization" through the adoption of the stock corporation system. But on the other hand, most of the state-owned enterprises are perplexed by the adaptation to a market economy. In particular, deficit enterprises, which are said to account for one-third of all state-owned enterprises, are actually embarrassed by severe circumstances that are endangering their very existence, not to mention the adaptation to a market economy. Although the relative weight of state-owned enterprises is declining gradually, given the fact that they make up the majority of the Chinese economy, one can scarcely think about the development of the Chinese economy in the twenty-first century without addressing the critical issues facing these enterprises – notably the adaptation to a market economy and the revitalization of these enterprises.

In the following sections, I will present a scenario for promoting reform by clearly discussing, from the perspective of the awareness of such problems, the significance and position of the stock corporation system in reforming state-owned enterprises in line with corporate rationale in business administration.

Details of, and problems with, the reform of state-owned enterprises

An examination of the trend in the reform of state-owned enterprises in China since the 1980s reveals that such reform can be largely divided into two phases. In the first phase, which lasted until around 1986, the central government decentralized managerial power and transferred profits to enterprises. As such, this phase represented the embryonic stage of the autonomous management. In the second phase since 1987, the managerial contract system was adopted and broadened, the stock corporation system, or the stock system, was promoted by a small number of excellent state-owned enterprises, and the foundational system was established through the Corporation Law (1988) and the Ordinance on Conversion of Managerial Mechanism (1992). This phase was, therefore, the development stage of the autonomy of management.

A basic policy for reforming state-owned enterprises runs through these two phases: "autonomous management" through the "expansion of autonomy of management," and "separation between ownership and management." This basic policy itself is valid. Ordinarily, various individual reform measures must be applied successively while adjusting to the enterprise's level of maturity of autonomy. However, there is no unified framework for this effort, and reform measures lack an organic linkage for mutual interaction. This problem not only exists between the managerial contract system and the stock corporation system but also is pronounced within each system. That is to say, in regard to the managerial contract system, various contract methods are being promoted monotonously, independently, and arbitrarily. Meanwhile, the stock company system was introduced and adopted on a trial basis by shelving the task of defining it in the so-called socialist market economy. As such, the stock corporation system is interpreted in various ways according to the member concerned and this raises questions about whether such introduction constitutes a means of raising capital (manager) or a means of reforming enterprises (government and academic circles). The various types of reform measures must be integrated and implemented so as to enhance gradually the autonomy of state-owned enterprises.

In order to surmount these problems, it is essential to draw up a scenario for effective reform based on a universal theoretical framework pertaining to the reform of state-owned enterprises, by taking into account China's special situation.

Universal framework for the reform of enterprises

With respect to public enterprises, represented by state-owned enterprises, a corporate rationale in business administration already offers a framework for universal progressive reform. The basis of such a rationale is to free the original form of management (pure public administrative business: management of business activities by a public administrative organization) of public enterprises, which are bound by the principles of politics, public administration, and public finance, from these restraints and realize the principles of management (raising the effectiveness of production in line with a market economy): that is, to broaden and reinforce the autonomy of management of public enterprises. "Expansion of the autonomy of enterprises," China's basic policy for reforming state-owned enterprises, conforms to this basic principle. It was for this reason that I said earlier that this basic principle is valid.

The question is how to make concrete progress in progressively broadening and strengthening the autonomy of enterprises. The stock corporation system cannot be suddenly employed by all enterprises. This is because the stock corporation system is a method to be adopted by private enterprises that have developed and improved substantially. Thus, even if this method is suddenly applied by public enterprises, which are at a stage of a low level of managerial autonomy, for the purpose of privatization, this effort would not produce the hoped-for effect. From this standpoint, the adoption of the stock corporation system requires the enterprise concerned to have a corporate structure of a private enterprise that can adapt to a market economy. Until this condition is met, enterprises should heighten their managerial autonomy through a system other than the stock corporation system. An example of such a system is the managerial contract system. It should be noted that, even within the managerial contract system, there are varied contract systems corresponding to the level of managerial autonomy. Specifically, the wrong order of implementation should not be taken. The correct order is as follows: first, the investment and output contract; second, the inter-locking two-items contract (the contract for the interlocking relationship between profit to be paid and technological improvement items, or between realized profit and total wages); third, the fixed amount of profit contract; fourth, the progressive amount of profit contract.

Under the universal theoretical framework, the process of expansion of managerial autonomy of public enterprises will be as follows: first, pure public administrative business; second, non-subordinate public enterprise (business by public administrative organization under the self-support accounting system: "separation between public finance and business management"); third, independent public enterprise (independent organization with its own corporation status: "separation between public administration and business management"); fourth, autonomous public enterprise (has virtually established autonomy of management: "separation between politics and business management"). In the last phase, autonomous public enterprise, "public and private enterprises converge" in the sense that autonomous public enterprises free themselves from the restraint of the principles of politics, public administration, and public finance and behave according to the principles of business management. Public ownership therefore becomes a nominal symbol of ownership.

If this framework is applied to the reform of Chinese state-owned enterprises, the managerial contract system will be used in the process up to the formation of independent public enterprises, and the stock corporation system will be used in the ensuing process. My discussion below will focus on the latter part of this process.

Suggestions for a scenario for reforming the management of Chinese state-owned enterprises

A major premise of the adoption of the stock corporate system is to broaden gradually the autonomy of enterprises through the implementation of the managerial contract system and to develop professional managers who can discharge the functions of autonomous management while realizing the transition to a corporate mechanism. Based on this effort, state-owned enterprises will be classified into the following three areas, and problems will be solved according to each area:

1. The core business and its related resources aggregation: direct area;

2. The operations that promote and support the core business and the resources for these operations: indirect area;
3. The various functions unrelated to the core business and aggregation of resources for these functions: societal area (such as social security systems).

Regarding the direct area, a necessary specified amount of resources will be organized. That area might be transformed into an independent stock corporation after its resources are evaluated by the appropriate independent consulting institution (such as a domestic or foreign consultant). During this time, businesses will be split up or merged if the need arises. The stockholders will, in principle, consist of the government, the general public (including B stocks), and employees. Surplus resources (including retired persons who are receiving pensions) and cumulative deficit, which were excluded from the formation of a stock corporation, will be placed under government control, along with the societal area (3), and dealt with as discussed below.

A bare minimum of the operations of the indirect area will be integrated into the new stock corporation of the direct area. But as for the parts with characteristics of a market economy, these will be treated separately as much as possible to form independent enterprises. With respect to the societal area, similar measures will be taken for feasible parts. More specifically, dining halls, hospitals, schools, nursery schools, and other facilities fall into this category – including the operations such as warehousing, transportation, maintenance, education, and training in the indirect area. In this case, the process of forming a stock corporation is in accordance with the case of the direct area. In regard to housing, however, it would be more appropriate to convert them into owner-occupied houses, rather than enterprise-owned, through sale to local residents.

The remaining portion (primarily social security) of the societal area, surplus resources, and the cumulative deficit transferred to the control of the government will be handled by the government in the following manner:

1. All social security, including pensions, will be reorganized into an integrated national social security system.
2. Of the pooled surplus resources, human resources are particularly problematic. The government will be responsible for including retired workers in the social security system and undertaking countermeasures against unemployment, as well as efforts to locate jobs, for other surplus human resources.

3. The pooled cumulative deficit and surplus resources other than human resources will be written off by the dividends and the sales revenue of government-held stocks. The management structure of new, and leaner, enterprises that have enhanced their autonomy can be expected to register an increase in preferred dividend, stemming from a rise in profitability and a surge in sales revenue of stocks.

The aforesaid measures need to be supplemented. First, regarding the ownership of stocks, two points need to be realized:

1. Preference shall be given as much as possible to employee stock ownership;
2. Government stockholdings shall be non-voting stocks (dividend preference stocks).

These initiatives will strengthen the incentive to improve performance through the participation of employees in management, do away with government intervention in management, and enable enterprises to exercise their autonomy. Furthermore, ownership centring on employees and the public is consistent with the principles of socialism. That is to say, although socialism holds that state-owned enterprises are "owned by the people," this is merely an ideological fiction. In reality, "government ownership" is tantamount to "party and bureaucratic control." By eliminating this gap between principle and reality, the people can be made the actual owner through privatization by way of stock offering. Nevertheless, in order to maintain this consistency, it is essential to restrict the stockholding and transfer by public individuals for the following reasons.

First, the control of an enterprise by specific persons needs to be basically prevented. Moreover, when earnings of an enterprise take an upturn, the government's equity share decreases because the marketability of stocks rises. These trends favour the securing of management autonomy. On the other hand, the right to control by specific stockholders may be formed through the heavy buying of stocks through the market. This must be prevented. In order to do so, it is necessary to implement restrictions on stockholding and the assignment of stocks by public individuals, similar to those employed by some countries during privatization.

Employees participate in management through the employee stock ownership. But under the principles of socialism, participation implies broad-based participation in decision-making, including the appointment of officers, such as directors. In an employee stock ownership, each employee will have the right to one vote. This system realizes management participation through stockholding based on democratic equality among employees. In addition, it gives rise to the allocation of results as seen in dividends for stockholdings. For these reasons, it can be expected that this system will provide employees with the incentive to improve earnings.

The conversion of government stockholdings into non-voting stocks is a systemic requirement for securing managerial autonomy. Yet, it is not a sufficient condition for the improvement of management performance. As a sufficient condition, it is desirable to adopt stock options as an incentive to managers, along with employee participation – an incentive to employees. As in the case of resource evaluation during conversion to a stock corporation, the details and conditions of this scheme should be determined by the independent specialist body. Unlike the managerial contract system, stock options are not bound by the government. Furthermore, because business performance is evaluated by the market, such an evaluation has outstanding objectivity and offers the best incentive to managers of companies that adopted the stock corporation system.

Some claim that cross-shareholding in corporate groups is a good measure to secure managerial autonomy. Though I do not wish to deny the impact of this measure, an important question is how to convert an enterprise into a stock corporation. If, owing to the scenario mentioned here, individual enterprises establish a set-up to display their autonomy and undertake cross-shareholding to protect each other, then there is no reason to oppose this. Nevertheless, Japan's experience has shown that, if cross-shareholding is carried too far, there is a danger that it would hinder free competition. Certain restrictions or conditions therefore need to be imposed. One such condition would be to convert stocks held by companies in the same industrial group into non-voting stocks, as in the case of the government. This would give rise to "silent, but stable, stockholders," and would better fulfil the intentions of advocates.

Conclusion: Outlook

Reform calls for clear ideas and the selection of methods in line with such ideas. The same can be said about the reform of Chinese state-owned enterprises. In reality, however, spurred by a wave of precipitous transitions to a market economy, various "reforms" are being implemented on a trial-and-error basis without adequately coordinating the concept of establishing the autonomy of enterprises with the various types of methods. Focusing on the concept of reforms, the impact of these reforms is winding its way through Chinese enterprises. But it is also a fact that such reforms are making progress. The stock corporation system is a typical example.

In order to adopt the stock corporation system, it is crucial to establish the appropriate business conditions; to go through certain steps to establish such conditions; and to develop the political, economic, and social environment. Furthermore, because the introduction of the stock corporation system into state-owned enterprises entails the reform of ownership, ideological disputes cannot be avoided in socialist China. Yet (putting B stocks and foreign capital aside) the conversion of state-owned enterprises into stock corporation is a switch from ideological people's ownership (in fact, government ownership) to realistic people's ownership (stockholder = the employees and the public as owners), and is not an issue that threatens the foundation of the socialistic system. If this switch becomes a problem because it gives rise to a disparity, there is a method that grants equal stock purchase rights like Russia's voucher system. In reality, however, this method widened the disparity, and thus ended in failure. Rather, as was done at the time of privatization of Volkswagen (VW) in Germany, it would be better to aim at "people's stockownerism" by allowing stocks to be owned widely and dispersedly, by restricting stockholding per person and the transfer of stocks.

Comments

Wu Jiajun

In Professor Mitsuo Morimoto's paper, the historical background, present condition, and future prospect of China's enterprise reforms were thoroughly analysed. In the article, the author divided state-owned enterprises into three parts – direct, indirect, and societal – and presented different policy measures respectively. These policies are targeted precisely for the difficult problems that need to be solved immediately in the process of present enterprise reform. Reading this, widely broadened my perspective.

It is Professor Morimoto's opinion that state-owned stock should be voteless preferred stock. I agree with his opinion and think that it will benefit the guaranteeing of earnings from state-owned property and the independent management of enterprises. But, until now, there has been disagreement about the above opinion. The responsible government departments think that state-owned stock should be generally common stock, otherwise the controlling power of the government would be weakened. However, in academic and business circles, there are more people who share Professor Morimoto's opinion. Some businesses have already put this into practice and have obtained good results. I believe that through practice, a consensus about this issue will be reached.

Professor Morimoto also considered that "the best way to bring enterprise autonomy into action" is "to give managers the right to buy stock in the company they manage." He thinks that the right to buy stock is also an optimum incentive scheme to the managers. Theoretically, I think that Professor Morimoto's opinion is correct, but we can't expect much of this idea. Because the existing capital stock in large and medium-sized enterprises is too large, it is impossible for managers to hold a large proportion of the stock. The result is that the effectiveness of the method mentioned above is limited to independent management and to stimulating improvements in management.

The goal of state-owned enterprise reform is to realize independent management and to assume sole responsibility for profits or losses. I have the following three considerations in relation to this paper. My purpose is to present an explanation of the enterprise reform, not to refute Professor Morimoto's article.

First, to create a modern enterprise system is the direction of the reforms in the state-owned enterprises.

In the twenty-first century, China's enterprise system will be directed toward building up a modern enterprise system. However, in today's China, there are still various arguments about what the modern enterprise system entails. A comparatively popular opinion is to regard the enterprise corporation system as the modern enterprise system. I think that this is an oversimplification, since the enterprise corporation system includes unlimited responsibility companies and limited partnerships, bearing unlimited responsibility, which fall behind the need of market economic development, and which therefore should not be seen as a modern enterprise system. China's state-owned enterprises, in fact, could be thought of as unlimited responsibility companies for which government bears unlimited responsibility. The essential characteristic of modern enterprise systems is limited responsibility. State-owned enterprises must be reformed into limited companies or limited responsibility companies. To do so, the state-owned enterprises for which the government bears unlimited responsibility need to be changed into enterprise corporations that bear limited responsibility with the property of the corporation.

At present, the state-owned enterprises can be reformed using various methods: (1) ordinary small-scale enterprises can be contracted, rented, sold, or changed into stock cooperation enterprises; (2) nationalized companies should be reformed into stock-controlling companies step by step; the core companies of enterprise groups could also be reformed into stock-controlling companies where possible; (3) state-owned large and medium-scale enterprises could progressively change to companies.

Second, the proportion of stock held directly by the state can be cut down sharply by utilizing corporate mutual stockholdings. This is the most effective way to achieve the independent management of enterprises.

For a large number of enterprises with professional competitiveness, mutual stockholding between corporations should be vigorously promoted and stock rights should be plural and dispersible. For example, one enterprise could join with another enterprise in order to increase the capital fund, while at the same time holding the stock of other enterprises with the capital generated. Doing so would result in a simultaneous increase of the capital fund, which is now simply held by each mutual stockholding enterprise, thus keeping state capital from changing hands. Of the total capital fund, the proportion of the original directly held state-owned capital will decrease. Corporate mutual stockholding, with the condition of plural and dispersed stock rights, is a "making-it-unreal mechanism." In this system, the power of control of the last owner will be weakened, allowing a condition where managers' control of enterprises can be realized, as well as (eventually) the independent management of enterprises. In the process of forming companies, if the "making-it-unreal mechanism" of corporate mutual stockholding works well, and the sole "administrative mother-in-law" is changed into a plural "corporate mother-in-law," we will be able to let enterprises participate mutually while weakening the direct interference of administrative organizations and realize the independent management of enterprises.

Third, to build up an "interest defence line" by readjusting interest relationships is a fundamental way for enterprises to assume sole responsibility for their profits or losses.

As state-owned enterprises belong to the state, a bankruptcy is, therefore, naturally a bankruptcy of state-owned property. Because of this, some people think that property rights should be divided among individual people in volume; if this is not done, then assuming sole responsibility for profits or losses is only empty talk. I don't agree with this opinion, and think that it is a kind of small owner-manager's view about assuming sole responsibility for profits or losses. In modern enterprises, many characteristics of the relationships of property rights have arisen that differ from those of small owners' management. The system of assuming sole responsibility for profits or losses is not really a simple institutional arrangement about property rights or, for that matter, individuals. For instance, the high salary, high bonus, high pension, high social intercourse allotments, and high social status of Japanese stock company managers have brought them real interest that is much higher than the actual company stock they are holding. This incentive scheme can stimulate enterprises to improve their management and form a "defence line" to keep the property rights from suffering losses. It is not suitable to believe excessively in the effect of dividing property rights among individuals in volume during the process of enterprise reform. The interest relationships should be adjusted in order to form an enterprise-based common destiny union and make the interest of managers and employers connect directly with the business of the enterprise. This is a defence line that protects the enterprise's property rights from suffering losses and is also a core problem in the debate about assuming sole responsibility for profits or losses.

My three considerations mentioned above are still controversial in present-day China. For example, some people take the negative effect of corporate mutual stockholding too seriously, which will bring about monopoly and limit free competition. On the other hand, I think that we must pay attention to the very basic viewpoint of this problem: that is, from the viewpoint of strengthening and improving the basis of market economy, corporate mutual stockholding has, indeed, the negative effect of limiting free competition. However, China's state-owned enterprises have been strictly controlled and completely monopolized by government; therefore, introducing the corporate mutual stockholding system should be regarded as progress toward the competitive market economy, not retrogression.

Comments

Oleg Vikhanski

The process of transformation of socialist countries' economies from central planning to the market is not only extremely complicated and difficult to implement but also is unique for every country: the experience of one country differs greatly from that of another. Nevertheless, there are some requirements for the process of implementation of transformation that could be common, to some extent, to every country. Russia has had fairly long-term experience of attempts to improve the national economy and to make it more efficient. Many times after 1965 in the former Soviet Union, many economic reforms of different kinds and reforms of management of the national economy and state-owned enterprises have taken place. But all these reforms failed, as it was impossible to install a market mechanism within the framework of a socialist economy. Only a radical change in 1992 opened the way for developing a free market economy in Russia. Negative experience of economic reforms in the Soviet Union makes me rather sceptical about the future of managerial reforms in China, as they look very much like managerial reforms conducted in the Soviet Union in the 1960s–1980s. This is a general comment on the chapter by Professor Morimoto. Being of this point of view, I would like to make some more comments on his chapter.

Professor Morimoto's statement, at the outset, that *the fundamental task for the management of twenty-first century enterprises in China is to adapt all state-owned enterprises to a free market system*, has a very deep and important methodological meaning. Two questions arise: the first is whether a free market system could exist without free and independent enterprise; the second question is whether the logic of creating a free market economy is (a) establishing the market system and then adjusting state-owned enterprises to it, or (b) privatization of state-owned enterprises and establishing independent companies and then on the basis of their activity creating a free market system. During the period of perestroika in the Soviet Union, Gorbachev and liberal economists tried to introduce an approach of the first kind for transformation of the central planned economy to the market system. At the beginning of their reforms they tried to improve management of state-owned enterprises by giving them more freedom in decision-making and then by introducing self-management and self-financing systems. But these management reforms failed because all attempts to improve management and to increase productivity and efficiency of state-owned enterprises were not connected with property rights. At the end of perestroika attempts were made by the Soviet Government to build a so-called "socialist market." In fact, these were completely unrealistic and resulted in the complete collapse of the economic system. From these facts can be drawn the conclusion that the process of creating a free market system should start with both institutional changes in property rights and radical changes in political and social spheres.

The comment of Professor Morimoto, concerning *the lack of an effective linkage between the expansion of independent and self-supporting management on the one hand and adopting of a stock system on the other hand*, from our point of view is extremely important as it emphasizes the core of the key contradiction that can create problems in the implementation of managerial reform in China. The elimination of the government's intervention in management and promotion of employee participation in management by so-called employee ownership can result in the disappearance of any effective control over management. Managers will become quasi owners. As a result, they will manage the enterprise for their own temporary interests rather than for the long-term interests of the enterprise itself. Now, as in Russia privatization was conducted on the basis of employee ownership, we have this negative result in almost all large-scale enterprises. In this case Professor Morimoto's theory that *a stock option, unlike the contract system of management which put restrictions on it, will be a great incentive for autonomous management*, appears to be absolutely correct and very valid.

Finally, I would like to mention that the very rapid growth of the Chinese economy during the last few years is the result of many factors. Among these factors there are such very important ones as major foreign investments and the very high degree of entrepreneurial activity of the Chinese people. But the state-owned industrial enterprises are still inefficient. This means that managerial reform of Chinese state-owned enterprises should be developed in a more radical way.

Session II summary

Yasuo Okamoto

The first theme covers the restructuring of Chinese industry and cooperation strategy in the automobile industry.

First, Mr Chen, a director at the DongFeng Automobile Group Economic Institute, gave a very detailed report on the development of the automobile industry, centring around the DongFeng Automobile Company. Comments on this report were then presented by Mr Fujino, a director of the Management and Administration Research Institute of Itochu Corporation, and Professor Tetsuo Minato, Aoyama Gakuin University.

I would like to summarize the discussion, while looking back on the post-war development of the Japanese automobile industry. In 1991, Japan became the world's No. 1 producer of automobiles, and the number of automobiles produced in that year was 13,240,000. In 1965, the automobile industry produced only 69,000 vehicles. Of these, the vast majority were trucks, and the Japanese automobile industry in the 1960s was in a very precarious situation. Just as Mr Chen points out for China, Japan in the 1960s had very small-scale production, and a variety of small lot production was taking place.

Against such conditions, during the 1950s, arguments had been presented that a country like Japan, with a very weak production basis, should not produce passenger cars. The Ministry of Commerce and Industry, the predecessor of the Ministry of International Trade and Industry, took up the stance of promoting passenger car production. The Ministry of Transport was against this and, instead, wanted to promote imports rather than domestic production. But the result was the promotion of the development of a domestic automobile industry, because the automobile industry occupies a strategic position in the economy as it is a comprehensive industry.

There are many questions as to how much the government contributed to the development of the international competitiveness of the Japanese automobile industry. If I had to point out two areas where there were contributions from the Japanese government, I would comment as follows. First, in the 1950s, Japanese passenger-car production technology was very poor; the introduction of passenger-car production technology from Europe was therefore needed. Since foreign currency was lacking in Japan, the Japanese government preferentially allotted foreign currencies to the automobile industry, in order to facilitate the introduction of European small passenger-car production technology. Second, in order to nurture the international competitiveness of the Japanese automobile industry, the Japanese government delayed the liberalization of trade and capital as much as possible.

Mr Chen reported that China has a policy of concentrating automobile production within three or four companies in the final stage. It is true that there are too many automobile companies in China. In the same manner, MITI in Japan had considered concentrating Japanese automobile manufacturers, since there are only three automobile companies in the United States. However, MITI was not as powerful as the Chinese government, and it could not mobilize the forces necessary. Nevertheless, we must note that Honda Motors and Mitsubishi Motors, currently strong passenger-car producers, did not produce passenger cars early in the development of the automobile industry in Japan. What I want to emphasize is that it was not the concentration that contributed to the competitiveness of the Japanese automobile industry. Rather, since there was very stiff competition in the automobile industry, it was possible for today's automobile industry to develop. As the development of motors has progressed since the 1950s, there has been overwhelming progress in passenger cars.

At the same time, export factors contributed greatly to the development of the Japanese automobile industry. The Japanese automobile industry exported 58 per cent of its passenger-car production in

151

1985; this is a major cause of trade friction. In the 1950s, Japanese passenger-car exports were near zero. In 1960, Toyota gave up on exports to the United States. Japanese passenger cars were totally lacking in international competitiveness in that, for example, they could not withstand high-speed driving, they were heavy, they had many problems, and they required much spending on repairs.

It took a long time for the international competitiveness of Japanese passenger cars to be formulated. Currently, the Japanese lean production system is famous in many countries. The Toyota production system was generalized by the MIT group. Toyota Motor Company began introducing parts of the system in 1949, and it was considered to be complete in the 1960s. First, it involved multi-job workers; then it added multi-process work. Then, team production, standardization of production, automation, and the so-called "just-in-time" system were completed. These contributed to strengthening the international competitiveness of Japanese passenger-car producers.

During this time, innovation among the Big Three automobile producers in America stood still. One of the factors that caused this was that the American manufacturers were slow to downsize; another factor is that the excellent Japanese passenger-car production technology surpasses that of the American automobile manufacturers in value and quality. These are major factors. However, today, there has been a remarkable recovery in the international competitiveness of the American Big Three manufacturers. A factor that has contributed to American recovery is the appreciation of the yen. American automobile makers established long-term contract relationships with parts manufacturers, and they learned design work and many other things from the Japanese automobile industry. In Europe, Volkswagen and Mercedes Benz have been learning the lean production system.

It is a very interesting problem as to how the Chinese automobile industry will go about learning the process. One should note here that one of the advantages for the development of the Japanese automobile industry was that it started development relatively late. This means that Japanese automobile makers could learn from the trial and error of the advanced countries. There was an opportunity for the Japanese automobile industry to select better production methods. Therefore, it is expected that, as China moves toward developing an automobile industry, Chinese automobile makers can tap into the advantage of starting development later than the automobile industries in Japan, the United States, and Europe.

The next theme covers management reform in the Chinese national corporations. First, Professor Mitsuo Morimoto of Aoyama Gakuin University proposed some questions about the direction of institutional reforms among the Chinese national corporations, concerning the transition to commissioned management responsibility, the downsizing of the national corporations, and the introduction of stock ownership in coordination with the other measures.

It was especially emphasized that it is necessary to recognize the possibilities of various responsibility systems, depending on the levels of autonomy of the national corporations. As far as the stock ownership system is concerned, a company system was proposed with stock ownership residing among many small stockholders, and the major force would reside with the employee stockholding system. This was a very bold and yet fresh proposal. Regarding this proposal, Professor Wu Jiajun of the Institute of International Economics, Chinese Academy of Social Sciences, commented that, although the national government is against the idea of making national stock non-decision-making priority stock, he personally is in favour of this. In the sense of promoting autonomous management, there is a proposal to promote the co-holding of stocks in order to lower the ratio of stocks held by the national government. Then, Professor Oleg Vikhanski, of the School of Business Administration at Moscow State University, made a realistic comment based on experience of the reforms in the former Soviet Union and Russia. He commented that, in general, he agrees with Professor Morimoto, but he has some questions about the transition to an employee stockholding system.

At the end of 1993, there were already 25 million stockholders in China, and it is said that the ratio of common stock to company assets is gradually increasing. In the background of this development is the fact that it is no longer possible to use huge amounts of national funds to cover the "red ink" of companies. Instead, it seems there is an intention to use the savings in the cities and agricultural villages, and the amount of the savings is said to be 2×10^{12} yuan, as sources for industry. At the same time, as to the form of corporate ownership, there is a considered judgement that it is desirable to have common stock and limited responsibility for corporations and, for this, it is desirable to have large- and medium-size companies.

However, there would be problems in realizing all of these conditions at once. In order to realize independent management of corporations as the market economy enlarges, it is necessary to allow management capabilities to grow at the same time. For the reforms in

153

forms of ownership to progress without the expansion of management capabilities would create much uncertainty about the survival and competitiveness of the independent corporations. In other words, unless streamlining and modernization of corporate management progresses simultaneously, corporate reform may end up as empty theory with the only reforms being in ownership structure.

However, contemporary corporate structures are very complex, and it is not possible to extract one, single, ideal type. For example, large Japanese corporations differ from large American corporations in various ways. The large stockholders in American major corporations are institutional stockholders, but the effective management of corporate heads is checked while at the same time they are provided with incentives such as stock options. However, as a result, a problem of major income differences among employees has emerged. Whether to consider this as a problem is a question involving a certain value judgement. In Japan, the income difference between management and employees is quite small, seven- or eightfold to tenfold; in the case of the United States, 70- to 80-fold differences are common. This problem should be considered as a management problem.

However, Japanese corporations are not stock-owner corporations, in that employee interests are considered first and stockholder interests second. In that sense, Japanese corporations are employee corporations. For example, the stockholder capital–profit ratio is very low and the dividend ratio is very low. In this sense, it has been questioned whether Japanese corporations are or are not capitalist corporations. As globalization progresses, in a sense, this is working as a reforming power on Japanese management and Japanese corporate structure.

It is said that about 45 per cent of the stocks listed on the Tokyo Stock Exchange are held in cooperation. When two companies hold each other's stocks, the management of one company cannot very well exercise checks on the management of the other company. This can be said to represent an erosion of stockholder rights in Japanese corporations. This has also led to the situation where an objective evaluation system of Japanese management is very unhealthy. However, it would be very difficult to make judgements as to whether Japanese management can really take over the American management structure – or whether it should do so.

It is under such circumstances that we should consider the direction in which China is heading. Professor Morimoto proposes, after much consideration, a common stock system with major forces residing in employee stockholder companies, which taps into the reality of socialism. There is a problem in this as to whether checks on management are carried out correctly. In this sense, we need to consider the forms that Chinese management and corporations are going to take. But it is not only China that is experimenting with this problem: Russia is facing similar situations; in the so-called capitalist countries, the United States and Japan are not necessarily satisfied with the current structures. In this sense, it is very interesting to question what the structures of corporations and management are going to be like in the twenty-first century.

Session III
Politics and society

6

Asia since the Cold War and the new international order: The historical perspective and future prospects

Satoshi Amako

Introduction

The term "Cold War" refers to the state of sustained tension, unaccompanied by overt warfare, that existed between two blocs defined by opposing ideologies and political systems – that is, democracy and the free market versus communism – and specifically between the United States and the Soviet Union, the two nuclear superpowers at their core. The Cold War in Asia underwent a gradual thawing process after the 1972 *rapprochement* between the United States and China, while the disintegration of the Soviet Union and Eastern Europe in 1991 led to the fundamental collapse of the Cold War structure. And although some of the major issues of the Cold War era persist (such as those involving Taiwan and the Korean Peninsula), we are now witnessing a trend toward the globalization of economic activity and the flow of information, with an accompanying shift away from ideological agendas. Thus, there is no doubt that we are entering a new stage.

This report will address the following three topics. First, I will review the basic characteristics of international relations in post-Cold War Asia. Second, I will focus on China as a country that has a major impact on international relations in Asia. I will assess (a) China's political, economic, social, and military position; (b) the Chinese world view and approach to foreign policy; and (c) several scenarios for China's own future after Deng Xiaoping. Third, based on those analyses, I will offer several possible paradigms of the new international order in Asia in the coming century, and at the same time present my own view of the region's future.

1. Chief characteristics of the political structure in post-Cold War Asia

(a) Asia has gradually evolved as an independent region, with sustained economic growth being a major factor in that evolution.
(b) While the enmities of the Cold War era are atrophying, relationships involving coexistence without reunification continue in force.
(c) Reflecting the new reality of post-Cold War political issues, the regional political situation is growing increasingly complex and diverse. This includes regional conflicts with a background of irrational factors, the politicization of non-political disputes, and the existence of psychological threats.

Let's take a look at some concrete examples of (a) – regional independence. Following Japan's development into an economic power in the 1960s and early 1970s, economic ties have evolved in a climate of prosperity unparalleled in other regions, due largely to the rapid growth of the newly industrializing economies (NIEs) and the Association of South-East Asian Nations (ASEAN) since the late 1970s, as well as to China's open-door policy and its links to Hong Kong. The good-neighbour relationships and peaceful coexistence necessary to guarantee these economic ties have evolved at the same time.

ASEAN, in particular, is playing an increasingly important role as an intraregional unifying and coordinating mechanism. This is something Asia has lacked until now. In July of this year the ASEAN Regional Forum (ARF) was held in Bangkok, bringing together 18 countries and organizations, including the United States, Japan, China, and the EU. The participants addressed the problems of the Asian region as a whole, in both the economic and political spheres, with particular emphasis on security. They agreed to work toward formulating confidence-building measures.

The typical forms of (b) – coexistence without reunification – are China–Taiwan and the Korean Peninsula. In both cases, the end of the Cold War has seen the division and confrontation engendered in Asia in the early 1950s gradually transformed into non-confrontation and coexistence. The nature of the relationship between China and Taiwan, in particular, has been altered by a rapid increase in non-political (especially economic) contacts since the mid-1980s, to the point where the two are now inseparably tied. On the Korean Peninsula, military tension has been greatly eased by South Korea's pursuit of the so-called "northern policy" since the mid-1980s, the North–South prime ministers' talks in the early 1990s, the simultaneous admission of the two Koreas to the United Nations, and the normalization of relations between China and South Korea.

Nevertheless, the evolution of such non-confrontational relations does not necessarily mean that reunification is any nearer in either case. In the case of China and Taiwan, for example, not only has Taipei rejected Deng Xiaoping's call for a "one state, two systems" arrangement, but a movement toward solidifying the Taiwanese identity has emerged, including the right of self-determination, and a scenario for reunification seems anything but close at hand. As for the two Koreas, the North's suspected nuclear programme has further undermined stability in the region, and this problem, coupled with the North's poor economic performance and the unsettled political situation following the death of President Kim Il Sung, has stalled progress on the reunification issue.

There are many examples of (c) – the increasing complexity and diversity of regional issues. They include the following: confrontations between China and ASEAN on the one hand and the Western nations on the other over human rights, environmental issues, and economic development; the mounting ethnic movements in Tibet and among the Uighur and other groups; territorial disputes in the South China Sea; increasingly serious trade imbalances that have become politically sensitive issues between China, Taiwan, South Korea, the United States, ASEAN, and others; growing arms exports within the region; and the emerging perception that certain nations are security threats, owing to ongoing regional frictions and the trend toward greater military spending.

China is deeply involved in areas (a), (b), and (c). In some cases the involvement is direct; in others, China exerts a strong influence. Let me turn, then, to China, the focus of my second topic.

2a. Characteristics of China's world view and approach to foreign policy

First, Beijing places a strong emphasis on the nation-state as the basic determinant of international relations. In other parts of the world, the spread of free-market mechanisms and information technology is leading to a breed of internationalization that has broad economic and social dimensions; in the political sphere there are increasing expectations that national barriers will be lowered through the universal recognition of human rights and democracy. In China, on the other hand, the former has been accepted but the latter has not, and the advocacy of human rights and democracy by outside forces is viewed by Beijing as interference in China's internal affairs and an infringement of its sovereignty.

This emphasis on the supremacy of the state has its roots in Chinese tradition (in the doctrine of *zhiguo pingtianxia*, literally, "ruling the state and maintaining peace throughout the realm"), as well as in China's modern history (in the harsh experience of invasion by the Great Powers, and the lack of individualism in relation to the state). Thus, even today, China's view of international affairs is marked by a firm belief in the centrality of relations between nation-states. International cooperation and peaceful coexistence are also viewed essentially as issues between nation-states. The Chinese position is noteworthy, given the prevailing mood in post-Cold War debate, which favours a UN-centred model of international relations with partial waiving of national sovereignty, and emphasizes universal, supranational values.

Second, there is a strong prevailing perception that "total national strength" determines the role that a nation plays and the influence that it wields in international affairs. In February 1990, Deng Xiaoping said that "to measure the strength of a nation, one must view it in a total and comprehensive way." In May 1991, Jiang Zemin emphasized that "international competition is ultimately a contest of total national strength." The phrase "a contest of total national strength" may very well indicate that Jiang sees international relations basically in terms of a power game.

Total national strength is determined primarily by the various elements of a country's resources, including economy, science and technology, national defence, foreign relations, culture; by its capacity for survival and growth; and by its relationships on the international scene. Since the promotion of reform and the open-door policy is intended to increase total national strength (see *Nanxunjianghua*, by Deng Xiaoping [February 1992]), it is undeniably a national goal of the Beijing government to achieve big-power status by bolstering the nation's strength.

Third, China's foreign policy emphasizes that multiple major powers are the central elements of the international political structure, and the country leans toward the view of an international order shaped by these powers. After World War II, the Chinese viewed the international order in the bipolar terms of the Cold War. This perception, one might add, reflects the Chinese consciousness of international class struggle – namely, the forces of socialism versus capitalism, and imperialism versus national liberation. But after the Sino-Soviet alliance soured, Beijing's view of the international order shifted, and the formula of the "three worlds" was born, the tripolar model of the strategic triangle. With the end of the Cold War, the present situation is seen as one stage in the transition to a multipolar world, with a structure that analysts describe variously as having "five poles," or "one superpower and several strong powers," for example. In any case, the Chinese view of the international system is best described as one based on a polarity of leadership among several major powers.

Fourth, China's basic approach in dealing with specific international problems has been through bilateral contacts, with a strong dimension of power politics. There was a period during the 1950s when solidarity with fellow socialist nations was of paramount importance, but otherwise the Beijing government has basically pursued an independent and autonomous foreign policy and remains firmly committed to maintaining this autonomy, at least where Chinese interests are at stake. In consequence of this, China has a strong aversion to third-party intervention, whether by another nation or an international organization, preferring to handle problems through direct negotiation or confrontation with the country or region concerned. At the same time, the traditional doctrines of *yiyi zhiyi* (playing one foreign power against another) and *hezong lianheng* (being united or split according to the circumstances) are strongly evident in Beijing's diplomatic negotiations, along with power-political thinking such as "the enemy of my enemy is my friend."

2b. Scenarios for China in the post-Deng Xiaoping era

In examining various post-Deng scenarios, I shall exclude the more extreme possibilities (i.e. the political chaos of a succession struggle, or collapse of the entire communist system) in order to focus on the basic characteristics of the different ruling systems likely to take shape depending on the basic direction adopted in political and economic policy.

Scenario 1

Under central initiative, top priority is given to maintaining nation-wide political stability while pursuing economic growth. In this case, the political system would move toward unified authoritarianism. The priority given to political stability would set strict limits on democratization. Scenario 1 is, in fact, the response chosen by the central leadership after the Tiananmen Square incident in 1989, and the situation today can be judged, on the surface, to be moving in this direction.

Scenario 2

The centre seeks both political and economic development simultaneously, while accepting the risk of some degree of political unrest. In this case, the political system would move toward democratic institutions approaching those of the West. This was the direction taken, to a point, by Hu Yaobang and Zhao Ziyang in the 1980s. The experience of Japan and the NIEs indicates that, sooner or later, stable economic growth makes political democratization inevitable. Yet the Chinese leadership seems unlikely to choose this direction within the next few years. The question is whether they will succeed in shifting gradually to scenario 2 after scenario 1 has been established to some extent.

Scenario 3

Those regions, especially on the coast, that have made real gains during the years of reform and the open-door policy begin to give top priority to their own regional interests, and a weakened central authority is unable to bring them back into line. In scenario 3a, regional leaders would then place political stability high on their agendas, and there would be a shift to rival local authoritarian, or cascade-type, governments. In scenario 3b, each region would seek political democratization along with economic development, and there would be a movement toward a federation type of democratic system. However, 3b is probably a scenario viable only over the long term.

In the short term (or the medium term, taking us into the first part of the twenty-first century), scenarios 1 and 3a are the most likely. In either process, those domestic policy makers who put state and national interests first will continue to prevail, and democracy is not likely to make significant progress. China's world view and foreign policy approach are also unlikely to undergo any major changes in terms of the characteristics noted in section 2a.

Let me now present my personal view of the international order in Asia in the coming century.

3. Paradigms of the new order and the impact of China in the twenty-first century

In terms of paradigms of a new order centred on peace and security arrangements, I would suggest five main possibilities: (1) a unipolar (lone superpower) model; (2) a new Cold War (bipolar) model; (3) a new great triangle model; (4) a multiple-framework, multiple-layered coexistence model; (5) a United Nations-centred model.

The unipolar leadership of paradigm 1 can be defined, in terms of contemporary reality, as an order maintained by the hegemony of the United States alone. During the Gulf War, a "new world order" was seriously considered both in the United States and elsewhere, given the demise of the Soviet Union. But there is little doubt that the Chinese would strongly oppose such dominance, and, given the total national strength of the United States today, China would not consider it feasible. Leaving aside questions of feasibility, we may note that the preceding analysis leaves open the possibility that the Chinese themselves may, in the distant future, pursue paradigm 1 with China as the lone pole. We should also remember that the notion of *huayi zhixu* (order between China and the barbarians) has long had a place in Chinese tradition.

Paradigm 2, a Cold War (bipolar) model, is predicated on China becoming a military superpower and the United States maintaining its strength. This type of thinking is particularly strong among Chinese military leaders, who are adamant in their opposition to American diplomatic pressure for *heping yanbian* (peaceful evolution) and human rights, and in their assertion of territorial rights. However, many of China's weapons are outmoded, and, in a contest of total national strength, the possibility that China could effectively rival the United States militarily is minimal over the short to medium term.

Paradigm 3, a new great triangle model, holds that in the near future the triangular relationship between the United States, Japan, and China will be the pivotal one in international relations in the Asia-Pacific region. He Fang contends that, since the Cold War

important changes have taken place in power relations and their groupings in the Asia-Pacific region, especially among the major powers. Competition and coordination between the US and Japan have replaced the US–Soviet rivalry as the chief factors affecting the regional situation, and the new triangle of China–US–Japan has begun to play an important balancing role in place of the China–US–Soviet triangle.

It should be noted, however, that the positions or roles of the United States, China, and Japan in the international community are neither homogeneous nor balanced, nor is the structure or nature of the bilateral relationships among them. Thus, while it is true that the new triangle has already become a significant factor in international relations, it seems premature to conclude that it is integral to the structure of a new order.

Paradigm 4, a multiple-framework, multiple-layered coexistence model, proposes that a number of different frameworks for interdependence and trust will be developed – at both the government and private levels – in areas such as politics, defence, economics, culture, and information. These frameworks would overlap and interlink so as to form an overall security mechanism. The coexistence of many forums at different levels is an example of the movement in this general direction. Such forums include the Asia-Pacific Economic Cooperation (APEC) summit, which has become the venue for the most comprehensive intergovernmental talks in the political and economic arenas; the Pacific Economic Cooperation Council (PECC), a similar framework in the private sector; ARF, which is expected to be instrumental in creating confidence-building measures for political and security matters; and ASEAN itself, which aims to form a community in the South-East Asian region.

Paradigm 5, a United Nations-centred model, seeks to create and maintain order by restraining policing actions by individual powers, forging the United Nations into a single cohesive centre, and giving it authority over the relations between states. This idea was seriously pursued at the end of World War II, and the debate has been renewed since the Cold War ended. But individual nations have widely divergent attitudes toward the United Nations, and there are also major constraints on its organizational, financial, and personnel resources. Thus, in the short run, conditions do not favour the realization of this model.

Overall, then, the optimum direction for the future is probably a combination of paradigms 4 and 5. There are several reasons for this. First, Asia is home to a wide diversity of political views and systems, economic levels and methods of economic development, cultures, religions, customs, and ethnic groups. Moreover, the potentially divisive issues are very complex. It would be difficult, therefore, to create a highly systematic, "one-size-fits-all" security framework and ensure that it functioned adequately. Second, the hub-and-spokes pattern of security arrangement, with the United States as the hub, has been changed owing to the dismantling of the anti-Soviet strategy, a decreased American military presence, and the rising independence of each nation in Asia. Third, any kind of polar structure (whatever the number of poles) ultimately tends toward a power game between the major powers, as typified by a struggle for hegemony. In such power games, the interests of the big powers are likely to override those of weaker nations, and the rivalry between powers tends to escalate too far. The attitudes taken by the United States and China will be crucial in determining whether a framework that combines paradigms 4 and 5 is to be created.

Comments

Chen Qimao

First of all, I would like to congratulate Professor Amako on his excellent summary and remarks on the situation of post-Cold War Asia and the emerging new world order. However, this does not mean I agree with all of his viewpoints.

My following comments will be limited to within the Asia-Pacific area, i.e. the East Asian and the West Pacific areas. Since Asia is so wide-ranging and complicated, it is impossible to analyse it briefly, and I noticed that Professor Amako's presentation concentrated also on the Asia-Pacific area.

With regard to section 1, there are two different perspectives to the situation in post-Cold War Asia. First, although there still exist in Asia a number of instability factors generated during the Cold War period, such as the unsolved historical disputes about territory and sea issues, and the increase in military spending, the overall situation in Asia today is fairly sound. The marked decrease in areas of tension, the relative stability of politics, the rapid economic development, and the widespread acceptance of collaboration and negotiation among the countries concerned, all make Asia a striking contrast to the post-Cold War European case, where political upheavals and economic stagnation are being witnessed. Many Chinese scholars share this viewpoint. Second, it is thought that the Asia-Pacific area may generate great turmoil or even become a new source of a world war (the Korean Peninsula, the South China Sea, among others) and therefore may not be safer or more stable than Europe. Many Western experts accept this opinion.

With regard to section 2, just as implied by Professor Amako, the key disagreement revolves around the role of China: will China become a force devoted to peace and stability in the Asia-Pacific area and even the world, or will it become a force of instability?

When the Cold War finished, some Western people concluded that China would follow the former Soviet Union into a state of turmoil and disintegration. Several nearby Asia-Pacific countries were also afraid of the resulting effects of turmoil in China. Since the autumn of 1992, owing to the increased opening-up of China, the reforms, and the faster development of the Chinese economy, people believing in a "threat from China" began to see it as a great undeveloped country which might be in a position to destabilize the existing balance of power in the Asia-Pacific area and seek control over the region once it becomes strong enough.

Although there are still many attempts to analyse the possibility of instability occurring in China, recent reports by the international media commonly tend to agree that the trend for China to upgrade itself and become a strong country is basically inevitable, despite the existence of many uncertainties, which unfortunately I will not be able to discuss here. In this comment I will only analyse the influence of a more fully developed and stronger China on the peace and stability of the Asia-Pacific area and the world.

China is a socialist country and pursues a foreign policy of independence and peace. This policy holds as a goal the defence of world peace, and depends on a lasting peaceful and safe international environment for the modernization of China. It treats the Five Principles of Peaceful Coexistence (mutual respect for territorial integrity and sovereignty; mutual non-aggression; non-interference in other nations' internal affairs; equality and mutual benefit; and peaceful coexistence) as its elementary principles when dealing with other countries. Professor Amako regarded China's foreign policy as strength diplomacy. However, I think that, in fact, every country establishes its foreign policy on the basis of its own strength, just as the so-called "weak country without diplomacy." Nevertheless, strength diplomacy is not the characteristic of China's foreign policy. As a matter of fact, China is a country that regards the Five Principles of Peaceful Coexistence very highly. On the basis of these elementary principles, not only does China resolutely not intend to seek a sphere of influence outside its own territory, it also opposes contending for hegemony and the distribution of spheres of influence between the superpowers. Moreover, China will not permit infringement of its sovereignty nor will China allow itself to be brought into the sphere of influence of another superpower. Indeed, China takes the issues of state sovereignty, independence, and self-reliance very seriously, not only because of its history of invasions by imperialist and colonialist powers in the past, but also because of the existence of unfair relationships between the strong powers and weak powers, the rich states and the poor states. Even in the post-Cold War world, China takes these issues seriously also, owing to the existence of hegemony and power politics. China still feels that its security faces a certain amount of realistic and potential threat, yet China has never intended to increase its security by damaging the sovereignty of other states. As an Asian country, China's interest is crucially related to peace and stability in the entire Asian region. In history, a so-called "safe region" established by the capitalist big powers for their own safety was usually held on the premise of invading or harming the territorial integrity and sovereignty of other countries. Derived from this premise, after World War II, the Soviet Union also built up a surrounding "safe region," and thus damaged the sovereignty and territorial integrity of its neighbours. The concept of a "safe region" and its establishment has been abandoned by China because it violates the foreign policy of peace. For the sake of safety, China is actively pursuing a good-neighbour policy in the Asia-Pacific area to establish good relations with neighbouring countries on the basis of the Five Principles of Peaceful Coexistence.

With regard to border and territorial disputes among other countries, China consistently advocates resolving the problems through peaceful negotiations or, when circumstances are not favourable, shelving the disputes temporarily and conducting common development, or maintaining the existing situation, avoiding military contact on both sides and opening a controlled border to develop friendly border trade. In recent years China has also actively participated in multilateral security talks in the Asia-Pacific region. Even though military expenditure in China has increased since 1989, to a great extent the purpose has been to counteract the effects of inflation, and to gradually replace out-of-date military facilities. The Chinese navy is used only for coastal defence, and it does not compete with the navies of the United States and Russia, nor with those of Japan and

India. The security of sea routes in the Asia-Pacific region is closely associated with the interests of many Asia-Pacific nations and should therefore be commonly discussed and resolved by the interested countries. China is not trying to control the sea routes of the Asia-Pacific region solely and is also incapable of doing so. The Chinese government has repeatedly declared that, now and in the future, China will not seek a sphere of influence, or fill a power vacuum, even if it were to become a strong power. This declaration is gaining the understanding and support of more and more countries.

Omnidirectional diplomacy is the characteristic of China's post-Cold War foreign policy, i.e. China is willing to develop good relationships with every country on the basis of the Five Principles of Peaceful Coexistence, including developed and developing countries, the United States and Russia, Arab countries and Israel, the Democratic People's Republic of Korea, and the Republic of Korea. Indeed, Mao Zedong said that drawing a distinction between ourselves, our friends, and the enemy is the most important issue of revolution. This doctrine may have been appropriate in the revolution and war era. However, as pointed out by Deng Xiaoping, instead of war and revolution, today's theme is peace and development. Also, it is not wise to draw a line between friends and enemies. This important change concerning China's foreign policy ought to be noticed by the world.

China's foreign policy of peace is determined by the property and interests of the existing Chinese government, rather than one specific government leader. Economically, China has lagged behind the developed Western countries for over 100 years and in the past several decades has even fallen behind the "Four Little Dragons" of Asia. At present, furthermore, China is faced with the challenge of the new world revolution of science and technology. It is a problem for the existence of China whether it will be able to develop its economy in a permanent, rapid, and healthy manner while at the same time gradually decreasing the economic and scientific gaps between itself and the advanced countries. China is also confronted by great population pressures (the current population of approximately 1.2 billion has an annual rate of increase of 1.1–1.2 per cent, or 14 million people). According to the calculations of Chinese scientists, the land area of China can support only a maximum population of 1.6–1.7 billion, and by the year 2025 the population of China will have reached this maximum, given the present rate of increase. Consequently, although China had almost resolved the problem of fully feeding and clothing its 1.2 billion people by the 1980s, this problem could reappear if the new process of reform, opening, and modernization is not achieved, or if China were to be involved in a great war or some other form of upheaval. This condition requires that China, not only at present but also in the future, must insist on a foreign peace policy of independence and self-reliance, so as to be able to pay attention to its internal construction. It is without basis to suspect that China will threaten neighbouring countries once it becomes strong. On the contrary, a strong China will become a strong force for defending peace in the Asia-Pacific region as well as in the rest of the world.

Turning to Section 3, when discussing the new order in the Asia-Pacific region in the twenty-first century, it is necessary to point out one basic fact: that is, owing to the political and economic development after the Cold War, the Asia-Pacific region has become the centre of an area bringing together the United States, Russia, Japan, the Association of South-East Asian Nations (ASEAN), and China. The United States is still the strongest nation with regard to national power in the Pacific area. However, the situation of the United States itself controlling the Asia-Pacific region has disappeared for ever, because of the relative depression of the economy and the overextended battle lines in the world, which have led the United States to apply a limited force in the Asia-Pacific region. There is a crisis and many questions to be resolved in Russia after the dissolution of the former Soviet Union. The influence of Russia in the Asia-Pacific region has been greatly weakened, but because it still has a powerful military force in the area, its influence cannot be ignored. China has increasingly become an important steadying power in the political affairs of the Asia-Pacific region, and its economic status in the world will progressively increase through the process of reform and openness. But until the end of this century, the gross national product (GNP) of China will still be relatively low, thus limiting its national power. China has neither the intention nor the ability to seek a leading role in the Asia-Pacific region.

Japan has become an economic superpower and is becoming a political superpower. It cannot be doubted that the influence of Japan will continually rise. However, because of the fundamental economic contradictions between Japan and the United States, various domestic restrictions on power in Japan, and also the opposition and resistance from concerned countries in the area, the intention to create a regional leadership by Japan or to lead by a union of Japan and the

United States will be difficult to realize. With the exception of Indonesia, the member countries of ASEAN are all medium or small in size. With their union and cooperation, their standing in the areas of politics, strategy, and economics is rising increasingly, and their right to speak about Asia-Pacific affairs is correspondingly increasing as well. Now, these countries are preparing to allow other South-East Asian nations (such as Viet Nam) to join them so as to create a large alliance including all the countries in the South-East Asian region. In fact, a multipolar state of quadrilateral and five-sided arrangements between the United States, Japan, China, Russia, and South-East Asia is now forming in the Asia-Pacific region. In this area, the various powers have achieved a condition of relative balance and mutual restriction, where no one country or country group can decide everything unilaterally.

In December 1988, Deng Xiaoping suggested building a just, reasonable, and new international political order based on the Five Principles of Peaceful Coexistence. I think that this suggestion conforms to the present tide of peace and development and meets the desires of the world's people, but it has far to go before this kind of new international political order can mature on a global scale. However, in the Asia-Pacific region, it is possible to form a fair, reasonable, and new political order by paying attention to the following interpretations:

1. The trends, i.e. the shift from tension to relaxation and the replacement of confrontation with dialogue, are developing increasingly. Various conflicts and hot points have been brought under control and tensions are subsiding. Peace and development have become decisive leading factors.
2. The economy is increasing steadily and the differences between South and North are gradually decreasing.
3. A multipolar condition has been formed and a variety of powers (including developed capitalist countries, socialist countries, and developing countries) are now in relative balance, thus strongly limiting attempts to create hegemony and to rely on power politics.

Owing to complications and a large diversity of politics, economics, social systems, cultures, nationalities, and religions in this region, the new Asia-Pacific political order will not be a unitary structure. Instead, it will be a combined bilateral and multilateral, multi-level, multi-structure and multi-channel system that is similar to the fourth model suggested by Professor Amako. It is still difficult at present to construct this system in detail. The important consideration is to

173

establish this new order on the basis of the Five Principles of Peaceful Coexistence, in particular the principles of mutual respect for territorial integrity and sovereignty and non-interference in others' internal affairs. This new order will pursue a policy of equality among small and large nations and will resolve problems through negotiations between the interested countries; that is, neither the superpowers nor the other large countries (for example, the United States, Japan, or China) will be authorized by the Security Council of the United Nations. In the quadrilateral and five-sided relations, there can be no doubt that the triangle relationship between the United States, Japan, and China is the most important. Nevertheless, China will not agree to establish a "new big-triangle-relationship order" that would enable those three countries to play the leading role in the Asia-Pacific region. The common affairs of the Asia-Pacific region should be dealt with through consultation among all the Asia-Pacific countries. By doing this, many bilateral problems will be resolved through peaceful negotiations between the interested countries. It should be mandatory that the internal affairs of one country are to be resolved by that country alone, rather than with the hasty and liberal interference of regional organizations, unless the stability and safety of neighbouring regions is being affected. China will do its part for the establishment of such a fair and reasonable new Asia-Pacific political order.

Comments

Khien Theeravit

First, I would like to thank the organizer of this symposium for inviting me to be here. May I also express my sincere thanks to both Professor Amako and Professor Chen for their instructive presentations.

I do not have any serious disagreement with the ideas of the speaker and the comments of Professor Chen, but I do wish to supplement some of the points being raised and offer a different perspective on some of the issues being made.

On the political structure of Asia in the post-Cold War years, the speaker suggests that the divisions of Korea and China remain problematic for East Asia, though the issues have been transformed to non-confrontation and coexistence. The Korean tensions have been eased, especially after the signing of the US–NK agreement in Geneva on 21 October. However, North–South dialogue for reunification at the summit level has been continuously postponed since Kim Il Sung's death, as Professor Amako has already mentioned; hence, it remains problematic. On the Taiwan problem as well, I am not optimistic. While economic relations may forge ahead, even across the Taiwan Straits, an attempt by Taiwan to establish its national identity is likely to cause tension sporadically in years to come between the People's Republic of China (PRC) and its friends over the issue of proper intercourse with Taiwan.

On the political structure of Asia in the post-Cold War years, I would like to add that the American military presence in Japan and South Korea is also a Cold War legacy that remains a source of abnormality for both stability and instability in East Asia. If tensions in East Asia continue to ease, I expect that there will be greater demands in Japan and South Korea for the dismantling of the American military bases. I am raising this issue in hopes that the parties concerned be well prepared to make a smooth transition.

It should be added as well that the collapse of the Soviet Union has had an extremely positive effect on peace and stability in South-East Asia. The absence of the Soviet threat in South-East Asia has effectively removed the fear of former Soviet allies in Indo-China. And that, in turn, has paved the way for China to normalize its relations with the Indo-Chinese states, and has facilitated gradual integration of the Association of South-East Asian Nations (ASEAN) and Indo-China.

On the question of the transformation of economic structure of Asia in the post-Cold War era, I may see things somewhat differently from the speaker. It is true that economic strengths in East and South-East Asia have been growing and regional economic cooperation seems to have been strengthened, but "regional independence" can hardly be realized. Instead, *global interdependence* is the trend. China is no exception: though its economic base is large and its potential for self-sufficiency considerable, it can hardly resist the trend of comprehensive globalization.

Concerning regional conflicts in post-Cold War Asia, besides problems inherited from the Cold War era, as mentioned earlier, the speaker adds to the list – ethnic, territorial, and trade conflicts. At present, trade conflict remains political in nature. But I would like to add that territorial disputes (e.g. the South China Sea, border disputes in mainland South-East Asia) and ethnic conflict (e.g. in East Timor and Myanmar) remain security oriented. Large-scale migration in various parts of Asia also persists as a source of regional instability. Ethnic conflict and migration will intensify in countries where greater freedom and liberty are being introduced. Both ethnic conflict and migration are also parts of China's domestic problems. What roles China has played (and will play) to resolve conflict and tension in adjacent areas such as the Korean Peninsula, South China

Sea, and Myanmar are matters of mutual interest to the people of Asia. I hope that China is well aware that its neighbours are expecting China to play a constructive role in these in the years to come.

Continuing with the regional security issue, which the speaker simply touched on in passing, is the question of arms build-up in East and South-East Asia. This is a popular topic discussed among scholars of international security affairs. People tended to expect substantial disarmament world wide after the Cold War, but this was not the reality. The expansion of the Chinese naval force is often cited as a potential threat to South-East Asia. In actuality, China is no exception in terms of armaments. Great military powers like China, the United States, and even Japan have shown no sign of spending less on arms. They can equally pose a threat to regional security. Even smaller countries, like those of ASEAN, continue to increase their military spending. I am afraid that they, too, can be a threat to regional security.

On the question of Chinese foreign policy in recent years, the primary Chinese concern has been economic in nature. Even in diplomacy, they are reluctant to pose as a great power in intervening in other countries' problems. Unlike the United States, China does not like to use the United Nations to intervene in others' internal affairs. However, China has never exercised its veto power in the UN Security Council. China may not like the US approach to dealing with various security issues in Asia, like the one with North Korea, but no indication has been made that it will differ significantly from Japan in allowing the United States to play a dominant role in the security of Asia.

What will happen to China's political structure after Deng? Professor Amako projects for us three-and-a half scenarios. The last half is a popular one: a movement toward a federal type of democratic system. He said that this will be viable only over the long term. As a student of Chinese affairs, I think that this is highly unlikely, even in the long term. To end a unitary system established since the First Emperor Qin would probably invite a civil war, or chaos similar to (or even worse than) that in the former Soviet Union. It is unlikely because, first of all, the Chinese Communist Party (CCP), with the monopoly of political power, would make a pre-emptive move to replace anyone in the key position who dared to challenge such a long-established tradition. Secondly, the People's Liberation Army

(PLA), still being controlled by the CCP, would decisively crush such a move. And, finally, China is very large, and one cannot expect outside help to distort the Chinese spirit. However, we should recognize that increasing numbers of economic entities of various forms have been, and will be, introduced – such as the five special economic zones and the economic development zones of the 14 coastal cities, and including Hong Kong after July 1997. Greater autonomy is being given to economic administration. This may eventually effect changes in power structure at the provincial level. If these changes are viewed as a form of federalism in the making then, yes, it will be possible. But then a redefinition of the term "federalism" is necessary.

As for the future of China in world affairs after Deng Xiaoping, I believe that whoever has the final say in China will, none the less, not have a free hand in reversing the present trends in both domestic and international affairs. I endorse Professor Chen on this point. It is possible, as the speaker's paradigm 3 suggests, that the United States, Japan, and China will establish hegemony over Asia. The process of joint hegemony might evolve automatically. However, I doubt China will be willing to play a part voluntarily in this joint venture. I believe that China will exercise its power through the United Nations coupled with the ASEAN Regional Forum, a new creation that attempts to promote peace and stability in South-East Asia by adopting so-called "preventive diplomacy" and by promoting confidence-building measures. I believe that Professor Chen and I agree on this point.

I have some further thoughts about China's roles in the new world order. In an effort to maintain peace in Asia, China may prefer to work through the United Nations, as in Cambodia. But China would hardly agree with other permanent members of the UN Security Council in deploying troops to seek peace by force. The Gulf War was a clear case of external aggression. China has agreed on this fact, but it none the less advocated seeking peace, or restoring Kuwaiti independence, through diplomacy. So, if there were a war in an attempt to denuclearize North Korea, one cannot expect Chinese participation on behalf of the United Nations.

I am raising this point because I think this is relevant to Japan. Japan has a peace constitution, but an increasing number of Japanese are demanding that the government send armed forces to keep peace abroad under the UN flag. They have circumvented the peace constitution by dispatching troops to a number of countries. They are not for fighting – not yet, at least – but the line between keeping peace by force and using force to fight for peace is thin. In so saying, I am not against UN forces opposing external aggression, but I am very much for the Japanese peace constitution. I used to think that, with the end of the Cold War, other countries would copy the Japanese peace constitution and the United Nations should work toward that direction. But the real world has moved in the opposite direction.

7

Prospects of social development

Lu Xueyi

Introduction

The contemporary history of China since the 1840s is essentially a history in which the Chinese people have dedicated their efforts to the country's modernization. It has been an ideal for generations of Chinese to build up a modern society and to become an advanced nation in the world. This dream has begun to come true gradually since the Chinese government adopted the reform and open-door policy in 1978, which puts economic construction as a premier task of the country. At the beginning of the 1980s, the Chinese government drew up a three-stage strategy for the realization of the country's modernization. The first stage was to double the size of the gross national product (GNP) of the year 1980, and to solve the problems in the people's clothing and eating habits. This goal was basically achieved by 1987. At the second stage, a further doubling of the GNP achieved at the first stage will be accomplished so that the Chinese people can enjoy a so-called *xiao kang*-level (fairly well-off) life at the end of this century. The third stage is to take another 30–50 years to establish a modern society in China, when per capita GNP will reach the level of the middle class in developed countries, and the Chinese people will have a comparatively wealthy life. Currently, the

Chinese people are devoting themselves to the realization of *xiao kang*-level life by the year 2000. The first half of the twenty-first century will be a historic period for the Chinese people to build up a socialist modernized country with Chinese characteristics.

The implementation of the reform and open-door policy in China since 1978 has brought about great progress and change to Chinese society. At present, China is in a period of social transformation, i.e. from a traditional society to a modern society, from an agro-based society to an industrialized society, from a rural-centred society to an urban-centred society, and from a closed or semi-closed society to an open society. The structural transformation from a traditional society to a modern society is a transitional period that all developed countries have experienced, which is not special for the development of socialist society. However, owing to the special historical, cultural, and resource endowment backgrounds of Chinese society, the transformation to a society with Chinese features differs from other transformations in some aspects. An important aspect involving those Chinese characteristics is that, in addition to the transformation toward a modern society, it is also necessary to accomplish the transformation from a planned economy to a socialist market economy, which should start with a series of reforms to the system.

Such a close relationship between social transformation and economic system reform is rarely seen in the modernization of other countries. Proceeding with social transformation from a traditional society to a modern society, together with system reform from a planned to a market economy, results in structural conflict: system friction, conflicts of interest groups, conflicts of roles, and a clash of senses of value occur in the transformation and interact with each other, so that the resulting complicated situation greatly increases the difficulties of social transformation. Moreover, this social transformation and system reform is being performed in a country of 1.2 billion people whose development is imbalanced. The difficulty, complexity, and arduousness of the social transformation and system reform are consequently not hard to see. While accomplishing the transformation and reform, special attention should be paid to systematic stability, coordination, and innovation. The reform and open-door policy since 1978 has significantly advanced this historic transformation. Past practice has verified that the reform and open-door policy is not only the self-perfection of the socialist system but also is the only way to establish a modernized socialist country with Chinese characteristics.

181

The coming 16 years (1994–2010) are, for the Chinese, the most crucial phase for building up a modernized country. In the past 16 years (1978–1994), a concrete political, economic, and social foundation has been laid for the achievement of social transformation and economic system reform, through concentrating national emphasis on economic development, determining and then implementing the reform and open-door policy to perform large-scale construction of economic and social undertakings. By the year 2000, the GNP will have reached double that of 1980. Nevertheless, per capita GNP will only have reached US$800–1,000, and China will have built up only a basic framework for the socialist market economy. It is not until 2010, when the GNP of the year 2000 will have been further doubled, that state power is expected to be reasonably strong. By the year 2010, a socialist market economy will be wholly established, and will progressively become perfect, mature, and formalized so as to put the development of economic and social undertakings on a more effective basis. However, it is just during these coming 16 years that the continuation of conflict between the old and new social structures and the friction between the two systems, conflict of interest groups, and the clash of old and new senses of value, as well as chance significant events occurring at home and abroad, will have great influence on reform and modernization, and there thus exist both opportunities and challenges for the development of Chinese society. This is why the next 16 years become the most important stage for China's modernization. At present, China is already at a stage of overall economic and social development and about to cross the threshold of becoming a developed and modernized country.

The advantageous conditions for the development in China are as follows:

1. A good foundation was laid in the past 16 years: that is, Deng Xiaoping's theory for establishing a socialist country with Chinese characteristics through conducting the reform and open-door policy has been extensively accepted by the majority of Chinese people.
2. The world political environment is favourable to China. The Cold War has ended, while a new world political order is being formed, and world development is right at a cross-point connecting the old and new worlds. At this extraordinary time, many knowledgeable people believe that the twenty-first century will be the Asia-Pacific century, and the advantages of geopolitics and geoeconomy,

moreover, provide a golden development opportunity to China, which is located in an important position in the Asia-Pacific area.

3. There is an increasing trend towards economic development in China. Because of the economic system reform and the orientation of a market economy, overall industrialization has been carried out in China. It is predicted that the years 1991–2010 will be a golden period for economic development, and the annual growth rate of the GNP during these 20 years will be about 8.25 per cent. By 2010, China is expected to change to a middle-income country from a low-income country with respect to per capita income and thus, with its great population, it will become one of the top nations in the world. Some foreign experts also predict that, if China could keep its current economic development trend, by 2010 it would become the fourth biggest economic power, just behind the United States, Europe, and Japan.

On the other hand, there are also difficulties for the development of China:

1. As a whole, the achievement from development has been greater than from reform in the past 16 years, although reform is the precursor of, and promotes, development. The planned economy, operated for nearly 30 years in China, has been thoroughly involved in various aspects of social and economic development. The reform started within the agriculture sector with success, and greater confidence was thus obtained for further overall reforms, including those in urban areas and industrial sectors. Initially, the urban reforms were predicted to come into effect within 3–5 years. However, in fact, an approach suitable for the reform of large and medium state-owned enterprises has not yet been found over the past 10 years. Many problems still need to be solved in the reform.

2. Comparatively speaking, both the development of the social system and social undertakings are behind the economic reform and development. Economic structure has been adjusted, whereas the social structure (such as the urban–rural structure) has not yet made a corresponding change. It is clear to see that the country is dedicating itself to the establishment of a socialist market economy, while the development of social undertakings and system reform are still in the exploratory and trial stage.

3. There was imbalanced development in China before this reform. In recent years, the disparities between the urban and rural areas, different regions, and occupations have further increased rather

than decreased. For example, the income ratio of urban to rural residents was 2.37:1 in 1978, 1.7:1 in 1984, and 2.55:1 in 1993. Meanwhile, the disparity among the Eastern, Central, and Western regions has also increased. A potential unstable factor exists if these disparities continue to increase and cannot be solved properly. The current policy adopted by the Chinese government is to take appropriate care of the inequality in society and the regions under the condition of efficiency superiority. However, many problems still remain in actually performing this policy.

Certainly, in light of the development trend, advantageous conditions are prevailing over disadvantageous factors. The economic development land reform trends, the favourable world environment, the advantages of geopolitics and geoeconomy, and especially the great achievement from the past 16 years' reform and open-door policy in China have all laid a foundation for the sustainable development of China in future. Moreover, the political stability and the activity of a billion people participating in the reform and development are also the great potential driving force for China's development. Therefore, it is reasonable to believe that, in the next 16 years, the Chinese government will continue deepening the reform and broadening the open door, and overcoming the obstacles and harmful factors confronted in the development, so as finally to achieve sustainable economic growth and social transformation in China.

Once the target of 1995–2010 economic and social development has been achieved, China will have passed the most crucial period of building up a modernized country and will be in a relatively smooth development period with much better development prospects. Along with a high rate of economic growth and adjustment of the economic structure, the social structure and relationship will also be greatly changed. As stated above, China is now in the stage of transformation from a traditional society to a modern society, and the reform and open-door policy has greatly accelerated this transformation process. As for the social transformation, some will soon be approaching the critical turning-point, while others will need a longer period. Since China is a country of great population and area and of imbalanced development, the social transformation will be accomplished step by step in different provinces, cities, and areas in a form of gradient rather than synchronous development. By the middle of the twenty-first century, China will have completed the transformation from a traditional country toward a modern country and have wholly built up a socialist modernized country with Chinese characteristics.

The following is an analysis and prediction about several important changes in the social transformation.

Population structure

At the end of 1993, China's population record was 1,185 million; the natural population growth rate for this year was 1.145 per cent with a total birth rate of 2.16 per cent. By the year 2000, according to a prediction based on the 1990 population census data, the total population will increase to 1,287 million. Furthermore, according to this prediction, China's population growth rate will be zero at the year 2033, and the total population will reach a peak of 1,519 million. Afterwards, China will enter a new phase of population decline.

In 1990, China's illiterate or semi-illiterate population over 15 years of age was 182 million, or 16.1 per cent of the total population, a 6.7-point decrease from the 22.8 per cent in the year 1980. This is an annual rate decrease of 0.84 per cent, which shows that great progress in wiping out illiteracy has been made in this period. According to 1990 population census data, the number of people graduating from university and college for professional training were 6.14 and 9.62 million, respectively, a 9,720,000 net increase at an increase rate of 160.1 per cent compared with the 6,040,000 people holding certificates of university and college for professional training in 1982, while the total population graduating from high schools and polytechnics was 89,880,000, a 23,350,000 net increase over the 66,530,000 of 1982, at an increase rate of 35 per cent. Overall, the cultural quality of China's population has improved significantly within the last decade. Nevertheless, the educational quality of China's population is still poor, and the number of people graduating from university is only 1.4 per cent of the total population, whereas in 1987 the proportion of educated people with university degrees in the United States and European countries was above 10 per cent of the total population, and above 5 per cent in the Soviet Union and Japan.

At the end of 1990, the population over 65 years old was 64.18 million, and accounted for 5.6 per cent of the total population. It is predicted that these elderly people will reach 88 million, constituting 6.8 per cent of the total population, by 2000, and will constitute more than 7 per cent of the total population by 2004, when China will become an "ageing" country. Further, by 2030, they will rise to 219 million and constitute 14.5 per cent of the total population, which is equivalent to the population for France in 1992. Based on data from different countries, it usually takes 40–100 years for the over-65 population to rise from 5 per cent to 7 per cent of the total. This means that the population ageing process synchronizes with social and economic development. For the figure in China to take only 22 years to increase from 4.9 per cent in 1982 to 7 per cent in 2004 can be attributed to the birth control policy of the Chinese government. However, the non-synchronization of the faster ageing process with relatively slower economic development will also lead to greater difficulty in supporting those old people.

China is a country with a huge population and has met many setbacks in the problem of population and birth control. From the early 1970s, Chinese central and local governments started to conduct birth control as a basic national policy on the basis of a series of policies concerning population control, improvement of population quality, and regulation of population structure formulated in the First National Meeting on Birth Control held in 1972. Although implementation of the birth control policy (especially "one couple, one child") at first met with great resistance and was not understood by many inside and outside China, the great success in the control of China's population over the past 20 years has won over most Chinese people. The birth rate and natural increase rate of China's population have decreased markedly, to a level lower than the world average. The ratio of China's population to the world population was 23.2 per cent in 1972, falling to 22.2 and 21.49 per cent in 1981 and 1991, respectively. And according to a prediction by the planned parenthood World Population of the United Nations, this ratio will further decrease to 21.27 and 18.5 per cent in 1994 and 2025, respectively. It should be acknowledged that China's effective birth control has made a great contribution to humanity: in the words of H. Marlor, Secretary-General of the International Planned Parenthood Federation, "China is a big country, and there is a great difficulty in conducting birth control. But the Chinese government did it very well." Also, just before the International Population and Development Conference held in Cairo this September, Dr Boutros-Ghali, the Secretary-General of the United Nations, said that China has made a very important contribution to the population problem and to the relationship between population and development.

There were very strong reactions to the "one couple, one child" policy at home and abroad, and some people overseas criticized this policy for different reasons when it was carried out in China. The policy is formulated according to the specific situation in China, and is also a part of the "birth control, well treated and well educated" policy. Moreover, even though conducting such a strict policy at present, China still grows by a net 14–15 million people annually. This is why Chinese people are gradually agreeing that is very necessary to conduct this policy in our country, which has a relative shortage of per capita land and resources and needs large-scale construction. On the other hand, some Chinese people and overseas friends are afraid of carrying out this policy because Chinese children in future may become spoiled, dependent, and irresponsible as the "little sun", or "little noble" of every "4 (grandparents)–2 (parents)– 1 (child)" family, owing to the particular Chinese tradition of loving children; this could be problematic when this generation grows up in one or two decades. It is, of course, necessary to do our best to avoid this potential danger to the future of China's society. In fact, one-child families have not been so common in China from the early 1980s: in other words, the Chinese government has permitted peasant families to have two children, according to the actual production and living conditions of Chinese peasants. For example, in 1989, the ratios of newborn babies born in one-child, two-child or over-three-child families to all newborn babies were 49.5, 31.2, and 19.3 per cent, respectively. The number of families with one child in urban regions is certainly much greater than that in rural regions. Moreover, a family with one child generally has advantages in the child's growth and education, with stronger material and financial support (this is particularly important for low-income Chinese families), so that the child is able to obtain enough nourishment and living conditions for health, and to receive better education for intellectual growth. Meanwhile, when this generation of children grows up, the realization that they bear the hopes and support of their grandparents and parents will arouse their sense of responsibility. Historically, the achievements and parents will arouse their responsibility. Historically, the achievements made by some eldest children and only children have been associated with their responsibility, trained in childhood. Consequently, I am confident that it is reasonable to believe that the next few generations of "only children" will be able to do much better for our modernization.

Employment structure

The labour force totalled 681 million in 1990 (males aged 16–59 and females of 16–54), and is forecast to be 774 and 865 million in 2000 and 2010, respectively. The peak is predicted to be in 2020, with a total labour force of 893 million. From that time on, the labour force will see a declining trend toward the predicted number of 840 million in 2030. The labour force will increase annually by 9.3 and 9.1 million during the periods 1991–2000 and 2000–2010, respectively. That is, in the coming few decades, the labour supply will be exceptionally sufficient and exceed demand in the long term; therefore, the employment market will still be in the prime of life. It is necessary to make timely use of this period to develop many more labour-concentrated industries so as to exploit fully this huge labour force in economic development and accumulation of property, and to prepare the necessary materials for the future ageing society.

The GDP (gross domestic product) for 1993 was 3,138 billion yuan. Out of the total volume, the share of primary industry was 21.2 per cent, secondary industry accounted for 51.8 per cent, and tertiary industry took up 27 per cent. China's economy, it is believed, will continue to develop at a relatively high growth rate in the coming 20 years, and the industrial structure will be correspondingly adjusted. The share of secondary industry is predicted to be 52.3 per cent in 2000 and 52.8 per cent in 2000, to 17.2 per cent in 2010. In contrast, the share of primary industry will continue to decline from 17.7 per cent in 2000 to 17.2 per cent in 2010.

In 1993, the employed population over the whole country was 605,900,000 in total: of these, 347,920,000 were working in primary industry, accounting for 57.4 per cent; 135,500,000 in secondary industry, accounting for 22.4 per cent and 122,480,000 in tertiary industry, or 20.2 per cent. Furthermore, 26.7 per cent (161,560,000) were in urban areas, while 73.3 per cent (444,340,000) were in rural areas. Among the people holding jobs in urban areas, 110,940,000 were in state-owned units, accounting for 68.7 per cent, 36,060,000 were in collective enterprises (22.3 per cent), 11,160,000 were in personal and private enterprises (6.9 per cent), and 3,430,000 were in other kinds of units (2.1 per cent).

From the above data, it can be seen clearly that the present industry and employment structures in our country are inconsistent. Out of the GDP for 1993, the share of primary industry was 21.2 per cent, but in the employment structure, primary industry accounted for 57.4 per cent; the GDP share of secondary industry was 51.8 per cent, but secondary industry accounted for only 22.4 per cent of numbers employed. This structure is obviously unreasonable; it results from China's current separated urban–rural control system. The people holding urban *huko* (household registration) are in comparatively full employment (in 1993, the unemployment in townships and cities for the whole country was 4.2 million – an unemployment rate of 2.6 per cent). However, the population in rural areas cannot migrate to townships and cities at will, although the annual increase in the labour force is 10 million, of which most hold rural *huko*. Because they all have cultivated land, they are naturally considered from a conventional viewpoint already to have got jobs. The increasing labour force is therefore concentrated in rural areas. Although industrialization and urbanization in our country have developed greatly over the past 10 years of reform and openness, the population holding jobs in rural areas increased by 137,960,000, from 306,380,000 in 1987 to 444,340,000 in 1993 – that is, the labour force increased by 9,190,000 in rural areas every year. This situation does not match the fact that the population of primary industry in the GNP decreased annually.

In the coming long term, the problem of employment in our country is expected to be very serious, and the task of solving this problem will be arduous. It is necessary both to achieve full employment, while retaining working efficiency and consistently improving the labour force quality, and to reform and readjust the present unreasonable employment structure between the urban and rural areas, and among enterprises, so as to coordinate the development of an economic society.

As for labour force supply, as predicted above, the annual increase in the labour force will average 9,200,000 from now until 2010. But among 444,340,000 of the rural labour force in 1993, the population engaged in agriculture was 347,920,000. Since there is only arable land of 1,434 million mu (960,000 million hectares; i.e. 4.12 mu per worker), full employment was obviously difficult. According to one estimate, there are now 150 million surplus workers in rural areas. To achieve the goal of changing 50 per cent of the rural surplus labour force into non-agricultural employment by 2010, it is necessary for 4.5 million people to migrate from rural to urban areas each year. This means that, over the next 20 years, employment or re-employment must be arranged for about 13.7 million people. This is an extremely hard task, because people dismissed from present state-owned enterprises and institutions during the reform must also be given the chance to get jobs again.

If the additional labour force can all obtain jobs in non-agricultural occupations and a part of the surplus labour force in rural areas can be transferred to secondary and tertiary industries, then by 2010 the employment structure in our country will be improved significantly. By that time, with a primary industry share of 34 per cent, secondary industry of 36 per cent, and tertiary industry of 30 per cent, employment structure will be basically close to the output structure. This goal is expected to be achieved, as long as we keep an economic growth rate of 8–9 per cent, insist on reform in the labour employment system, fully promote the township transformation and urbanization, and develop tertiary industry step by step.

Owing to the development of the market economy, a more loosely planned system, the promotion of competitive interest, and stimulation of higher incomes, the labour force began to flow from the middle of the 1980s on a larger and larger scale. The characteristics are that the labour force moves from rural to urban areas, from inner Western to Eastern Coastal areas, from undeveloped and poorly developed areas to developed areas, from enterprises with lower marketing to those with higher marketing, from state-owned enterprises to non-state-owned concerns, and most noticeable is that the surplus rural labour force moves to cities and townships as well as secondary and tertiary industries – a phenomenon called "farmer-labour tide".

After the policy of the "household responsibility system" was implemented, farmers' initiative for production was aroused. Consequently, the available arable land came to seem insufficient, and many farmers left for cities and townships, and for secondary and tertiary industries, to find a way of developing production and increasing their wealth. In 1984, the Chinese government made two important decisions – one to promote the growth of rural enterprise, the other to permit farmers to go to townships and cities to engage in manufacturing and commercial activities. Since then, rural enterprises have developed significantly. By 1993, the labour force in rural enterprises had reached 112 million, an increase of 60.7 million over that for 1984. Many workers are said to have departed from the land while staying in their home towns: that is to say, although having become mainly engaged in second and tertiary enterprises, they are still living in their home countryside or village. Another part of the surplus rural labour force has gone to cities or different townships for work and commercial activities – a migration beyond province, district, and township boundaries. With the achievement of city reform and rapid development of various public utilities in cities such as services of construction, transport, environmental sanitation, and tertiary enterprise, the urban labour force is not enough to meet current needs. Meanwhile, the heavy, tiring, and dangerous jobs that the city labour force dislikes doing also need the extra force from rural areas. At the end of the 1980s, the labour force moving into cities and townships was about 30 million a year, with a decrease in 1989 and 1990 and an increase again in 1991 and 1992, when it finally caught the attention of society as the so-called "farmer-labour tide". This flow reached 60 million by the spring of 1994.

The central point of the "farmer-labour tide" is the transfer of the surplus rural labour force from rural areas to cities and townships, to secondary and tertiary enterprises. The kind of transfer certainly exists in a period of social transformation and has been experienced in all industrialized countries. Our country is now in a period of social transformation with a high rate of increase in the economy; however, the former planned system, *huko* system, and labour employment system have not been reformed correspondingly. Consequently, this special "farmer-labour tide" has appeared as a special form of surplus rural labour force transfer. It has contributed a great deal to making the structures of urban–rural industry and employment more reasonable, and has pushed the labour force to the places and enterprises. For large- and middle-scale cities and developed townships, which have absorbed most surplus farmer-labour, their economy has grown most rapidly, prosperously, and actively; thus, the Zhejiang Delta area has absorbed about 6.5 million farmer-labourers, and the Yangtse Delta area has absorbed about 5 million farmer-labourers. The areas that supply surplus rural labour have also been repaid, in capital, technology, as well as information, and so on. For instance, 6 million have moved out of Sichuan Province (4 million out of Henna Province, 3 million out of Anhui Province); over 6 million yuan (even more than the investment used to support agricultural development by the provincial government) has been remitted to Sichuan Province from post offices, banks, and other sources every year. However, there is also an unfavourable side to the "farmer-labour tide". Because this large-scale transfer of surplus labour force was basically spontaneous, it has exerted great pressure on transportation, public security, civil administration, family planning, and the management of cities and townships, and has resulted in a lot of social problems. At present, the governmental departments concerned have given attention to these problems and public opinion has also changed. Unlike the previous common opinion that farmer-labour was so-called "*mangliu*" (blind migrants) and was therefore restricted, repelled, and driven out, the people are now generally agreed that the advan-

Lu Xueyi

tages of this movement are more significant than the disadvantages. The public security departments have prepared to reform the *huko* control system of townships; the labour departments have also brought the transfer of labour force into their working plans; and the departments concerned are discussing and drawing up policies and methods to remove the negative influences induced by the "farmer-labour tide", so as to make the transfer of surplus labour from rural to urban areas, to secondary and tertiary enterprises, in a more orderly and unhindered way, and to make the employment structure and urban–rural structure more reasonable.

The urban–rural structure

China's reform and open-door policy started in rural areas and progressed rapidly. The rural reform changed rural society greatly and provided experience and the physical foundation for urban reform. However, the areas are also the focal points of China's difficulty in counting its reform, to develop and accomplish modernization. At present, there are still 850 million living in rural areas, accounting for 72.4 per cent of the total population. To change the greater part of them into workers and regular employees is expected to be a long and arduous process, and a lot of obstacles have to be surmounted.

From the beginning of the 1950s, a planned economy system began to be practised and a dualistic social structure that sharply separated urban and rural areas was gradually formed. In this structure, industry was built up in cities and agriculture took place in rural areas; urban residents lived in cities and farmers lived in villages; the *huko* of non-agriculture and agriculture were controlled respectively, and the transformation from agriculture *huko* to non-agriculture *huko* was severely limited. Before 1978, peasants engaging in non-agricultural work were limited and the slogan was "The hearts of people turning towards agriculture, labour force returning to farmland." However, the hearts of people turning towards agriculture made up only 28.4 per cent of the GNP, with the rural population making up 82.1 per cent of the total population and a rate of urbanization of only 17.9 per cent.

Since the reform and open-door policy in 1978, industrialization has grown rapidly, especially in rural areas; rural enterprises with rural industry as the main body have been built up. As result, the industry output value accounted for 48 per cent of the GNP in 1992 and agriculture accounted for only 23.8 per cent. However, because

192

of the limits of the *huko* system and other reasons, until 1992, out of 1,171 million of the total population, the people in rural areas were still up 72.4 per cent, the rate of urbanization being only 27.6 per cent.

During the process of modernization in China, the existing important problem is that the urbanization process has seriously lagged behind industrialization. In 1992, the rate of industrialization of China was 48 per cent, while that of urbanization was only 27.6 per cent, or 20.4 per cent less, and over 12 per cent lower than the rate of world urbanization (40 per cent). This backward situation is unfavourable to the development of modernization; economic scale benefit; the development of tertiary enterprises; the improvement of science, education, and other social utilities; the formation of agriculture scale management; and also the development of agriculture, which has caused a lot of social problems. The "farmer-labour tide" is one of the problems induced by the fact that many of those in the surplus labour force in rural areas have gone to cities for jobs. In the winter of 1993, the government made the following decisions: utilize fully and reconstruct the present small townships; build up new townships; reform the *huko* system of small towns gradually, and permit peasants to migrate to townships to engage in manufacturing and commercial activities in order to develop the tertiary enterprises of rural areas and to promote the transfer of the rural surplus labour force. By implementation of this new policy, hundreds and thousands of peasants will move to townships and cities, and this will greatly accelerate the process of China's urbanization.

In 1993, there were 560 municipalities and cities (3 are directly under the central government), 196 prefecture-ranked municipalities, and 361 country-ranked cities. There were 15,233 towns, with country governments located in 1,795 towns. Moreover, there were 32,956 market towns where town governments were located. In the same year, there were 333,051,000 people and 100,750,000 families living in cities and townships. From now on, the number of cities and townships will continue to increase, and all these municipalities, cities, and towns are expected to increase in both population and space. It is predicted that, in the year 2000, the population in cities and townships will be over 500 million (about 160 million families) and the rate of urbanization will be 40 per cent. In the year 2010, 690 million Chinese will be living in urban communities, taking up a percentage of nearly 50 per cent of the total population by that time.

Currently, there are three opinions on development strategy concerning realizing urbanization in China: one is mainly to develop townships; the second is to develop primarily middle and small cities, while the third is mainly to develop townships. Each of the three opinions has its own grounds. A lot of people working in practical departments think the best policy is mainly to develop townships, and now this policy is being carried out. I basically share this opinion. To my mind, the way to develop rural areas includes three steps: first, to promote the household responsibility system; second, to develop a town and township enterprise; third, to build townships. This process can be considered logical. Early in the 1980s, the slogan "Leaving the land but not leaving the village; entering the factory but not entering the city" was presented. Developing townships played a positive role in breaking through the urban–rural barrier at that time and supported the development of town and township rural enterprises. However, it is only a temporary transition period. If town and township rural enterprises are built up, quite a lot of farmers will have really settled down in townships. It is only a quasi-dualistic society structure (or so-called three-dimensional society structure), in which over 20 per cent of the population live in cities, 30–40 per cent in townships, and 30–40 per cent in rural areas. This is only an assumption, because this is only a transfer without migration of the population and is only a step toward urbanization. Town and township rural enterprises themselves will develop to become modern enterprises in the future of the urban–rural structure in China; the dualistic society structure must be changed, and most residents should settle in cities in order to achieve regional modernization. The so-called regional modernization means that, in the bigger areas formed by nature, geography, natural resources, environment, economic society, and historic traditional culture, a megalopolis or a large city as a centre takes some middle and small cities as intermediaries to connect many more townships and villages in the same district, to form a radiating network. As a result of this radiation, all economic and social utilities in this area are led to a coordinated growth so as to achieve industrialization, urbanization, and modernization of this whole area. In the world, there have been many examples of regional modernization. In China, several large areas are gradually coming to regional modernization earlier than other areas: these include the Beijing–Tianjing–Tangshan area, the Shanghai–Nanjing–Hangzhou area, the Guangzhou–Shenzhen–Zhuhai area, the Shenyang–Anshan–Dalian area, the Qingtao–Yantai–Weifang area, and the Fuzhou–Quanzhou–Xiamen area.

Regional patterns

China is a country with a vast territory and a great population, uneven distribution of natural resources, and significant regional disparities in economic and social development. Modern industry coexists with hand agriculture, while economically developed areas coexist with vast undeveloped and poor areas, and a small amount of scientific technology at an international level coexists with hundreds of millions of illiterate and semi-illiterate people. These significant disparities in area development have been caused by objective natural resources and a long period of history.

There are significant regional disparities in China's population and natural resources distribution. A line drawn from Aihui County in Heilongjiang Province to Ruili County in Yunnan Province would divide China's 9.6 million square kilometres of territory into two parts of equal area. However, 90 per cent of the total population is concentrated in the south-east area, where there are relatively few energy and mineral resources. In the north-west part, however, only 10 per cent of the total population reside because of the dry, cold weather and lack of water, while a greater part of the nation's mineral resources are found, such as coal, natural gas, petroleum, metals, and rare earth metals. There are gorges, highlands, and grassland. This separation of natural resources from the population results in great difficulties in the rational distribution of production and coordinated growth of the economy and society. The political and economic centre of the Chinese nationality was originally in the north central plains. After the Northern and Southern dynasties in the fifth century A.D., the heart of the economy turned to the southern area; from then on, the Yangtse Valley economic area gradually replaced the Yellow River economic area, to become the heart of China's economy. For state defence and other reasons, the political and military centre is still in the north, and thus a separation of the economic centre from the political heart has been formed. From 1840, aggression by foreign capitalism began from the trading ports in the southeast coastal area, with its good agricultural foundation and vast population. This area had also had the most developed foreign trade in the times of the Tang–Song dynasties, and grew rapidly with a relatively well-developed commercial economy around cities such as Shanghai, Hangzhou, Ningbo, Xiamen, Fuzhou, and Guangzhou. Some modern industry and commercial enterprises were then built up.

After the founding of the People's Republic of China, large-scale industrialization began in the 1950s. To meet the needs of the international environment and national defence, during the periods of the first and second Five-Year Plans and the regime of the Third Frontier construction, most projects were carried out in the interior and the north-east of the country. Moreover, some industrial, scientific, and educational institutions were moved, with establishment of manufacturing bases in cities in the central and western parts of China, such as Baotou, Shijiazhuang, Zhengzhou, Luoyang, Xiangfan, Shiyan, Xianyang, Baòji, Mianyang, and Xichang, thus contributing to a certain extent to improvements in production capacity distribution and area structure. Some problems remained, such as the role of coastal cities, the industrial base not being fully used, and the economic benefits not being so good.

Since implementing the reform and open-door policy, the strategy of China's economic development has turned to economic benefits and the focal point of economic construction has moved to the coastal areas. First of all, special economic zones were established in Shenzhen, Zhuhai, Shantou, and Xiamen, and soon 14 other coastal cities were opened, including Dalian, Tianjin, Qingdao, Lianyungang, Shanghai, Ningbo, Fuzhou, Guangzhou, and Beihai. With the superiority of original capital, technology, qualified people, and fundamental institutions in these areas and the introduction of foreign investment, advanced technology, and modern management, these areas developed rapidly. In order to give full play to comparative regional advantages and strengthen the direction of macroeconomic construction, depending on the growth level of the economy and technology, geographical structure, and resources distribution of the region, the country was divided into three economic belts – east, central, and west. Eleven cities in the eastern area, including Beijing, Tianjin, Hebei, Shandong, Jiangsu, Shanghai, Zhejiang, Fujian, Guangdong, Guangxi and Hainan, were defined as developed areas; the nine provinces and regions in the central area (Heilongjiang, Jilin, Shanxi, Henan, Hubei, Hunan, Jiangxi, Anhui, and Shaanxi) as poorly developed areas; and eight provinces and regions in the western area, including Sichuan, Yunnan, Guizhou, Gansu, Xining, Qinghai, Ningxia, and Xinjiang as underdeveloped areas. Certainly, this kind of division is only relative and the factors of geographical structure and administrative regional division were considered to a large extent. In fact, a province in China is very large, such as Sichuan Province with 100 million people in 0.56 million square kilometres, and it also can be divided into three types, according to developmental stage – developed, quasi-developed, and developing areas. So the division only approximately shows the current economic developing level of various provinces and regions.

Over the last decade, the coastal cities have benefited from the policy of reform and open door and have taken the lead in relaxing policies and developing a market economy, so that the economy in these areas has grown fast, while the central area has followed them. As a result, the former regional disparity has been significantly increased. From 1982 to 1992, the total output value of industry and agriculture in Guangdong Province increased from 41.5 billion to 492 billion yuan; per capita farmer's annual income increased from 182 yuan to 1,307 yuan. Meanwhile, the total output value of industry and agriculture in Guizhou Province increased from 10,190 million to 44,620 million yuan; per capita farmer's yearly income increased from 108 yuan to 506 yuan. Thus, in 1982, the total output value of industry and agriculture for Guangdong was 3.07 times that for Guizhou Province, and had increased to 11.03 times that for Guizhou by 1992. In 1982, per capita farmer's yearly income was 1.69 times that in Guizhou and had increased to 2.58 times by 1992. This is only an average comparison between the two provinces and for a precise comparison between counties, cities, townships, families, and persons, the disparity would be much more marked.

On the basis of large-scale construction over the past decade, the eastern coastal area has strengthened its economic power, basic facilities, and self-development ability, and improved its investment environment so that it has absorbed not only overseas capital and technology but also a large amount of talented people, labour, and capital from the central and western areas. As a result, the existing regional disparities in China's economic and social development will continue for a relatively long time and the gap between the eastern area and the central and western areas will be further enlarged, rather than reduced.

In the process of industrialization, this interregional disparity is unavoidable, owing to the pressure of market forces, and is also helpful for economic development in some specific periods, since it forms a graded state of development over the country that results in a wave of lasting economic growth with regard to the progressive adjustment of industrial structure and enlargement of market capacity. However, this disparity, especially the income gap between different areas, must be controlled within reasonable limits; otherwise, it would cause various social contradictions and lead to instability in social and economic development. Special attention should be paid to how to choose a suitable opportunity to speed up the development of the central and western areas – in particular the north-western and south-western areas where minorities are living – with the aid of governmental macro-readjustment. In fact, various preferential policies implemented by the central government to accelerate the pace of development of rural enterprises in the central and western areas since the 1990s have come into effect, and some rural entrepreneurs of the eastern coastal area have also been seeking development in the central and western areas. Through many years of geological prospecting, it has been found that there are very rich petroleum, natural gas, coal, and other mineral resources in Xinjiang and exceptionally abundant amounts of coal and natural gas in Inner Mongolia. The Chinese government is aiming at the construction of transportation, communication, and basic facilities in these areas for the future large-scale development of the north-western area. With the objective of building up a socialist modernized country and achieving common prosperity across the country, by the end of this century and the early part of the coming century, the Chinese government will transfer the strategic economic emphasis to the development of the central and western areas so as to balance progressively the geographical structure of the economy. This transfer is to increase the total social and economic level in the central and western areas and, furthermore, is a new economic growth point for the increase of the whole national economy.

On the whole, China is currently in a historical period of transformation from a traditional society toward a modern society. In the first half of the twenty-first century, China will achieve this transformation to become a socialist modernized country, and this chapter only describes some major aspects of this transformation. The actual transformation must be more complex than that described here, and there must be many tortuous and difficult processes, even reversals, needing to be solved in accomplishing the transformation. However, for the Chinese people, the direction and means of achieving the transformation are clear and the objective of building up a socialist modernized China is certain to be achieved.

Comments

François Gipouloux

Professor Lu Xueyi is correct in emphasizing the double change – in economic system and social structure – occurring as the process of Chinese modernization. To be sure, Professor Lu has captured the essence of the dilemma caused by the changes underlying the tremendous transformation of the Chinese economy. The reform and open-door policy is not merely a means of adjusting the numerous deficiencies borne by this highly bureaucratic and inefficient economic system; it is a maelstrom in which no sector of Chinese society has been left untouched. Such a dramatic change in less than two decades has seldom occurred in modern Chinese history, ever since the irruption of Western powers, in the mid-nineteenth century. It has brought high growth and greater affluence to coastal areas, to some parts of the countryside, and to urban residents. It has also brought a great deal of instability and uncertainty. Let me concentrate my comments on the following points of Professor's Lu presentation.

The urban–rural divide

Although the revenue gap between urban and rural residents was wider during the Maoist era, 16 years of continued growth have not narrowed the urban–rural gap in China. Erosion of revenue, and fiscal abuses by local authorities, have led to unrest in rural areas, as spectacularly illustrated by the riots in Sichuan Province in May 1993. But the problems are not limited to the revenue gap or fiscal extortion. Growth and economic reforms have also led to an erosion of the traditional means of social control. As millions of peasants are seeking a better life in cities, or simply a way of escaping the growing hidden unemployment in the countryside, the *huko* system, or the assigning of residence through administrative control, has gradually unravelled. The gap dividing the urban from the rural population in China is not only an economic one: it is also an administrative one, used and reinforced by the Chinese Communist Party (CCP) in the early 1950s. Even today, those born in rural families can never become anything more than peasants, and must marry peasants. Access to a better education or health care is also denied to rural residents. However, there is no new system allowing for the accommodation of millions of peasants in the cities. They are usually employed in the burgeoning Town and Village Enterprises or the construction sector, have low wages and precarious labour conditions, and also form the bulk of urban delinquents.

The same erosion of the mechanisms of social control can be noted in the cities. The *danwei* – the polyfunctional unit that provides workers with a welfare system "from the cradle to the grave," according to the Chinese expression – is actually under pressure from economic restructuring, while workers have found many other ways to earn money. The widespread egalitarianism, so strong among Chinese workers, has been put into question. The social compromise that has been found between the authorities and the workers – low productivity but long-term employment, and low wages but the right to laziness – has been shattered by economic reforms without the emergence of a new form of social compromise. This leads me to the second point.

The deficiencies in the rule of law in China

The transformation of a highly hierarchical society into one ruled by the law is a lengthy and painful process in China. The large-scale development of corruption in this no-man's-land stretching between plan and market is also an illustration of this deficiency.

Regional imbalances

The current gap in revenue between Shanghai and the poor regions of the south-west – Yunnan Province, for instance – is 8 to 1. Has the sustained economic growth we have witnessed during the past 16 years led to a better economic integration of China by weaving together various regions with distinct specializations? Or has it caused a fragmentation of China's national unity? After all, China has never had a unified market, and its economic history shows just how strong its local entities' autonomy has been. As history shows us, national disunity has occurred much more from ethnic or religious conflict than from uneven economic development. However, the development of "economic warlordism," with interprovincial trade wars, in China is an alarming phenomenon.

Let me express, in that context, some of my reservations concerning two particular points in Professor's Lu presentation.

The first concerns the projections he makes of industrial growth in China. Nothing is more misleading than the mere extrapolation of figures. This is true for economics in general, and is highly risky in the case of China. The Chinese government itself recognizes that its statistics are often distorted, even false. A fundamental characteristic of economics is fluctuation. And, indeed, China has registered steep oscillations in its growth over the past 15 years. Every "boom" has been followed by an abrupt "bust." The root of these devastating swings lies in the poor control of macroeconomic tools such as taxation and monetary emission.

Another point made by Professor Lu concerns consumption patterns. It is true that China enjoys a high rate of saving. But, with a single glance at the official statistics, it is rather difficult to get a clear picture of Chinese consumption patterns. In the coastal cities, for instance, the per capita revenue is skewed for a multitude of reasons – tax evasion, moonlighting, and non-monetary advantages. Perhaps another reason is China's high rate of consumption for a low-revenue country. This has led to the traditional difficulty of transforming savings into investment. It can also be seen in the outflow of Chinese capital, and the lack of investment in the countryside.

Conclusion

Social development cannot be reduced to a mere modernization of the economy and of its management; it requires the ability to mobilize social and cultural resources in order to reach economic objectives. What has been remarkable with the high growth rates of the Japanese and, to a lesser extent, Taiwanese and Korean economies, is not so much the fact that growth was strong but that it was stable. This is lacking in China. Moreover, modernization has often, if not always, been conceived as Westernization. Nobody could deny that we are now witnessing a process of economic and social development that has been clearly divergent from a Western pattern for more than two decades. China, too, given its rich history and cultural variety, is certainly going to create an original market economy or capitalist economy.

So what will China become in the twenty-first century – the new giant of Asia, or a crumbling empire, torn by political divisions and creeping civil war? Or a confederation ruled by the law instead of charismatic leaders? Communism is dead in China, too. But nationalism also seems to have lost its appeal. There are many Chinas, not only the one within the territorial entity which is termed the People's Republic of China (PRC), on the mainland, but also outside – Hong Kong, Taiwan, and Singapore, for example. As frontiers blur in a global world, so has the configuration of China. What we are witnessing, in this process, is a new conquest of the centre by the periphery. The old debate, on whether China is a nation or a civilization, is taking on new relevance in such a context.

Comments

Hiroshi Okuzaki

Population structure

This September in Cairo, Egypt, the United Nations hosted an international conference on the world population problem. One conclusion was that, in order to control the rapid population growth, a serious view must be taken of the standard of education. What is the percentage of educational expenses by the Chinese government? Compulsory education does not last long. After all, it is most important, I think, to elevate the standard of education.

Industrial structure

If China can remove several obstacles, she will continue to grow at a rapid rate. The first of the obstacles is the highway problem. What is the total length of national roads in China? What is its ratio per square kilometre of the area of China? What is the percentage of asphalt-surfaced roads? The second is the railway problem. What is the total length of railroad in China? What is its ratio per capita in China? The third is the water problem. For example, what is your expectation of the amount of water necessary in the year 2000? A shortage of water would give a mortal wound to the agriculture and industry of China. The fourth is the problem of forest conservation. The Chinese proportion of woodland is very low compared with the rest of the world. The woodland ratio per capita is lower still. Chinese rivers have no forests in the upper reaches, so that dams will be of no use in 10–20 years. The fifth is inflation. According to Japanese newspaper reports, China now has a problem of 20 per cent inflation. The explosion of inflation will deal the Chinese economy a serious blow.

Urban–rural structure

It has been reported that the acreage under cultivation is on the decrease in China. This will result in a decrease in agricultural output, which may cause farmers to migrate to urban areas. In this case, a large quantity of food will be needed. Inevitably, food prices will rise acutely. Is it possible for more than 100 million farmers to migrate to the urban areas?

Regional patterns

Free competition is incompatible with equal division. The Chinese government and people may need to abandon their equal-division mentality. It is not known how to modernize such a large country as China. I think, perhaps, that the country should adopt a federal system.

Other problems

These include the following:
1. Contamination of the environment;
2. Contradiction between Chinese world strategy and economic policy;
3. Elevation of the educational level;
4. Improvement of student conditions;
5. An awareness of responsibility for present conditions in China;
6. A moral society based on the rule of law.

8

Chinese democracy and constitutional development

Lucian W. Pye

Introduction

Optimists about China's prospects keep their minds concentrated on the economy and set aside speculations about political development. The leadership wants to keep it this way as it cheers on the idea that "to get rich is glorious" and that any talk of democracy is a certain threat to stability. Yet any long-range view of China, particularly one that extends into the twenty-first century, must include considerations about the prospects for constitutional democracy. Can the Chinese remain almost alone in the world in resisting the apparently inexorable trend of democratization?

For a hundred years, enlightened Chinese intellectuals have had visions of their country practising democracy. The leaders of the Reform Movement in 1898, Kang Youwei and Liang Qichao, for a brief 100 days seemed on the verge of putting China on the path of becoming a democracy based on a constitutional monarchy, but the reactionary forces in the court were too strong. Yet the need for reform was so apparent that, by 1905, after the shock of the Boxer Rebellion and the example of the Japanese victory over Russia, even the reactionary Empress Cixi recognized that change would have to come, so she appointed a study group to travel to Japan, the United

States, Britain, France, Germany, Russia, and Italy in order to plan for a Chinese constitution. (The mission was delayed when a revolutionary, who would have none of a constitutional change which would have left the Manchus in power, blew up their train as it was about to leave Peking.) The mission eventually proposed that China should adopt the Japanese model.

Ultimately, the goal of democracy through a constitutional monarchy proved to be unacceptable because the existing dynasty consisted of alien rulers, the Manchus. The Qing dynasty had to go, and there was no Han family who could be an alternative ruling house. All that existed was the radical option of China instantly becoming a republic. The sorry state of China's floundering after the 1911 Revolution proved that merely proclaiming the existence of a republic would not produce democracy.

Indeed, one can readily make the case that, if China had not had the misfortune of being at the time ruled by an alien dynasty, it might have matched the successes of other constitutional monarchies, from Britain to Japan, in both modernizing and becoming democratic. But with that more gradual route blocked, the Chinese had only the radical option of claiming they were now to be a democratic republic. The chasm between China's traditional bureaucratic imperial system and a functioning parliamentary democracy was simply too great to be spanned in a single leap. From the end of the Qing, China's rulers of the day have promulgated one constitution after another, but the results have been a continuation in the unbridgeable gap between constitutional declarations and actual practices. The Chinese tradition of rule by men and not by laws has thus remained unmodified in spite of the series of proclaimed constitutions. The limited impact of constitutions is dramatically demonstrated by the fact that, in every one of the 11 most authoritative constitutions since 1908, there have been unqualified provisions for freedom of speech, press, and assembly – rights that the Chinese people have at no time really possessed.[1] The repeated inclusion of such guarantees of freedom in each successive constitution points to the unrealized aspirations of thinking Chinese. No outsiders, and certainly no Westerners, imposed these human rights values on the Chinese, and therefore they represent ideals that Chinese would like to have but have as yet not been able to realize.[2]

With such a record of failures, why should anyone take seriously a paper on Chinese democracy and constitutional development in the twenty-first century? The optimistic answer is that China is on its way to becoming another of East Asia's economic "miracles," and social theorists from the time of Aristotle have said that, when an economy produces a middle class, conditions are right for democracy. And it is not just theorists who believe so but also Western policy makers, who have long justified foreign aid as the way to get the necessary economic growth which will, in turn, transform authoritarian regimes into democracies.

Of course, Deng Xiaoping is betting that exactly the opposite will happen and that economic success will preserve one-party rule and the dictatorship of the proletariat. Rather than trying to determine who will be right – for, as Confucius once said, we are told, "Prediction is difficult, especially with respect to the future" – I shall, in the time allotted to me, focus on what would have to change for China to become a constitutional democracy in the twenty-first century. By identifying critical problem areas we (hopefully) will have a better basis for speculating about China's political prospects. In particular, I want to analyse five major problem areas that currently present obstacles to the kind of political development that lovers of democracy would like to see take place in China.

First, however, a qualifying consideration to protect my diagnosis, and this is that history is full of the unexpected, so what today may seem almost impossible could turn out, almost accidentally, to be easily achieved. After all, the Soviet Union seemed to have been an unshakable monolith, but then it all came tumbling down when just a little scope for freedom was allowed. In short, nothing would please me more than for history to prove that I have been unduly pessimistic, and that I have seen mountains where only molehills existed. I also want you to keep in mind that, by focusing on the problem areas, I run the risk of seeming to be a killjoy who is only interested in bad-mouthing the Chinese. I hope you will understand that this is not the case and appreciate the risk I am taking. The alternative of speaking only of positive developments, and there are many, would result in producing a boring recital of wishful thoughts.

I want you also to keep in mind that in every generation of modern Chinese there have been heroic bands of believers in democracy. This is true not just of the dramatically visible leaders of the May Fourth Movement, the "big character poster" writers at Democracy Wall, and the students in Tiananmen Square but of brave hearts even when repression has been most severe. With these qualifications in mind, let us recognize that, in looking to the twenty-first century, our task of analysis is to identify those obstacles that must be overcome if the aspirations of China's democracy-lovers are to be realized.

China is not a coherent nation-state system

The first major problem area relates to a distinctive characteristic of Chinese society that sets it apart from other countries and ensures that it will have a different pattern of development from most countries, and which therefore makes forecasting about China more problematical. This unique characteristic is that China is not a coherently structured nation-state in that its social, political, and economic developments are not integrated or reinforced as they usually are in most national systems. What happens in the Chinese economy is not necessarily transmitted into comparable political and social developments. Indeed, what happens in some parts of the economy may have little or no effect on other parts of the economy. Social trends here are not matched by social trends there, and even significant social and economic developments will not necessarily be felt politically. Major societal developments, which in other countries would have instant and predictable consequences for public life, may not cause any political repercussions. Instead of pulls toward equilibrium, China abounds with contradictions. Thus, for example, on the one hand there is the new China of flashy entrepreneurs in their Italian suits, Mercedes Benz automobiles, five-star hotels, and cellular telephones; on the other hand there is the China of failing state enterprises, listless workers, rural poverty, and a demoralized educational scene.[3] There seems to be no need to resolve the contradictions between what is permitted, indeed expected, in the Special Economic Zones (SEPs) and what is allowed elsewhere. If what is allowed in the SEPs is good, then why not allow it everywhere? Where else would it not seem odd to proclaim the ideal of "one country, two systems"?

Sun Yat-sen complained that China was like a plate of sand: it didn't hold together and it lacked structural form; it was made up only of individuals and family groupings. What was troubling Dr Sun was that China was not composed of a set of interacting social, political, and economic systems so that changes in some area would produce predictable changes throughout, as all the elements seek to find a new equilibrium; trends in China do not necessarily become accumulative. At any time there are many positive signs of development as well as negative ones, but there is no telling as to how they will add up, and thus both optimists and pessimists can find grounds for their outlooks. At the same time, the national mood can easily go through exaggerated swings from states of joyful, self-confident optimism to dark depression as the result of what turn out to be only superficial developments.

A key reason that China has this problem is that, as I have said elsewhere, China is a civilization pretending to be a nation-state. What binds the Chinese together is their sense of culture, race, and civilization, not an identification with the nation as a state. More of this phenomenon in a moment, but here the point is that the unity based on being a civilization produces the contradictory effect that China can not only appear to be changeless – indeed, impervious to all influences – but also undergo startling and dramatic changes, with little lasting traces of what went on before. Mao's China goes, Deng's China comes, and there seem to be few connections – and who is to say that equally dramatic and unexpected changes will not come after the Deng era ends? Changes (especially in the political realm), even profound changes, may have little impact on the Chinese psyche because the people's sense of identity is not rooted in the political sphere of the nation-state. Policies can zig and zag, and what officials declare to be abominable one year can be praised in the next, and the public does not seem to be perturbed by the contradictions.

The fact that the various systems are not coherently integrated, as in conventional nation-states, means that there are no clear levers of control to direct change, no recognized pressure points for guiding society-wide developments. Even the state authorities lack a precise control mechanism; hence their constant reliance upon brute coercion. To get things done, it becomes necessary for the leadership to mobilize indiscriminately the entire population. Thus, what in other nation-states can be handled by routine administrative actions can, in the case of China, call for mass mobilization campaigns.

Moreover, the rulers in Beijing can issue their policy decrees, but the provincial or local authorities may only pretend to obey if the policies do not suit them. The Chinese political art of feigned compliance means that pretentions can smooth over what in other systems would be sharp tensions. Therefore, in China, contradictions can abound. As the wits in Beijing like to put it: "The leaders lie to us, and we lie to the leaders; the leaders know that we know that they know that we are lying, and the people similarly know that the leaders know that the people know that they are lying. So everything is normal."

Yet, paradoxically, this loosely structured characteristic of Chinese public life also makes it possible for the top leader to utter a few cryptic remarks and the whole society will go off on a different tack. Thus in January 1992, Paramount Leader Deng Xiaoping only needed to make a visible visit to South China and mumble some praises for the SEPs to trigger a new leap forward for the reforms and China's current get-rich-quick capitalism.

Unfortunately, this characteristic also means that one cannot be confident that economic progress will produce the political consequences that would be expected in other societies. Thus, it is surprisingly easy for freedom to exist in the economy and non-freedom in the political realm.

Merchants without political demands

This brings me to the second problem area, that of the Chinese merchants' tradition of avoiding politics, which in modern times has contributed to the emergence of a middle class that remains remarkably apolitical. The theory that economic development should bring in its wake a more liberal political process is premised on the historical experiences of Europe and Japan, where the rise of merchant classes in the cities challenged the absolutist authority of lords and kings and produced parliamentary rule. In those countries, the dictates of the market and the concerns of the merchants supported the need for more pluralistic political systems, where interests could be represented and the rule of law would prevail. Chinese history, however, has, to date, been quite different. In China's Confucian tradition, the merchant was seen as being near the bottom of the social ladder, having no rights to challenge established authority. Instead, it was the task of the merchant to accommodate his interests to the dictates of the Confucian moral order. Indeed, the very idea of articulating any special interests was contrary to the Confucian tradition, which held that the supreme value was selflessness and the ultimate ideal was a willingness to engage in self-sacrifice for the good of the collectivity. The Chinese, of course, acted in terms of their individual interests, but individualism was not an ideal and, therefore, they could not openly articulate their interests.

The result was that, in traditional China, a genuine political economy never really surfaced, in the sense that the political arena never reflected the diverse economic interests of the society. Wheat-growing North China and rice-growing South China were all ruled as though they were the same. The differences between the cities and the countryside were not politically recognized. Instead, it was assumed that the supreme ruler operated in the best interest of everyone, and to assert any particular interest openly was to be crude and rude. Consequently, interests had to be submerged and operate out of sight. Instead of openly asking for changes in the law, mer-chants had to seek exceptions in their individual cases. The tendency, therefore, was toward various forms of personal favours that in other cultures would be seen as forms of corruption. Thus, historically, Chinese merchants did not band together to influence the law-making authority of government; rather, they sought individually to influence the law-enforcing process in the hope of winning exceptions in their personal cases.

The process of modernization in China also failed to produce strong economic interests that could be openly expressed politically. This was, in large part, a consequence of the treaty port system, which sheltered the growth of a dynamic commercial class but which, however, gave it no scope for open political activities. In Shanghai, in particular, but also in the other foreign concessions from Tientsin to Canton, there were communities of modernized Chinese who resem-bled middle-class people in every respect except for being totally apolitical. They continued to operate in the old merchant tradition of avoiding politics and leaving the role of government to others. The same behaviour pattern also characterized the Chinese who went down to South-East Asia and became prosperous business people in Singapore, Malaysia, and Indonesia. In these colonial areas the Chinese sought to make money and avoid politics. The result has been a modern continuation of the old tradition of an apolitical, neutral merchant class.

This pattern has continued with the get-rich-quick entrepreneurs of the current Deng era. Thus, with only a few exceptions, almost all of the successful private entrepreneurs and business people remained silent during the period of the Beijing Spring and the democracy movement. After the repression at Tiananmen, the business commu-nity in China quickly praised the values of stability and economic progress and avoided all discussion of politics and democratic de-velopment. The possibilities for corruption have, in a perverse way, eliminated any need for the new capitalists to challenge state authority in order to protect their interests. As in traditional China, it seems wiser to stay on the good side of government by remaining silent about political matters and to work quietly behind the scenes to get necessary favours.

Given this tradition, the big question for democratic development in the twenty-first century is whether the growing Chinese middle class, which has been hell-bent on making money, will, in time, feel it necessary to become more openly involved in making political demands. Up until now, those who have benefited the most from China's impressive economic development have sided with the Party leadership in opposing all moves towards pluralistic democracy. The fact that the most successful business people in Hong Kong have not been active in pushing for democratic development there does not augur well for the healthy development of a politically active business class in China itself. On the other hand, in Taiwan there has been a significant involvement of business interests in the political process. In part, this development took place because it reflected the more basic divide between the mainlanders who came over after the defeat of the Kuomintang and who monopolized government, and the local Taiwanese who have tended to dominate the economy. As the pressures for political involvement from the Taiwanese community became greater, the business community willingly became more active.

The need for a civil society

The phenomenon of the politically uninvolved merchants is part of a much larger problem – that of the failure of China to develop a strong civil society that could challenge and constrain the state and provide the basis for a democratic political process. Historically, the Chinese bureaucratic empire totally dominated Chinese society, and there were no autonomous power groupings within the society who could overtly operate as significant checks on the state. What groupings there were, such as the clans and the secret societies, tended to operate much as the merchants did, privatizing their interests rather than asserting them as a part of society's claims on the government. China never had the benefits of the competing authorities and the divided powers that feudal Europe and Japan had. In Europe there was the historic role of the Church in limiting the power of the state, and in both Europe and Japan there was the tradition of powerful nobles and lords, with their great houses, castles, and autonomous estates, who could check the authority of kings and shoguns. In China there was no constraint from society on the power of the emperor, only his personal morality in upholding the Mandate of Heaven. The only stratum of society that could challenge the state authorities was that of the Confucian intellectuals. It is true that the Confucian scholars were expected to criticize authority if the mandarin officials did not conduct themselves according to Confucian norms. However, this also meant that the scholars were on the side of established authority and not a force for change.

This tradition of the intellectuals being the main source of criticism of authority has persisted until recent times, but, as Tiananmen showed, whenever there is a direct confrontation, the state can all too readily suppress students, writers, and thinkers. The state's control of the mass media has also been near total; therefore, this important institution for democratic development has not matured in China to the point that it can become a representative of society and a check on the authorities.

There are certain signs, however, that the foundation of a civil society may be taking shape in China. Increasing numbers of professional associations are forming. There are also the beginnings of a self-conscious legal profession, which will, in time, need to assert itself more actively as a challenge to the state. Furthermore, the geographically uneven pattern of economic development has created the basis for local interests that may increasingly wish to make special claims. Therefore, it is not inconceivable that, in time, local and provincial leaders will challenge those at the centre and thereby produce the basis for a more pluralistic and competitive form of politics. It is noteworthy that, even in the 1920s and 1930s, the provincial assemblies did begin to assert some of the interests of their constituencies. Indeed, it is noteworthy that Taiwan's successful democratic development grew from the seeds originally planted in the practice of having local elections, a practice that is now taking place in the People's Republic. The state, however, has been alert to the emergence of professional associations that might challenge its authority; in response, it has sought to co-opt such developments. Consequently, the most likely development would be some forms of corporatism in which the state would play a role in the organizations. This has already been the pattern with the state-sponsored labour unions. In time, interest can become an autonomous force, even in corporatist arrangements, but the development is likely to be slow and uncertain.

213

The need to replace a moral order with a political order

If a stronger civil society is to bring about democratic development, China will have to make the great modernizing break of moving from having a government that is, in theory, based on a moral order to having a government based upon a political order. In all traditional societies, the basis of legitimacy for governmental authority was the concept of a moral order. More often than not, the moral order had a sacred dimension to it, in that the religion of the society usually supported and gave authority to the rulers. With the emergence of modern society, with its greater degree of diversification and hence its competing interests, the moral order had to give way to the emergence of a political order characterized by politics within the framework of a rule by law. In modern societies, the mechanism of the political process, with its need for compromises and accommodations among freely competing parties, operates to provide order and stability, much as the market does for the economy, and thereby replaces the system of a moral order that was appropriate for a more simple state of society.

In the case of China, the traditional moral order was exceedingly powerful, based as it was upon the sophisticated concepts of Confucianism. Confucianism was, indeed, unique in that it gave China, at a very early stage of history, a strong secular dimension to its myth of legitimacy. In modern times, the erosion of Confucianism generated an almost frantic search for a new moral order, a search that resulted, in time, in China's turning to Marxism–Leninism as a new moral order to replace the Confucian order. Certainly, Maoism was an extreme form of rule by moral dictate. Correct behaviour became all-important, and all interests had to be denied or submerged in the name of upholding the interest of the Party, the state, the "people."

The lack of any differentiation between the basis for state legitimacy and that for private morality has meant that the erosion of Marxism–Leninism–Mao Zedong Thought has created a loss of faith that not only has weakened the legitimacy of the state but also has produced a general decline in moral standards. Deng Xiaoping has staked the future of his regime on the belief that the idea "to get rich is glorious" will have enough appeal to provide it with the necessary legitimization. But the erosion has also produced a social crisis as standards of honesty and general integrity have declined. Everyone is suddenly expected to look after himself or herself, in very private ways. The Chinese leadership is fully aware of this problem, as it has mounted "anti-corruption" campaigns and called for the development of a "High Socialist Civilization," but the regime is still too closely tied to its discredited Marxism–Leninism roots of legitimacy for it to be able to inspire a revival of private morality.

There are many reasons why China failed to make the modernizing transition from a moral order to a political order system, but not the least important of them is the Chinese tradition of idealizing the collectivity over the individual. First the Confucian tradition and then Marxism–Leninism decreed that any articulation of private interests was an abomination. Once a culture accepts the proposition that there may be many diverse interests in the society, then there develops the need for people to learn the arts of accommodation and compromise. Adversarial relationships become civilized and people learn to disagree without becoming disagreeable. When such a cultural change takes place, the society can practise genuine politics and the basis has been established for pluralistic democracy. As long as the government pretends that it is ruling in terms of a moral order, any disagreement with it can be interpreted as a subversive act, deserving of harsh repression.

Today, the Chinese leadership, even as it allows economic competition and diversification, continues to insist that, politically, it represents the interests of all the people. It continues to pretend that within the Party there are no élite factions and hence there is no basis for legitimate politics. As long as this pretension continues, the élite will see any assertion of interests by the people as a threat to stability. This hypersensitive fear of disorder will last until China makes the transition to having a public realm based on the play of political interests.

The search for a new basis of legitimacy

All of these considerations point to the overriding importance for the Chinese to find a new basis of political legitimacy to replace their outmoded Marxism–Leninism–Mao Zedong Thought and Mr Deng Xiaoping's Four Cardinal Principles. Ever since the Cultural Revolution, the Chinese have been experiencing a genuine crisis of faith as the leadership grapples with how to fit what is happening with its successful economic reforms into its pretensions that China has remained a socialist country committed to the development of Communism. The leadership continues to talk about its goal of building "Socialism with Chinese Characteristics" but, in fact, it uses the slogan as a rationale to prevent the articulation of possible alternative visions for China.

It is true that Westerners generally exaggerate the importance of faith and beliefs, whereas in China, a society with a less strong religious tradition, it may be quite enough for people to behave as though they believed in their Communist ideology. Lip service can be a suprisingly powerful force in a culture which has, as we have seen, raised feigned compliance and pretence to a high art form. Yet in time China will have to work out some new vision of what it is seeking to achieve as a nation. The goal of just economic development is not enough to provide the basis for effective government.

It is generally assumed that nationalism will replace Communism as the guiding principle of Chinese political life. The problem, though, is that, as of now, there has not been a version of Chinese nationalism that could set standards and provide specific values for legitimizing a political system. The Chinese sense of self-identity is, of course, extremely strong, based as it is upon a powerful traditional civilization. There is also a strong sense of Chinese racial and ethnic identity. What is lacking, however, has been the identification of particular elements of that culture that are to be singled out and associated with the ideal of China as a nation-state. What has passed for Chinese nationalism in modern times has been xenophobic fits of passion over having been humiliated by other powers. Anti-foreignism is not a viable basis for the development of a healthy sense of national identity. The Chinese government has frequently declared that acts of other governments will "hurt the feelings of the Chinese people," but anger at others is not the essence of modern nationalism. For nationalism to be the basis of state legitimacy, it needs to specify the particular ideals, values, and aspirations that set off that country from all others, but which also will command respect in terms of the norms of the international system. True nationalism cannot only provide guidance for the people as a whole: it must also have the power to restrain élite behaviour. The leaders in upholding the national ideals must also recognize that there are certain things they cannot do because it would violate national principles. At present, China has no such national principles: the people can only react to perceived mistreatment and offences against the collective sense of honour.

Chinese popular culture is rich in the potential raw materials for forming the sentiment of a modern nationalism, but, as of today, Chinese nationalism remains shallow in terms of having a distinctive set of values, ideals, symbols, and myths. Thus, it is not clear what is the specific content of the self-image that the Chinese wish to project in their relations with other nation-states. The Chinese know that they have a great history; they also feel that they have not been treated right by foreign powers; but they have not been able to spell out in specific terms the uniqueness of their identity as a nation-state.

Unfortunately, right now, China lacks any coherent process that might operate to identify those elements of Chinese civilization and culture that modern Chinese would like to have as the guiding principles for their sense of nationalism. What is needed is the opening up of a dialogue within China so that different points of view can contend with each other in trying to spell out what should be a future vision for China. In the past, this has been a task left to intellectuals, who have, since the May Fourth Movement, tended to reject most of traditional Chinese culture and opt for foreign values and ideals. The articulation of a healthy version of Chinese nationalism calls for the participation of all elements of Chinese people. There needs to be spontaneous and autonomous expression of the potential elements that people want to have included in their sense of national self-identity.

Conclusion

Thus, in a paradoxical way, I come to a surprisingly positive conclusion about the prospects for Chinese democratic development. For, in spite of all the obstacles and problems I have identified, I arrive at the ultimate conclusion that China now urgently needs to go through the experience of creating a new and stronger sense of nationalism, and this can only come about through an open dialogue of all the Chinese people. And what would such a process be but democracy at work? That is to say, the creation of a modern sense of Chinese nationalism must go hand in hand with the emergence of some form of democracy.

The various problems that I have identified as obstacles to democracy turn out, in fact, to be major obstacles for the realization of a true sense of Chinese nationalism. The leadership at times seems aware of this problem, as it acknowledges the existence of a moral crisis and the need for a healthier sense of civilization, but it shies away from opening the society up so as to allow popular forces to define a new spirit of national identity. The process of redefining the soul of China cannot be indefinitely delayed, because widespread scepticism has already given way to increasing cynicism that will in time become alienation and then nihilism – and the negative spirit of nihilism cannot give birth to the constructive values and ideals essential for a strong sense of nationalism.

Thus, the future of China as a great nation does require a transition to some form of democracy. Fortunately, the terrible turmoil China has gone through during the last four decades has largely exhausted both the leaders' and the people's tolerance for authoritarianism. Therefore, the time for democratic development may not be far off.

Notes

1. The history of Chinese constitutional experience is reviewed in Andrew J. Nathan, *Chinese Democracy* (Berkeley: University of California Press, 1985).
2. In recent years there have been some Asians, not so much from China but more from Singapore and Malaysia, who have tried to make human rights a narrowly Western set of values and to argue that Asian values are communitarian, not individualistic, and thus authoritarian governments in Asia should not be criticized. They often suggest that Confucianism justifies this distinction between West and East. Yet, there is nothing in Confucianism that idealizes authocratic, authoritarian government.
3. A vivid description of the contradictions in contemporary China is to be found in Orville Schell, *Mandate of Heaven* (New York: Simon and Schuster, 1994).

Comments

Jiang Ping

Professor Pye understands the political and social conditions of China very well. His research on the development of democracy and the constitutional framework in China is based on an analysis of the foundations of contemporary Chinese society. It includes some new opinions and poses some provocative questions. The conclusion of his research is therefore objective and reasonable.

First, it should be recognized that it is just the development of the market economy rather than economic development in general that gives a premise to the development of democracy and the constitutional framework. It is inevitable that the market economy will limit the strong governmental power and develop a consciousness of right, equality, and participation in civil society. The modern enterprise system bred by the market economy requires, of necessity, a suitable modern state. Democracy and a constitutional framework are the basic characteristics of such a modern government. Therefore, the orientation and pace of the development of democracy and the constitution in China will move forward, should the policy of developing the market economy be continued. However, the pace of development will be limited by many factors. I would like to clarify my own opinions on the five constraining factors, as described by Professor Pye, as follows.

1. The imbalance between the economy and politics

It is an objective fact in China that reform of the political system lags behind reform of the economic system. The Chinese government is currently confronted with dealing properly with the trilateral relationship between development, reform, and stability. The government has insisted that development is the goal, while reform and stability are the driving force and premise of development, respectively. If development and reform seriously affect stability, then stability will become the most important, since it is involved with political power. The essence of the relationship between development, reform, and stability is simply the relationship between the economy and politics, in which the economy should obey politics. The problem of political democracy is the core problem in the reform of the political system, and is also a sensitive problem associated with the stability of political power. An important reason for the collapse of the Soviet Union has been attributed to the reform of the political system going beyond the reform of the economic system. Consequently, reform of the political system should take place at a relatively slow speed. There is also a fear that a greater imbalance between the speeds of economic and political reform may lead to a dangerous situation in the current reforms.

2. The role of the entrepreneur in the progress of democracy

Until now, there has been no general concept of the "entrepreneur" in China. A number of entrepreneurs are the leaders of state-owned enterprises and have been appointed by the government; therefore, they can even claim to be a part of the government. On the other hand, the middle class, the entrepreneurs who are independent of the government, have never become a strong political force and, even today, have yet to recover their historically prominent position. Throughout world history, the middle class has been the primary representative asking for democracy and a legal system, but this is not the case in Chinese history. In China, however, the middle class has gradually been absorbing a group of young and middle-aged people with a high degree of culture, excellent management abilities, and their own political opinions. Their success will increase their wishes for a role in the creation of a political democracy.

3. Civil society in China

A government with strong powers has long existed in China. Such a government has interfered not only in politics in general but also in the economy as a whole, extending control even to issues of family life and personal affairs. Thus, China is far from forming a real civil society. However, the market economy has allowed China to undertake the separation of government from civil society. Professor Pye indicated that "historically, China lacked strong feudal lords and nobles whose competition for power established the foundations for pluralistic politics in Europe and Japan." First, this means that the competition for power between the feudal lords and aristocrats in a country lacking a democratic tradition, such as China, leads finally to a situation of separatist warlord regimes and war, rather than to the development of democracy. This has been verified by Chinese history and can also be seen in some African countries. Secondly, pluralistic politics and multi-party systems are forbidden under the current political system in China. The meaning of political democracy in China is, therefore, different from that in the West. Although still disputable, it cannot be neglected that the Chinese People's Political Consultative Conference (CPPCC), similar to the mediation system for settling economic disputes, is a form of democracy.

4. Traditional society

Professor Pye's claim that China continues to be essentially a traditional society is in agreement with the current real situation in China. Traditional society has never been a democratic and legal society: in other words, it is a society with a poor democratic and legal system. During the past several thousand years of Chinese history, the legal system established itself comparatively well, whereas the system of democracy suffered from great inadequacies. A legal system with inadequate democracy always meant that the country was controlled through personal wishes instead of the law. A legal system without democracy is very dangerous. A typical example of the indefinite expansion of power is the feudal official who said, "The emperor's law controls people whereas I control the emperor's law." Large-scale legislative activities have been going on in China. By the end of this century, about 150 important laws will have been issued. After that the situation of depending on related laws will be thoroughly changed. However, the problem of administering and obeying the laws will not be able to be solved within the near future. In addition to the non-synchronization of political and economic reform mentioned above, the non-synchronization of the establishment of democracy and legislation, and of the legislation and the administration of law, clearly shows all the problems that need to be solved during the transition from a traditional society to a modern society. One characteristic of traditional society is the lack of a democratic consciousness and the absence of a legal system. All Chinese, except the modern intellectuals and civil servants in economically developed areas, have a very weak consciousness of democracy. It is more important and practical for many Chinese to have more opportunities to become rich, rather than to participate in democratic politics.

5. The consciousness of nationalism

A crisis of belief exists to some extent. During the opening of China, two trends – a strengthening and a weakening – existed simultaneously in the realm of the consciousness of nationalism as well as the consciousness of patriotism. The solidification of the Chinese nation is concrete and necessary. In present China, there is no social function that will result in dangers such as original religious doctrinairism, autocratic monarchy, chauvinism, and anti-foreigner sentiments similar to those being confronted by other countries. But the feudal familism, the system of over-concentrated power caused by the unification of party and government, and the power abuse of officials as well as the lack of a corresponding supervisory system, may be seen as obstacles to the development of democracy in China. All of these obstacles are waiting to be dealt with in the future.

The development of democracy and a constitutional framework in China is a progressive process. It is almost impossible to return to the days of the Cultural Revolution, because the current social foundation is completely different from that time. On the other hand, it would also be impossible to administer a Western-style democratic system in China in the near future, because the internal structure of Chinese society is not capable of being changed in such a short time.

Comments

Isao Kaminaga

The analysis by Professor Pye of the past, present, and future of democracy in China is suggestive and really challenging. I would like to make a comment on his chapter from the viewpoint of law.

He persuasively points out that, in spite of a Chinese belief in democracy, there have been five major problem areas that continue to impede the growth of constitutional democracy, one of which – the fourth one – is that China is essentially a society where legitimacy has been derived from a moral order, but now China is seeking a new basis of legitimacy. He goes on to say that this could be found through a process of popular participation in a collective dialogue and a process of defining the content of Chinese nationalism.

This is definitely some form of democracy. What is, however, the actual form of popular participation in a collective dialogue in the context of constitutional democracy, and at what level? Does he mean, by popular participation in a collective dialogue, that some form of political process or some form of the legal system will result? How can we recognize this process in the frame and structure of the Chinese Constitutional Law? Could a legal system of freedom of information accompany this process?

There is no doubt that it will be increasingly and urgently necessary for China to improve its legal system, especially the administrative legal system, in order to realize constitutional democracy by the rule of law, and not by the rule of man. The Japanese Constitution provides democracy by the rule of law, but we must be careful how we evaluate the real aspects of the Constitution. The Administrative Procedure Act, which became effective on 1 October 1994, has no provision to make the administrative process democratic. We have not enacted a Freedom of Information Act. It would be important for Japanese and Chinese people to disclose legal issues publicly and to exchange opinions with each other if we are to share in the value of constitutional democracy.

Session III summary

Takeo Uchida

When I visited China in 1979, immediately following the beginning of the reform and open-door policy, my friend in the Chinese Academy of Social Sciences who was hosting me told me about four considerations that I must take into account in order to understand China: first, China has a long history; second, China has a huge population; third, China is a socialist society; fourth, the Cultural Revolution still continues to provide aftershocks. About 15–16 years have passed since the reforms and open-door policy began. During this period, the Cold War ended, and we are coming to a point where we must take other important factors into consideration.

In this sense, the first report by Professor Satoshi Amako, entitled "Asia since the Cold War and the new international order," discusses the future of China in a comprehensive manner from the point of view of the relationships with the environment surrounding China. It sufficiently deals with audience interests. Professor Amako points out that the Cold War was following a process of dissolution when China and the United States approached each other in 1972, and the structure decisively changed after the collapse of the Soviet Union and Eastern Europe in 1991. Although important issues associated with the Cold War linger, such as the unresolved problems of Taiwan and the Korean Peninsula, the understanding is that continued globalization and de-politization of the economy and information will steadily progress in this region. It is quite impressive that Professor Amako named such changes as the road to "non-confrontation and coexistence without reunification."

Professor Amako expects that the Chinese "state-centrism" and emphasis on "supreme national power" in the political sphere will not change. He also points out that the Chinese diplomatic paradigm is basically headed toward power politics. We cannot but be driven toward pessimism with such prospects. Against this backdrop, Mr Chen pronounces that China cannot help but promote peaceful coexistence in all directions, and China must abandon hegemonies and strong power politics toward outside countries in order to concentrate on domestic building. This really put us at ease. Professor Theeravit said, in the concluding comments, that interdependence in the Asian region has been slow to develop, and world-sized interdependence will be a factor in deciding the future of China.

The second theme deals with problems that accompany Chinese modernization, and Professor Lu of the Chinese Academy of Social Sciences gave a report entitled "Prospects of Social Development." Professor Lu presents a fine analysis based upon detailed data concerning social change associated with the movement from traditional to modern society. The audience accepted this in a straightforward manner. He then went on, from a macroscopic viewpoint, to examine population issues, employment issues, the relationship between urban and rural areas, and the current state of regional differences. Furthermore, he went on to describe the measures taken by the Chinese government to address these problems as a discussion of policy issues. Based on these data analyses, Professor Lu concluded that China will certainly achieve modernization.

However, Mr Gipouloux of the French National Centre for Scientific Research was somewhat sceptical about such a forecast. Mr Gipouloux pointed to the possibility of turmoil that may lead China to destruction in the process of moving from traditional society to modern society. He pointed out that there may be a necessity to revise the forecast projected from the data presented by Professor Lu, given the magnitude of the fluctuations in the Chinese economy. Professor Hiroshi Okuzaki, who commented last, changed the direction of the conversation and expressed concern that modern China is ignoring human resources such as scholars and students. He proposed resurrecting religion, especially the mores of Confucianism.

The third theme is "Chinese Democracy and Constitutional

Development," presented by Professor Pye, who holds an important position in terms of studying political progress and comparative politics. Professor Pye discussed the reasons why individualism and political freedom do not grow in China from the point of view of historical and cultural factors (the tradition of placing importance on human control rather than legal control.) He went on to stress the necessity of democratic and constitutional development in order to create a sense of nationalism and a civil society in China. He further proposed that, for the success of democratic development, it is urgent to develop a civil society and an intermediate stratum of people with secure occupational foundations. He pointed out that China cannot be placed in the category of a nation-state, because China is a civilization instead of an institution. His comments strongly urge us to change our attitudes.

Then, Professor Jiang Ping commented that there is a lack of democracy in China and a discrepancy between political reforms and economic reforms. However, Professor Jiang argued that the highest priority is placed on "stability" in China, and there is a problem with rapid democratic development in that it will destroy stability. Professor Jiang's comments put a condition on the opinions of Professor Pye. Professor Kaminaga commented that, in order for constitutional democracy to be established and take root in China, improvements in the administrative legal system are necessary. He further emphasized that liberalization of information is a prerequisite to developing a legal system.

Session IV
Panel discussions

Panel discussions

Is the vision of "optimism in the economy and pessimism in politics" a correct one?

Itoh: The panel discussion, the third unit of this international symposium on "China in the twenty-first century," will be a summarizing unit following the keynote speeches and the three research sessions. Now I'd like to introduce the coordinator, Professor Yamamoto.

Yamamoto: Today is the last part of our joint international symposium by Aoyama Gakuin University and the United Nations University. So far on Saturday and Sunday, we have had two keynote speeches, followed by three research sessions whose subjects were "The Chinese Economy in the Twenty-first Century," "Chinese Management in the Twenty-first Century," and "Chinese Politics and Society in the Twenty-first Century." In these sessions, we had reports and discussions on eight themes. Before proceeding to the panel discussion, first I'd like to fill you in on what has been debated by introducing you to some highlights of the discussions. The first keynote speaker, Mr Rong Yiren, Vice-President of the People's Republic of China, told us about the three phases of China's modernization, which China has been tackling as an important task since the 1970s. According to this speech, China has quadrupled its gross national product (GNP) compared with that of 1980, which was in the second phase, and now the government is aiming to bring living standards up to a certain level by the year 2000. Furthermore (he said), preceded by a few decades of hard work its economic level will reach that of other mid-advanced countries in the first half of the twenty-first century, at which point they will have basically completed their task of modernization. Regarding the targets of China's economy, we were given more details from the participants from China in the subsequent research sessions.

Another keynote speaker, Helmut Schmidt, the former Chancellor of the Federal Republic of Germany, suggested that in twenty years' time, China's total GNP may exceed that of Japan and may even surpass America's. But, he said, it will only be possible under certain conditions and mentioned five "if"s. In short, the first "if" is, "if it can avoid internal disturbances like the ones that happened before." The second is, "if it can provide enough industrial and social infrastructure, such as transportation and communication systems, which promote coastal-area development to expand into inland areas." The third "if" is, "if it can alleviate the enormous burden of armaments and of military industry." The fourth one is, "if it can maintain the current high level of foreign investment." And the last "if" is, "if it can succeed in getting inflation under control."

These and other "if" issues were also mentioned and debated in various forms in the following research sessions. Among them, one of the hottest issues was how economic development and political modernization, in specific terms, democratization, will be linked to each other. In other words, the question of whether they can continue enjoying the fruits of their reform policies, first introduced at the end of the 1970s, well into the twenty-first century, largely depends upon the political possibility of whether they can develop a political system that utilizes people's talents and energies for wider and higher social development.

One reporter indicated the importance of considering China's political problems because we cannot necessarily be optimistic about them, though we can about China's economy. Concerning this point, we also received some frank opinions from the Chinese participants. They said, for example, that rash and drastic change in its political system might even complicate the problems China is now facing: therefore, only according to the circumstances will China have to carry out reforms and make progress.

Through this discussion, I think we've reached a common under-standing of which matters to consider, if not the same understanding of the matters. This is a brief summary of the discussion.

Ishikawa: We've been hearing a lot of rich discussion going on, much richer than we had expected, as a matter of fact. First, I would like to express my appreciation of the speeches and discussion and also the participation from the floor.

I've been listening to the discussions from an economist's point of view, since I am one. But opinions put forth by political scientists and sociologists gave me a great deal of food for thought.

Especially I felt the comments on the political aspect were very severe. A few years ago, it was unthinkable to witness a scene where, in this kind of public setting, these politically severe comments on China could be made and also accepted by Chinese participants with a great deal of open-mindedness. This demonstrates how the rela-tionships between China and Japan, and other countries, have grown more peaceful and brought about two-way communication.

I would just like to add a few things as an economist. The com-ments from the economists are optimistic about the Chinese economy or about society or China at large. On the other hand, in the political dimension, people see China rather pessimistically and severely. That gives the impression that economic understanding of China is a bit superficial, as someone has already pointed out.

There was also a comment made from an economic point of view saying that it is not hard to deal with economic problems, but, rather, the problems of politics – especially about how policies are goings to be taken and how politics work in deciding policies – are, in the final analysis, most important. Although this comment was made from an economic point of view, as an economist myself I'd like to stress that there is another side of things to consider.

After all, since the world of academics is divided into many dis-ciplines, the aspect that economists deal with differs from that of sociologists or political scientists. It's important to look at the differ-ent aspects, but we need to consider the timing of this comment. It was made at a time when China had just started to get good results after going through 16 years of a series of hardships and overcoming difficult problems. But, for these past few years, its growth rate has been over 10 per cent. Both the rate of savings and the investment rate are also very high. Since the comment reflects this kind of bright side and is future-oriented, it might give you that impression.

233

But various people have pointed out that China also has a variety of difficulties concerning its future. Especially Mr Liu Guoguang's well-compiled report verified this point. Therefore, I can't accept, without reservations, the judgement that the economic overview on China is overly optimistic.

Another thing to say is that one of the reasons for the contention that economic analyses are superficial (which I think is most likely just a misunderstanding) is that economists choose statistical figures and numbers freely and base their judgements solely on those data. In analysing the connections between different variables extracted from the data, economists boldly, without reservation, employ neo-classical economics or other kinds of Western economics that are premised on well-developed market economy systems, only to draw simple conclusions.

Like any other developing economy, one of the important features of the Chinese economy is that a market system hasn't been developed. Aren't economists ignoring this point? Economists' papers may have given you this kind of impression. But analyses of today's Chinese economy are not as naïve any more.

The significance of the Chinese economy is that its task is more than just shifting socialistic economy to a market-oriented one: it also includes developing a less-developed economy by way of industrialization. This significance has already been shown in the past history of socialist economics and is also clear in the prospects for the twenty-first century. Economists are aware of this point.

One more thing to say is about the comparison with the Russian economy. The task for the Russian economy is only to shift its planned economy to a market economy, but China's task is more than just that. It needs to industrialize its fundamental economic structure as well as to change its system.

Therefore, economists are aware that these two things – namely, changing the system and developing the economic structure – are the inseparable two combined tasks for China, and we are doing our analyses with this awareness. Concerning this, participants from China made their points by using rich analytical vocabularies, far richer than a few years ago. We can find many phrases like "we must create a market economy system," and analytical methods, both of which were never seen in papers written by Chinese people just a few years ago.

In a nutshell, economic analyses must face many difficult problems and are actually facing them. And we are well aware that, in the light of analytical problems, there are still numerous uncertain and unstable factors involved in the analysis of the future.

Strange: I am a political economist, which doesn't count with many of the economists, but nevertheless I guess I am the non-expert in the Panel in that I have never been to China and I don't pretend to know much. But just one observation and one question that I would like to pose very quickly.

The first is that what strikes me is that we are all supporters of the Chinese team, if you can speak in football terms. We want them to win. We realize that there is a crossroads in their political and economic development. And we are on their side in the same way that we are on Mandela's side or on Solidarity's side in Poland. We really want them to succeed and I hope that they realize this. I don't know that we are in favour of the old man at the top and some of the *nomenklatura*, but certainly we are on the side of the people. And we wish them the comforts and the conveniences that we have, the freedoms and the opportunities, particularly for students, that we have here in Japan, in America, and in Europe.

I think there is no better proof of this, than the fact that a Japanese university chose to celebrate its birthday by selecting for discussion not Japan in the twenty-first century but China. It couldn't have a better proof and I hope that the Chinese appreciate this.

My question is, I have heard a lot of very wise and expert things in the last couple of days. It occurred to me to wonder whether the Chinese visitors were listening. It strikes me that very big, continental countries often have a deafness and blindness to what smaller countries do. The Russians used to have this; the Americans, if you will forgive me, still have it. I think the Chinese also need to listen and learn from the experiences of Singapore or of Korea, of Brazil or India, Switzerland or Sweden. They shouldn't be so stuck-up and proud that they think they cannot learn from other people.

So we'll come to the lessons later.

Liu: Anyone talking about the future of China will probably have to consider a great many "ifs," and that includes images rather than scenarios of the future. I would like to give two of my own impressions.

First of all, I believe that wherever development is happening in China, the process involved is an irreversible one. The Chinese are not going back to the sharing of the same rice bowl. I think it is the first time in Chinese history that people have tasted the fruits of economic growth, and thus no matter what difficulties they may encounter, the process of development will continue.

Secondly, one issue that I thought was not well discussed these last two days is the realization that China is a gigantic country with an area that exceeds that of Europe. I can therefore foresee that, no matter how capable the management, because of China's long history of coexistence between the backward and well-developed regions, and the traditional and so-called advanced sectors, disparity will be a major issue in management. This is a great task that has never been experienced in other countries, for example, even Japan: the population of China is ten times that of Japan. Therefore, no matter how capable the new ideas may be, China will face limits with respect to this disparity. This disparity will continue for a long time, and will contribute to the political system and uncertainty in the future.

Yamamoto: Professor Strange mentioned how big countries often fail to listen to others, but, as the word "insularism" suggests, small countries do not necessarily bring about good outcomes. Anyhow, America achieved its fame as a big country so....

Cline: I want to address the question of whether large countries are blind. I simply want to highlight two or three of the concepts that came out from some of the key economics papers.

Professor Perkins essentially said that China has grown extremely rapidly because they have a high savings and investment rate, which is 30 per cent of income. Before 1978, they had very inefficient use of that because of political turmoil. After 1978, they moved to a market system and they became efficient and suddenly those high savings rates translated into high growth rates. That's the first point.

The second point is a question of how long this is going to continue. Professor Perkins cites the example of Japan growing at 10 per cent for two decades. He says you could go on maybe for three decades. And he and Professor Pye essentially said the real obstacle could be a political disruption rather than economic potential.

I just like to raise some questions about whether China could really grow at 10 per cent for three decades. Historically, over the last century, growth per capita in the United States and Europe has been of the order of 1–1.5 per cent per capita. China's growth rate of its population is about 1–1.5 per cent. So from that historical experience, the total growth rate would be more of the order of 3 per cent, not 10 per cent. This is just a bit of a cautionary note.

And the other thing that Professor Perkins mentioned was that, because of China's size, a 10 per cent growth will begin to put very serious strains on the world resources and trading system. And that's a point that I want to refer to in the second part of the Panel.

Wong: I would like to echo or share the opinion of the young lady sitting next to me. Young because I was at LFC 30 years ago, and she is now still at LFC in the school of economics.

First, I think that relevant topics are being presented. China is already making an impact today, not to say in the twenty-first century, especially from the standpoint of South-East Asia. I would like to emphasize the same point that was raised by Professor Strange, that we hope China's economy will continue to go well. When the Chinese economy is doing well, there are lots of opportunities in terms of investment and trade.

China is a stable factor of this region and can also be a anxiety factor if the Chinese economy is not doing very well. It will have a negative impact on all of us in the Asia-Pacific region. But from the opinions of various experts, during this two-day conference, we can see that the problems faced by China are really enormous. It is a big continental country. Not even a continental country I think, as Professor Pye mentioned. China is not really a country, it is a civilization. China is so big, the problems she is facing and will face are enormous. China is trying to reform its traditional economy, changing from a socialist system to the market system. And that is not easy, as has been experienced by the Soviet Union and others.

China is modernizing its institutions, introducing laws, and building up infrastructures, so there is radical change. History has never experienced such a big economic entity, modernization, change, industrialization at the same time at such a high speed. So we will have to continue to engage our attention for years to come.

Ahn: I would like to share my view about the future of China. It seems to me there is no doubt that, come the twenty-first century, China will become the superstate of the world. But much more important is the question of whether or not China will become a democratic and benign country. It is much more important to examine what kind of China will emerge in the twenty-first century.

It is my view that there are two imperatives at work in China. What I call political imperatives are working toward nationalism, sovereignty, balance of power, Leninism, and political stability. On the other hand, economic imperatives are working toward reforms, the open-door policy, interdependence, and liberalism.

237

So, political imperatives are really working toward what you call a realist view of the world or, in Chinese terms, socialism with Chinese characteristics. However, economic imperatives are working toward a liberalistic view of the world, or a liberalistic view of the economy.

So it really depends on which imperative should prevail. In my view, it is highly desirable that the economic imperative should prevail over the political imperative. Should the economic imperative prevail over the political imperative, the future of China is promising. In the twenty-first century it is highly likely that there will be a decentralized China; perhaps there will be a United States of several Chinas. Being more democratic, capitalist, and liberalistic, China will be less dangerous.

Finally, it is very important for us to engage China in world affairs. As far as military expansion is concerned, I think the West should try to contain the Chinese imperative towards militaristic expansion or hegemonism. But, on the other hand, I think we should try to keep China engaged in economic activities, so that China also can abide by international laws.

Liu: The results of this conference were abundant. We've discussed corporate management, social, political, and economic problems, which are relevant in today's China. The suggestions made in this symposium were very helpful. Thank you very much.

The experts of Japan and other countries shared their experiences on problems in corporate management and others, especially in the field of economic reformation. We've had a good experience and it will help us a lot.

Susan mentioned at the end how China, being a large country, has failed to listen to other countries. China actually had this problem in the past. We call this self-complacency. Through being dogmatic, China perhaps became about 100 years behind the world's leading nations. We know keenly what it means to close the doors and be behind. Therefore, presently a new foreign policy. This foreign policy is not just limited to the opening of economy, investment, and trading markets: it also opens up cultural aspects. In the last few years, we have been deepening and widening our relationship in each area. Exchanges among people and mutual visits are being positively held. Also, we are sending exchange students to Japan, the United States, and Europe in order to acquire advanced experience. This is why China is in the middle of change, not the same old dogmatic country.

Chen: I came from Shanghai; by participating in this symposium, I've gained a lot. Experts from Japan and other countries have taught me many things. I've learned a lot especially from the analysis of Chinese economy by Professor Ishikawa and the analysis of the restructuring Chinese corporations by several Japanese experts. Those analyses contained many valuable things and I was enlightened by them.

Obstacles to an economic nation: Population, employment, political stability, withdrawal from poverty, differences

Yamamoto: Now let us move on to the second part. The topic of discussion should focus on the domestic movements in China, considering China's economic reform, economic growth, and other related social and political problems. After that, the topic of discussion should move on to the problems of China's internationality, politics, economy, and security.

Ishikawa: In addition to the statement referring to the economic kick-off: "the economy is doing well, but politics is a problem," China's economy has a problem in its structure. Structural problems arise from the fact that China's economy has not yet become an advanced economy. In other words, productive elements or productive resources are still imperfectly used, here in China's economy. They may be left unemployed, or excellent resources existing in other areas are unused because of a bottleneck somewhere.

One example of structural problems is the population employment problem. The size of population employment was reported during yesterday's conference by Professor Liu. Excess labour that still exists is mainly in the rural community. Although excess labour was absorbed because agricultural growth expedited the industrialization of the rural community, there are quite a few left who have not been absorbed. In the recent economic liberation, it was this aspect of excess labour that overflowed into the cities without being noticed.

In the last 30 or 40 years, China designated cities as sanctuaries for building the country. By doing so, China had prevented shifting the problems of the economy of rural communities to the economic and political growth of the cities. As a result of this, excess labour existing in rural communities did not flow into cities and create various economic and social problems. Under such circumstances, slums that existed in every developing country were non-existent in China.

However, conditions are changing recently. If such problems increase, they will have a great impact on China's policy and political decisions. In this sense, political movement would be limited and, depending on its management of economic problems, political problems might become severe.

The inability to manage excess labour can be related to the rise of the military during the war with Japan, or to other similar events in our modern political history. In this sense, the problem of excess population is important, and of unavoidable importance for China.

Another issue is the restriction of exports. China has been achieving its economic growth through expediting exports. The greatest factor for economic improvement in the last 10 years is the increase in exports. The question of whether such a high rate of exports can continue was concisely mentioned by Professor Komiya yesterday.

In short, foreign markets do not have enough room to absorb the tremendous amounts of products exported by China. Therefore, China must keep in mind that its trade situation will rapidly worsen if China were to strengthen its exports.

Furthermore, other problems, such as the trade friction Japan is now facing, will start to appear. These problems are important elements for the economic problems limiting the political problems.

Yamamoto: A big wall which must be overcome was mentioned. I would like to discuss the second issue of export restriction when international aspects are discussed later. Population pressure is a problem relevant not only to China but also to the developing nations. In this sense, this issue is the core of the worldwide North–South problem as we move to the twenty-first century. Inclusive of this matter, perhaps concerning the Chinese domestic politics or economics, what would be the most strategically important issues?

Ahn: I offer my view about the implications of economic development. What the Chinese call socialism with Chinese characteristics actually means capitalism with Chinese characteristics. What they call socialism has lost the meaning of Marxism. In fact, China is trying to practise Leninism without Marxism.

Now the question is whether this Leninism without Marxism can be sustained. If, indeed, China should follow the example of East Asian development, as Professor Dwight Perkins suggested yesterday, then it is my view that China has to abandon Leninism some time later on.

For the time being, the legitimacy of the previous Chinese system rests on performance. Currently, the Chinese seem to be justifying

Leninism in order to sustain stability. They are saying that stability is essential in order to accelerate economic growth. Then what if the economic growth cannot be sustained?

In other words, this is what we call development dictatorship or bureaucratic authoritarianism. This establishment cannot be sustained when performance cannot be sustained.

Therefore, it is not certain what would occur after Deng Xiaoping passes away. So there is a great deal of political uncertainty in China. One way or the other, there will be a generational change.

One thing that can be said is that political stability depends on economic performance. It will depend on top élitists' ability to sustain unity and stability among themselves.

Liu: I would like to talk about the economic problems of last year. The IMF tried to measure the actual growth of the Chinese economy. So they measured China's gross domestic product (GDP) by the currency exchange rate and by the purchasing power parity. When calculating by the exchange rate, China is tenth in the world; if calculated by the purchasing power parity, China comes in third place, behind the United States and Japan. When further calculations are made, China is reckoned to surpass the United States and Japan fairly soon.

Various people have shown interest since this result was released. Each of these two ways of calculation has its own distinctive meaning, such as its objective, use, and limitation. Generally, the actual economic power of developing countries is rated relatively low when it is measured by the actual exchange rate. On the other hand, the economic power of developing nations is rated relatively high when it is measured by the purchasing power parity. I'm not going to get deeper into this, but China's economic power is growing rapidly. How we look at it, and how it will influence the world's politics and economy, is yet to be discussed.

Personally, I don't think it's sufficient to judge a nation's economic power and its growth standard only by its economy's total amount, GNP and GDP. The Chinese economy is growing quickly, but increase and quality are low per capita.

According to the rudimentary statistics of the Chinese Social Institute, developing nations are overrated even if measured by the purchasing power parity.

In such a calculation, the GDP of China per capita will be $10,570 in the year 2000 which is slightly above average. Even in the year

2020, it will only amount to US$35,000. The GDP per capita in Japan for the year 2000 will be 5.4 times that of China, at $56,580.

China has great differences compared with the United States and Japan. Not only is income per person low, differences of income among regions are widening, too. The differences amount to as high as six to seven times, when comparing Shanghai, the city with the highest income, and Guizhou, the region with the lowest income. Some foreigners tend to measure China's economic growth based on wealthy regions such as Shanghai, Beijing, and Guangzhou. This is why the results are sometimes overrated.

However, there are still several minority regions and their surrounding regions that are not self-sufficient. There are many less advanced regions not far from Beijing. Therefore, China faces tremendous pressure as it tries to escape from poverty. This point must not be ignored when measuring China's economic power.

In terms of industrial structure the total amount of China's economy is growing rapidly, but in terms of its modernization it is far behind. Let us take a look at the percentages of the employed: 58 per cent work in primary industries, 22 per cent in secondary industries, and 60 per cent in third-level industries. In developed countries, primary industry consists of only 5 per cent and third-level industry consists of more than 60 per cent. This difference is large. Currently, the type of industry that is growing relatively quickly is intensive labour. High-tech industry and high value-added industry have just started in China.

While considering the structures of cities and rural areas, China is far behind the developed nations in city planning. In 1993, China had 28 per cent of its population in the cities and 72 per cent of its population in rural areas. These numbers are the exact opposites of the developed countries. In the developed countries, more than 75 per cent of their population lived in cities and less than 25 per cent of their population lived in rural areas. China must shift its large agricultural labour population to a non-agricultural industry.

This is such a huge problem that it won't be solved in 20 or 30 years. It will most likely take about half a century to solve this problem.

When referring to examples of level per capita, regional gaps, and industrial structure, and the structures of cities and rural areas, China's total GDP does in fact attract the attention of many others. However, the task of modernization remains difficult. More about this aspect can be explained by citing various examples. Such examples are in the management level, technical level, infrastructure, and environmental quality. As a whole, a huge gap exists between the developed nations. Right now, we have set a three-step development plan. We will enter the third stage of development in the year 2050. At this stage, we will have reached a moderate level of modernization and approach the developed countries. Chinese people do not say this out of modesty: this plan of original development was set by considering China's actual circumstances. In the year 2050, China will finally achieve modernization. Thus, when we rate and judge China's economy, we must seek the truth by sticking to facts and considering everything as a whole. By doing so, we will attain precise results.

China's economic development and its linkage to international society

Liu: Next, I would like to express my opinions on the influence China's rapid economic growth may have on the world's politics and economy. The world faces two problems – peace and development. Concerning the development problems – China possesses one-fifth of the world's population. So if China, with more than one billion in population, stays poor and backward, it will be a white elephant not only for China but also for the world. Endless upheavals and problems of emigration would occur. In any country, especially for Asian countries, these problems are unfavourable. Therefore the development of the Chinese economy itself will contribute to the development of the whole earth.

However, the increase of China's development and power is what is more important. It will present big chances and large markets for the world economy and the leading countries of the world, by exports and investments toward China.

The increase of China's import–export trading since the economic reform has been amazing. In the 15-year span from 1979 to 1993, foreign trade grew at an average of 18 per cent a year. Further use of foreign capital is expected to expand.

China has already become the world's second capital-absorbing country, right behind the United States. It is estimated that, in the year 2000, China's total amount of import–export trade will add up to $40 billion. The commutative total of exports is expected to reach $100 billion. Thus, the absorbing power of this huge market is stunning. Increasing the income level and ameliorating the investment environment would affect the leading economic countries in Asia-Pacific region and the world by receiving more goods and investment.

Therefore, they are profitable for the prosperity of the Asia-Pacific region, as a primary pump for the leading nations, and for the increase of employment.

Finally, from a political viewpoint, I would like to talk about the influence of China's economic development on the world. China's economic development is favourable for Asia, the Pacific economy, and the world's economic development. Therefore, most people in the world welcome the rapid growth of the Chinese economy. Now, we must anticipate the fast-growing Chinese economy and adjust our policy accordingly.

However, there are many others who have different views. They interpret the formation of a Chinese economic zone, including Taiwan and Hong Kong, as a new challenge to separate the world's power sphere. Due to this fear, some people are diverting from China.

These cautions and checks are divorced from reality. In order to achieve development, China needs peace and a stable international environment. While China takes an independent peaceful foreign policy, it is most important for China never to voice its supremacy and never to become a boss. Mr Deng Xiaoping supports this policy and so do all we Chinese people.

Although China will develop in the future, it will not voice supremacy and become a boss. This policy will not change. Thus, one need not worry about China becoming the core of the power sphere. After Hong Kong and Taiwan are returned to China, the relationship with the continent would be managed with the rule of "two systems, one country." This is a problem of peaceful unification within China. The others had imagined problems of a totally different nature.

Currently, China is playing an important role for stability and peace in the world's politics. This power of ours might be small for a while, but if 1 billion people are able to feed themselves and China's economy grows, China will become a very great power for world peace. The development of China's economy would contribute greatly to world peace and to the stability of society.

Yamamoto: A very important point was mentioned on the evaluation of China's economic development. You've warned of the danger of discussing only the total amount of GNP and absolute costs. The size of the GNP per capita, the quality of the economy, and the structure of the economy is what is really important.

In the second half, you've warned us of a so-called large Chinese economic region, including Taiwan and Hong Kong. There are many viewpoints which emphasize that.

Regarding the development of the Chinese economy, the media are seeing this as Greater China. There is even a viewpoint that includes all the Chinese people around the world and captures them as one big economic surge or economic sphere. I believe we could hear some useful stories on this subject from Professor Wong.

Wong: As a result of China's successful economic reform open-door policy, the Chinese economy has become highly integrated with the other Asia-Pacific countries. For example, today the Chinese economy is exporting more than half of its goods to the Asia-Pacific region, and more than 80 per cent of the investment going to China originates from the Asia-Pacific region. So you have this global integration, particularly with the two neighbouring economies, Hong Kong and Taiwan.

Most of Hong Kong's trade is now with China, and most of Hong Kong's manufacture is going across the border to Guangdong. It is the same with Taiwan also. So you have this rise of so-called Greater China. Now, the Chinese scholars from Taiwan and Hong Kong or even from Mainland China prefer to use the Chinese term of *hwaian chingchi* trend, which means Chinese economic circle, or sub-China economic circle: in general, Western scholars prefer the term "Greater China."

Now, I think Professor Liu has mentioned that scholars and officials from China – from Beijing – avoid using this term. I think he is quite right, because the term really is the reminiscence of Japan's wartime term, "the greater East-Asian prosperity sphere." So, they don't like to use this, because, indeed, it misleads people: it implies that China can be an aggressive expansionist power and so on.

Chinese from South-East Asia, Taiwan, Singapore, Malaysia, and Thailand also would not like this term because, again, it is misleading. In short, they assume or imply that overseas Chinese have not been integrated in their local societies. I am from Singapore. We call ourselves Singaporean. We don't like to be called Chinese from China. So in fact we don't like the term "overseas Chinese."

I used to argue about it: "Why don't you call yourself 'overseas British'? Indonesian-Chinese would be Indonesian for six generations; some Western journalists still call them 'overseas Chinese.' So, in that sense, we may call President Clinton, 'overseas British'." So these terms are confusing; we don't like it.

Of course, you see from an economic point of view that it is becoming a reality. You have this integration, trade, investment, and so on. For example, the nominal term of total Chinese GNP is about US$500 billion. If you add the GNP of Taiwan and Hong Kong, that will give you roughly about US$800 billion, which is about a quarter of Japan's GNP.

Of course, Professor Liu mentioned if you use PPP (purchasing power parity), then Chinese GNP is underestimated. Then you see, in a total economic sense, it is a very powerful concept. Most people will refer to Greater China to include only Mainland China, Hong Kong, and Taiwan. However, if we included overseas Chinese, about 20 million in South-East Asia, and 5 million in North America, Australia, Europe and so on, altogether there may be about 50 million Chinese outside Mainland China. If you count all of them, it is a very powerful economic entity.

However, I think this is a misconception because integration is very artificial: it is an integration without political agenda. The integration itself is market difference; it's driven by market forces. It is not a kind of integration you will see in the European Community (EC) or the Association of South-East Asian Nations (ASEAN). So, it is very loose. China itself is not integrated very well economically.

So this concept of "Greater China" does not make sense from a political angle. It also doesn't make sense from the economic standpoint. "Greater China" is not a cohesive, powerful entity. So I think people may continue to use it to serve their own purposes. To me, it is just part of the overall economic integration process, which is going on in the whole Asia-Pacific. Japan, and even Korea, are integrating with China. Also, ASEAN economies are closely integrated with Japan. So the same process is going on, which is the market difference. I don't think it has any political meaning at all, particularly as China itself is very loose and considered to become more so. Especially after Deng Xiaoping's old generation, the young generation may not be able to hold Mainland China itself together as a coherent political body.

So I think "Greater China" is only a common term used by certain agitators, I mean, political commentators and so on. It doesn't have economic substance.

Yamamoto: An explanation was made for a very important problem. China is an old country. Also, it is difficult to look over everything because of its size. For this reason, China has always been surrounded by various myths. A so-called China Market Myth has been told since B.C., thus: Western merchants always hoped Chinese people would make their sleeves one centimetre longer. It is important to distinguish myths from reality.

For example, Professor Liu indicated the enormous pressure facing China, with 80 million poverty-stricken people, when it tries to escape from poverty. We tend to forget these problems when we are dazzled by the recent economic boom.

Liu: I would like to add just a brief supplement to what Mr John Wong said. Professor Pye, in his excellent paper yesterday, spoke of China as a civilization instead of a nation-state, and said that the formation of the nation stage will take a long time. On the other hand, to speak of the so-called Chinese-economic-influence area, including the overseas Chinese, is, I think, misleading in the sense that there is a global economic integration happening. You can't just exclude the Chinese element, particularly in South-East Asian economic cooperation and division of labour. Behind this I don't think there is a political agenda which will create a separate group within the South-East Asian economy. I think it is very important to take note of this fact, otherwise it can be taken as a suspicious political signal to many of the ASEAN countries and the West.

I would like to return to some of the issues raised earlier, particularly that raised by Professor Ishikawa regarding rural labour migration, which is a very tough issue. I just want to make a few additional points. In the information society today people catch signals very quickly. When China starts to have more mobility, such as sector mobility and regional mobility, the momentum will continue. Professor Ishikawa made a fine presentation of a five-sector model, indicating that rural China also has fine potential for development with existing capital investment; there is, however, a time gap between the decentralization of development and the rush of people to the coastal areas. Professor Pye also noted that China's rate of urbanization has reached 28 per cent. Speaking as a kind of expert in this area, I think the trend in urbanization is a peculiar phenomenon that can be expressed mathematically as a logistic curve. When it reaches about 30 per cent, the urbanization rate rises very fast. This has been experienced in Japan, and Korea, and many other parts of Asia, and I think China will be no exception. With China's open-door market and more nationwide integration of economic systems, this urbanization trend and mass migration to the major cities will be a serious issue, which also reflects the problem of regional disparity. But with a big country like China, one of my biggest worries is (and I may be exaggerating) that when a province like Guangdong, with a population of 60 million people, has Hong Kong added to it, it could be equivalent to the Thai economy, with a strong export sector and urban infrastructure. When such a province enjoys a high growth rate, there will obviously be a problem of increasing regionalism, and the province will wonder why it should transfer what it has gained through its economic growth to backward regions. This, I think, is a very serious political matter. And here is a very serious management issue at the regional and central levels. With the population rushing to the cities as attempts are made to solve the disparity problem, provinces, for example like Guangdong, will want to continue their economic growth with an accumulation of local resources, which I believe will become an important issue.

There is one more point I want to make. We have mentioned that China is a gigantic country. Yesterday, Professor Komiya rightly pointed out that China's combined value of exports and imports has reached more than 30 per cent of the GNP, which means all of this growth is heavily dependent on direct foreign investment. This is linked with China's export capability, which is twice as high as that of Japan. So in this sense the current high growth is very dependent on the expansion of external markets. I am sure others will join in a discussion on whether China, as a gigantic economy, can continue to enjoy free access to international markets without limitations. This was also the past experience of Taiwan, which is a smaller economy, and Korea, with a population of 40 million. But with the kind of capacity to be built up in the coming years in China, this will probably be another bottleneck.

I may be overcautious, but I would like to mention the impact of a gigantic economy on the international economy. I believe Professor John Wong also quoted, as one example, Lester Brown of the World Watch Group, who asked recently, "Who will feed China?" At China's current population growth, once rice productivity in a country like China exceeds 4 or 5 tons per hectare, it has almost reached the limit. This has been experienced by Taiwan, Korea, and Japan, which at a certain level became net importers of grain. Japan, for instance, over the last 50 years has converted more than 50 per cent of its farmland into urban areas or areas for non-farm use. And this is also happening in China. So this is one example of how another issue is raised when a gigantic country transforms and begins looking to the world market for the supply of grain, not to mention the future supply of different types of energy other than coal.

This is why I disagreed with Professor Perkins yesterday when he said that size does not matter. I believe it is a tremendous issue to be looked at, beside the environment and other issues.

China's intentions in international power politics

Yamamoto: From now, let's discuss the international aspect. What kind of impact will China's economic growth have on regional security and political perspective? Surrounding regional countries will see great opportunities as China's economy grows. However, at the same time, there are concerns that this economic power may be transformed into military power.

Ahn: Speaking of China's role in East Asia and the Pacific, my view is pretty much the view that Professor Amako presented yesterday. If anything, it seems to me that there were great common grounds between Professor Amako and Professor Chen Qimao. If you exclude Professor Chen Qimao's rhetoric about five principles of peaceful coexistence, basically they agree on one point, that China wants to play a major role in East Asia.

It seems to me that China finds it extremely uncomfortable with the United States without any counteracting force after the end of the Cold War. So China is greatly worried about what the United States will do in East Asia. Therefore, it is my view that China is faced to seek a balance of power policy in its foreign policy, notwithstanding the official line that it is seeking peace and development, as Professor Liu suggested moments ago.

So the aim of Chinese foreign policy is to balance American power by making a coalition with the other powers, if necessary. So, as you know, there seem to be two views on Pacific cooperation. One view is that Asians should organize among themselves a view of re-Asianization of Asia by Asians themselves. Typical of this view is a view presented by Mahathir. As you know, in this morning's *Asahi Shimbun*, Mahathir says that he is against the idea of setting a timetable for a free trade zone in Asia or the Pacific. The Chinese tend to support Mahathir's view in order to curtail American attempts at hegemony.

But, on the other hand, there is a view that East Asia and North America should combine to make a Pacific Rim community. This is the view advocated by people like Funabashi of the *Asahi Shimbun*, what you call Pacific Globalism. Therefore, the Japanese are some-what wavering; they are sitting on the fence between these two viewpoints – the global Pacific viewpoint and the "Asia for Asians" viewpoint. The Chinese tend to support ASEAN's view and Maha-thir's view.

Now, having said this, on the whole the Chinese role in East Asia has been constructive. It is my view that China has played a very constructive role on the North Korean nuclear issue. But then, on Korea, as you know, today Li Peng is visiting Seoul but, at the same time, three days ago the Chinese pulled out their representative from the military Armistice Commission at Panmunjom. Therefore, the Chinese seem to play South Korea against North Korea, North Korea against China, and Japan against the United States. This is typical of the "using barbarian against barbarian" tradition.

So, to make my remarks short, I think it's inevitable that China wants to be a major player in relation politics. If indeed, as I said, there are two broad imperatives, one is the political imperative that is working toward nationalism, presence of power, sovereignty, and non-interference. However, the economic imperative is working toward reform, open-door policy, interdependence, and a borderless economy like that emerging in South China.

So it is very important for the United States and Japan to curtail China's attempt to play a hegemony role. According to this morning's paper, again, Sam Huntington of Harvard said that China is spending something like $90 billion for military expenditure. Should this trend continue, we must worry about a Chinese attempt to play a hege-mony role. So, on the whole we hope that China will abide by inter-national norms, presumably along the line of liberalism and inter-national regime.

Cline: My comments will focus on the implications of the size of China in the world economy. The central factor about China in eco-nomic terms is that China has one-fifth of the world's population. In much of the twentieth century, when China was in poverty and the economy was closed, its population was basically irrelevant to the world economy.

That is no longer true today, and it will be even less true in the future. Already, China's exports of about $90 billion are the largest of any developing country and if you add Hong Kong, the total is close to $200 billion. Now this is only 6 per cent of world trade but it is growing very rapidly and is highly concentrated in labour-intensive manufactures that are sensitive in the industrial countries.

Large countries are not marginal actors. In economic terms, their own actions can affect the market prices. It seems to me that we have to think about the future of the Chinese economy, not as China acting as a marginal entrant to the world economy, but as having effects that shift the world economy.

There is some possibility of this outcome in trade. There is even more possibility with respect to its impact on raw materials and global pollution. If China would continue to grow at something like 10 per cent per year, we could imagine large impacts on world demand for raw materials.

In 1990, China exported 500,000 barrels of oil per day. By the year 2000, it is expected to be importing 1.3 million barrels of oil per day. If it continued to grow at 10 per cent a year, by the year 2030 conceivably China could be importing more than 40 million barrels of oil per day. That is not going to happen because there is not enough oil: the total world oil production is only about 50 million barrels per day. Instead, under that scenario, there will be a very high upward pressure on oil prices as a consequence.

Consider copper and other materials associated with expansion of the electrical infrastructure. China currently plans to add annually close to 20 GW of installed capacity to today's annual capacity of 180 GW. That's comparable to the annual additions of electrical capacity in the United States over recent years and far above what China was adding in the first half of the 1980s.

Well, let's consider agricultural markets. We've already heard on the Panel the reference to the calculation by the World Watch Institute. According to the calculation, as incomes rise there is more demand for meat, and that has a multiplied effect on demand for grain. Because of land limits, China's grain imports by the year 2015 could exceed the global export availability of grain that is currently observed today.

What it really says is that we have to consider whether China could contribute to a revitalization of the question raised originally by Malthus, more recently by the Club of Rome. In the past, Malthus and the Club of Rome were wrong. The physical resources were not a limit to growth. I think we will face that question or that issue once again.

Considering global pollution in the area of carbon dioxide emissions, China has vast resources of coal. Coal is very polluting in terms of carbon dioxide, which causes global warming. China already accounts for 11 per cent of world carbon dioxide emissions. By the year 2100, it is expected to contribute to one-quarter of world emissions. If the international political groups become serious about the problem of global warming, one could imagine China being on a collision course with other countries on this issue.

Trade sensitivity is another area that we will have to watch. China has what would seem to be an almost unlimited supply of low-cost unskilled labour. Thus, it's natural that the focus of trade would be on production of labour-intensive goods. However, that puts pressure on individual sectors and unskilled workers in the industrial countries. It is a contrast to the trade between industrial countries, which tends to be intrasectorial trade or intra-industry trade and has much less adjustment pressure.

It is misleading to say that China's exports are only a few percentage points of world consumption because these exports have been concentrated in those sectors. They would be concentrated in the future, given the natural comparative advantage, if things are left to their natural tendency. Now, there is already an academic debate in the West about whether trade is contributing to the concentration of income in the United States. Over the past 10 or 20 years, unskilled wages in the United States have been dropping, and the gap between unskilled wages and skilled wages has been widening.

There is an academic debate about whether trade with developing countries has been a source of that trend. However the answer to that debate may be looking backward, we have to expect that, if we look forward and see China entering into this process on a mass scale, then the influences could be larger for the Asian Tigers today.

Already China confronts protectionist responses in such areas as textiles. US negotiators are cutting China's export quota growth from the beginning of 1994. The US trade bill implementing the Uruguay Round Table agreement is aimed at China's re-selling of Hong Kong quota materials, as a device to limit these imports. Once China enters the General Agreement on Tariffs and Trade (GATT), China confronts the "grandfather clause", so-called Article 35. This was applied against Japan in the past – the right of existing members not to extend the concessions to new members.

Now, one of the most challenging issues of this trade connection is the income-distributional implication. We have an interesting problem here. The natural trade connection is wonderful for world industrialization because it gives opportunities for Chinese workers to improve their status. It is potentially corrosive for income distribution within the industrial countries. So we have questions of ethics and politics. The politics of trade could force an increasing confrontation between essentially the upper classes in the industrial countries, who can benefit from the cheaper products, and the unskilled group, who have the impact on their wages.

This political diversion was fairly evident to some extent in almost every national debate. There, there was an alignment of labour unions and human rights groups on the one side, but on the other side there was a very powerful incentive to keep trade open to China because of the potential market for US exporters. Secretary Ronald Brown, on his trip to China in September, gave glowing accounts of the potential market for such exports as US aircraft and electrical power equipment.

Clearly, these politics of trade pose a challenge of achieving a result that is equitable, that is efficient, and that does not, in contrast, go in directions that are inequitable. In practice, that implies that the United States and other industrial countries will need to keep their markets open. If there is going to be equity involved, they will need to allocate spending on re-training of unskilled workers who are likely to be affected by imports from China. Now, there is also an irony in that China has become a locomotive of the world economy. If you take the trade share and the growth rate of China, Asia, and the four countries with newly industrializing economies (NIEs) and add them together, their contribution as a locomotive to world demand is greater than, or equal to, that of the United States individually or that of the European Union.

For example, if the growth of this area is something like 7.5 per cent compared with the growth of only 2.5 per cent in the United States, then that display more than offsets the fact that the absolute scale of the imports of this East Asian group is only about two-thirds that of the United States. So we have an irony that this area is becoming an important growth pole for exports for the rest of the world.

In sum, China's human and economic size, I think, will make it a source of both economic opportunity and economic tension for the industrial countries in the coming decades. For the Chinese leaders, there is a challenge to design a development strategy that is compatible with both international and domestic environmental sustainability. For industrial country leaders, there is a challenge to harmonize the opportunities for gains from trade with China and at the same time to maintain domestic equality. They must also avoid putting undue pressure on the unskilled group. For leaders of all sides, there will be a challenge to ensure the growth in the twenty-first century and not let it wind up defeated by the Club of Rome or by Mr Malthus. The solution to that, of course, once again will hinge importantly on technological change.

Yamamoto: We just heard you speak on security, relating it to both politics and economy. This becomes an international problem as China gains power. In relation to the security problem, the discussion should focus on the relationship between ASEAN and China.

As ASEAN is starting its dialogue on security of other countries in the Asia-Pacific region, China is also playing an important role in the security aspect. ASEAN has decided to take the leadership of the first ASEAN Regional Forum, which is going to be held at Bangkok in July next year.

Wong: ASEAN's relations with China have come through transformation from Cold War to *détente*. This year, for the first time, China was invited to be one of the partners, so there must be a new era.

ASEAN itself as an organization is changing, because now you have a bigger body, the East Asian Economic Caucus (EAEC) concept proposed by Mahathir of Malaysia and the even bigger council of the Asia-Pacific Economic Cooperation (APEC). So how does China fit into this? How do ASEAN and China stand?

For everybody in South-East Asia, if you talk about security, peace, and stability, it will be meaningless to neglect China. China in whatever terms is most important, just as Japan in economic terms is most important for the region.

The ASEAN view has also changed in a sense that ASEAN views China's economic growth as primarily good for the ASEAN region. It's also beneficial as to the region's growth in terms of providing more trade and investment opportunity, as well as a kind of stabilizing force. As I said, I endorse Professor Strange's view that all ASEAN countries, including Indonesia now, hope for China to continue to do well in terms of economic growth.

From the ASEAN point of view, economic growth is the most important bottom line: with growth you can have change, democracy, peace, and stability; without economic growth, there will not be stability. This is the most important point when we report on China.

Strange: First of all, we would like to say something about Professor Cline. I am amazed that an economist would ignore the factor of price. The demand for oil from China will go up. So, if the price rises, the Americans may not like that because they are used to using a lot of cheap oil and wasting a lot of it. They should have put a tax on petrol a long time ago the way the Europeans did, but they didn't have the guts to do it.

So I think the same thing applies to cereals. I have some advice on the internal effects on China, I think you should have tariffs on imported cereals into China. Don't take any notice of the Americans when they say they are in favour of free trade because they are not. They just don't like the way the Europeans protect their farmers. The Chinese need to protect their farmers.

Professor Wong has been absolutely right, and the other people who have referred to the rural–urban problem. You have got to look after the farmers and the only way you are going to do it is to protect them.

The other point on which I do agree with Professor Cline is that manufacturing exports from China are going to create problems for governments and for factory workers. It's a great opportunity for the managers of firms, including Japanese firms. It's going to be tough on the workers. Eventually, it is going to put pressure on the life employment system. The students who are about to graduate had better be aware of that.

Now, I think nobody has said much about money. Economists always pay too much attention to trade. In China, there are domestic problems of inflation and taxes. I think you probably can learn something from Latin America about the effects of inflation and the value of things like index-linked bonds and various sales taxes, for example VAT. I think you want a tax on petrol, energy, and a value-added tax on luxury goods.

I think there is a great deal of room for further discussion between the Chinese and other people as to the experience of fiscal problems.

I would now like to discuss questions of security. I don't believe that nuclear weapons or war between states, whether they are developed states or even developing states, is really a problem any more. So a lot of people in strategic studies in international relations are really looking closely at employment. So they will go on worrying about how many missiles the Chinese have.

I think the Chinese, like the North Koreans and Ukrainians, regard nuclear weapons as an important insurance policy. They don't need an awful lot of them, but they do need some. However, it doesn't mean to say that it's a threat to anybody, including Taiwan.

I think the significant thing is the absence of war between India and Pakistan. Despite all the trouble about temples, both sides have been very determined not to get into an escalating war situation. This is for a very simple reason – that the competition between states is about market shares and not about territory. Market shares are not gained by going around threatening other people. You get them by being efficient, by being adaptive, by being all the things Singaporeans, Koreans, and Taiwanese are. And the Chinese Republic should learn from that.

So, the only question, of course, is what do you do about the army? It does seem to me that most countries spend far too much on their military forces. The Cold War is over; we don't really need so many men under arms. We don't need so many arms. We need to control the arms trade. The army in China, like the army in South Africa in the past, is directed against its own people, not against anybody else. So I think the message that should come from the outside world to China is, cut down on the army, cut down on the pile of generals and maybe we can all live in peace.

The final point I would like to make is about the uncertainty. Everybody has mentioned that the risks are in politics and that opportunities are in economy. That's absolutely right. I think it's worth it because we are in Japan and Japanese firms are, many of them, very interested in expanding their manufacturing on the mainland of Asia.

The Japanese firms should remember a couple of things. One is that the Chinese have no reason to love any of us foreigners, beginning with the Opium War, the Boxer Rebellion, and the 1930s. Don't be surprised if you are not always terribly welcome or if you have to make special efforts to be welcome.

I remember an Italian firm I spoke to, who said, "When we go on a construction job in Africa, we always take a hospital with us." That is very sensible because it was open to everybody in the region to come and use Italian doctors. I think that's sensible. It's doing something for the locality that is socially useful. I think the Japanese firms should do this. I think the other thing that is peculiar about Japanese firms more than American firms, is that there is a sort of racial exclusiveness in Japanese management that will have to change. If you want to avoid the risk, and there will be political risks in China, you had better make sure that you have a local partner. You had better also pay attention to local managers by promoting them in your joint ventures on the mainland. I think this is terribly important.

Chen: I would like to speak on the safety of the Asia-Pacific region and on the influence of China. I think it's safe to assume that the safety of the Asia-Pacific region is stable. The economy is displaying stability, too. However, there are also pessimistic views. There is a possibility that a serious upheaval may occur in this area. As a key question, the problem of evaluation of China is included in this view. That is to say, whether China is a factor for stability or instability in the Asia-Pacific region.

I would like to emphasize here that China actually has a big part in preserving stability in the Asia-Pacific Region. I will explain this in two ways.

First of all, there is the success in China's reformation, modernization, and opening up. This, in itself, is a contribution to the stabilization of the Asia-Pacific Region. As you all know, China has a population of 1.2 billion, and there is an annual growth rate of 1.4 million. If there were to be civil unrest, similar to that in the former Yugoslavia, or a serious economic crisis, as in the former Soviet Union, or some political disorder extended over a long period of time, or if a serious famine were to occur, who would be the one to help out China? Would the United States be able to do it? Would the United Nations? Nobody would probably be able to do it. Say refugees started to flow out of China – for example, 10 per cent would be 120 million, or even 5 per cent would be 60 million. What country would be able to take in all these people? For this reason, the success in reforming, and opening up, for China could only be said to be a contribution to the Asia-Pacific Region.

The other point is that China is a socialist state. As Professor Ahn said earlier, China's distinctive socialist state may well turn into a distinctive capitalist state. I would like to point out here that the Chinese people hope for a prosperous and developed China and that the Chinese people are working hard to achieve this. We hope to maintain the structure of society, and to become wealthy together. We do not wish to choose the road of capitalism that would separate the rich and the poor. I believe these hopes of the Chinese people could become reality.

China practises foreign policy in its own independent way. This policy will preserve peace in the world, will be an advantage to the modernization of China, and has a basic goal of creating a peaceful and safe environment for a long time to come. Our five fundamental principles are respecting others' land and national sovereignty, prohibiting invasions and intervention in domestic affairs, and reciprocal equality. Peaceful coexistence is also our basic policy. For these fundamental principles, China is not going to widen its sphere of influence other than on its own land.

We will also not allow powerful nations to fight for influence. It would go without saying that we will not permit any large nation to violate our national sovereignty, or let China be put under any influence. Historically, some large nations, including the former Soviet Union, tried to build a safety bloc for their own sake, but this sacrifices the land and sovereignties of other countries. I believe this goes against the basics of peaceful diplomacy; therefore, China vehemently opposes this. We, China, for the sake of our safety, are pushing forward a good-neighbourly diplomacy. With our neighbouring countries – including Japan, ASEAN, North and South Korea – we are building a good, friendly relationship.

As for disputes for land, China would like to solve them in a peaceful manner through discussion as much as possible, to put aside the conflicts we can't solve for now, and develop natural resources together. If that is not possible, while avoiding military measures as much as possible, we will maintain the present condition, and start border trade at the border areas that are open now, which in fact are under control.

In the coming years, China will begin talks about security in the East Asian region and will eagerly participate in economic cooperation in the Asia-Pacific Region. If an economic bloc were to be formed in this region, I would hope it would be an open, and not a closed, economic bloc.

Since 1989, China has moderately increased the military budget. This is mostly to offset inflation. For example, China increased its defence budget by 20 per cent this year and, as you all know, China's inflation rate reached 20 per cent this year. Therefore, this 20 per cent increase has been offset due to inflation. All except a small portion of it went to renovating outdated arms equipment, but only for the Chinese navy that protects adjacent waters, and not to reinforce naval strength out in the sea. Therefore, China's naval strength is nowhere close to America's or Russia's and is far weaker than those of Japan and India in comparison. China also has never once thought about acts like protecting sea lanes. China's leaders, as I have been emphasizing repeatedly, do not believe in China situating itself in a power vacuum.

Even if China were to become a powerful country in the future, it will not advocate that power. I believe that what Mr Schmidt said earlier, in the keynote speech about China's economy, was too high an assessment. Mr Schmidt said that, by the year 2010, China would have outgrown America, but this is too much of an optimistic view. Chinese and American scholars have been carrying out joint research, and I would like to offer you all the data they have come up with. The result: China's economic scale in 2020 will be proportionate to America's. By then, China will have a population five times greater than America's. Therefore, the living standard then would be substantially lower than America's. Plus, this estimate is based on each of three decades. During the 1990s, there is an 11 per cent increase each year; in the first decade of the twenty-first century it is 8 per cent, and the next 10 years are estimated to have a growth rate of 7.6 per cent. In other words, whether China will be able to keep the 8 per cent growth rate in the twenty-first century is something I myself am sceptical about. In order to maintain the 8 per cent, we will have to solve a series of problems.

I am opposed to opinions that claim China will become a superpower. The Chinese define a superpower as a country that possesses far more power than other countries, always trying to lead, or a state that would advocate their might. It is impossible that China will become a country like that. From what I understand, even the present President of America, Clinton, says (as I said earlier), under the circumstances of the world, America will become a ordinary nation from what it was – a superpower. China has no intentions of becoming such a superpower, and doesn't posses the ability to become one.

Yamamoto: I believe there are three problems with the issue of security that has been discussed now. Unlike the situation in Europe where, during the Cold War, there were two sides that were confronting each other, the security situation in East and South-East Asia is much more complex and multilateral. A problem would occur if China faced an economic depression, and it is said there would be concerns if the military budget were to increase.

This is probably said because many people believe that it is a historical principle that an economic power would become a military power. We have seen that Japan has so far become the first example of an economic power that hasn't become a military power. Although still in the process, there is an undoubted belief that, if China were to gain economic strength it would turn into a military power. Plus, the fact that we do not know for sure the strength of China's military, is probably what is causing the anxiety.

The third concern is America's movement. Is America going to end its presence in Asia and listen to its own interests? Or is it going to continue to face resistance if it were to intervene too much? But there is also a dilemma in this region, that if America were to abandon Asia completely, it would create numerous problems.

Another concern is what kind of role Japan is trying to achieve in this region. Earlier, Professor Ahn told us that Japan is being a bystander, but the security talks among several countries in this region have just begun, and the fact that China is joining in is a very important and encouraging change.

Now for about 20 minutes I would like to hear questions from the floor.

Vikhanski (*OECD*): I would like to follow up on what Professor Ishikawa and Professor Cline said, which is about the ability to absorb Chinese exports by other countries in the future. This point has not been discussed much. China's economic development, I would say, is shifting toward the domestic mechanism. In other words, instead of relying completely on exports, they are focusing on domestic areas. From the point of view of OECD countries, they are already absorbing numerous exports. If the burden were to become greater, there is fear that instead of going along with internationally agreed rules, like GATT, power play would decide the subjects in the international markets.

Asia has a high growth rate, but this point may be the weakest subject. North America already asserts its voice in unison. It has complete and efficient politics, plus economic strength. Countries of Europe, too, will speak their voice together through the European Council, taking into consideration that they have small disagreements in the region.

But in the Asia-Pacific Region, we do not hear voices like this. Regional unity in this region is based on direct investment overseas and trading relationships, and is not based on political agreement.

Chen: I agree with you. In other words, the political situation. For example, the non-tariff barrier was a problem that was seen in the past. I am not saying that China should close its market. I hope there is no misunderstanding. Professor Strange might have a different opinion. I believe that the protection of agriculture is not the solution. What I have said is that, if China were to import 40 million barrels of crude oil a day, that would raise the price of oil.

Another example, to depend on exports, and China's dependency on exports in its GNP is very high, therefore it is often said that China is weak and fragile, but I think this is an exaggeration. This is related to what Professor Liu said, which is about the monetary exchange rate. In other words, owing to the rate of exchange, the domestic GNP is underestimated, and its vulnerability due to its exports is over-valued.

What this means is that the equation of political negotiations once again must carefully reconsider the strategy. Namely, to consider its impact on unskilled workers, it probably won't lean toward the protection of them.

Amako: Throughout yesterday's and today's discussion China's future as related to politics and economics has been the one main topic. Politically related, it is pessimistic; economically related, it is optimistic. I didn't feel there was enough discussion about the significance of their relationship, so I would like to offer some explanations.

Probably the stability of politics is being stressed, but what is the physics behind it that ensures that it is stable? For one, it is a communist state. The other is probably its military strength. On top of that there is the leadership of Deng Xiaoping. Another system that ensures its security, seen from its functional aspect, is the People's Representative Assembly system and the administrative bureaucratic system.

Then, how is the unstable factor going to be considered? I believe there are many factors of instability, lately the issue of economic reform – for example, the inconsistency in the growth of the economy; this is the issue of differences in prices and price itself. Then the inconsistency in social growth: this has been stressed many times, about the growing population and the problem of unemployment. Or the growth of disparity of interest between each social class. Or the growing disparity of interest between the central and regional state which in some cases leads to confrontation. Politically, there is a

261

demand for more political participation, or the decline of legitimacy in the communist party. There are situations like this, I believe.

When I think about the system after Deng Xiaoping, how would China be able to adjust its policy-making system, after this possible element of instability? In other words, the adjustment mechanism must be enlarged on several levels. To think about it, the system that guarantees stability, which I have just mentioned, and as a function, the People's Representative Assembly and the administrative bureaucracy, is the only system that would work.

I believe there is a big problem with this. I understand that China is today searching for the mechanism for its interest adjustments, economically and socially, but how can they guarantee their stability if they don't find this? In the end, with the decrease of the communist party's legitimacy, we can guess that it would become a military-reliant condition.

The idea that the issue of the threat of military strength goes along the line of economic development, which relates to Professor Yamamoto's earlier issue, was disputed by Professor Wong and Professor Chen, and I basically agree with their view. Rather, if a situation of military reliance were to come up to maintain their system on the line of domestic instability, that would be an extremely important problem. Therefore I believe that the change in the system, of finding the interest-adjustment mechanism, is probably the most important point to consider for the political and economical relationship.

Floor: This is for Professor Cline. An important opinion, the issue that many Chinese people should notice, is that intensive labour products are maintaining a very high growth rate. It was said that this would intensify trade friction and would cause disorder and tension between countries. Professor Ishikawa also mentioned this. I believe this is an issue that we must be very careful about.

But Professor Ishikawa mentioned the proposal on the development of the domestic market concerning this issue. I think this is a magnificent idea. As the professor from the OECD said earlier, it is necessary to expand the capacity of the international market or the domestic market. We must cool the tension through this expansion. I would like to know what Professor Cline mentioned earlier about what we must do. What can the Chinese, the Chinese government do? What is necessary for the general public, what must be done? Unless there is a solution, there is no road for us to proceed.

Pollution would occur if China's growth rate were to increase. Then, as the growth rate increases, would it be acceptable for China's per capita income level to be maintained at 300 dollars? Should this be continued?

Cline: Now, concerning the problem of the material for the intensive labour industry, we must keep in mind the issue of growth and development in each sector. Therefore, if other conditions are fixed, then numerous products, dispersement among many areas, and multi-lateralism will be sought out. Therefore it is important not to concentrate on just one thing, not to just concentrate on the industrialization of the intensive labour system.

It is good to focus on domestic markets for this meaning, but I do not believe it would be good to become protective and grow introvertedly. That is because Latin America had a bad experience – an inefficient experience – through that. We can say it is a model that didn't really obtain success.

Then the issue of pollution. Should they get money from developed countries, and lessen its impact on the environment? For example, the developed countries will keep their promises about pollution that is caused by coal. This means that the promise made at the Rio Summit, Earth Summit – resources of alternative energy, and the alternative energy strategy – is all supported. Or is it fine for the per capita income to be kept at 300 dollars? China, as a right, must keep developing its economy. This is not just for China, but relates to other countries' interests also.

Therefore, what China must do is (and likewise for developed countries that make demands on China) to consider what must be looked at. For example, there would be less focus on retraining. Retraining is necessary also. Many domestic political policy aspects will come up. These might have an effect on the economic aspects. I think it is important, to handle the problems of domestic inequality with a will. But I myself do not believe that this will hamper China's economic growth.

Ishikawa: As a Japanese, when I look across this auditorium, I contemplate what I thought about this academic session. I myself, and those who were adults during World War II (and I do not believe there are many who were adults before the war, but, including those people), we have a guilty conscience toward China. That is the basic mentality of our generation when we deal with China.

I am saying this because, from now on, Japanese will be associating with the people of China. This must be done more actively, and although this may sound insensitive to the Western nations, for us it is a very urgent problem and dealing with countries far away is not much of an issue. We must make our friendship more active. I associate with students, and today's young students (I believe people in their 30s, 40s, and 50s are the same also) do not feel the same way about China as we do. In a sense, they are very magnanimous, and the association with Chinese is more, should I say, nonchalant and does not give any different impression from talking to people from other countries. They, especially, do not possess that special emotion that we have when they come in contact with Chinese people. This kind of attitude is something we must find ourselves, and I would like the young Chinese people to find, or to make, a common language that can be used by us when we associate.

What I mean as a common language is, as we enter an era of globalization, we need an internationally accepted general concept that has a universal value. This can include democracy, rule of law, constitution, or the term "human rights." I am sure there are many opinions but, if ideas like these became a common language and became the basis of an unbiased relationship between the younger generation of Japan and China, and if this could be done developmentally, we would be very relieved.

Yamamoto: Thank you very much. I would now like to end the panel discussion. Being on "Expectations of China in the twenty-first century," I am sure we have left many opinions unsaid. But we have six more years to the twenty-first century. Considering the fall of the Berlin Wall, and the fall of the Soviet Union probably was not expected by anybody six years before it happened, it would be much more important to point out precisely and understand which problems to work on toward the twenty-first century.

For that, I believe that there were many things that were learned from today's panellists.

Chairman: The coordinator Professor Yamamoto and each panellist, and people who participated from the floor, I thank you very much for a fruitful, productive discussion. We, too, when we think of China in the twenty-first century, didn't have the slightest idea of Japan as a huge Chinese market. We have contemplated these issues for the

264

sake of a much more peaceful twenty-first century, and the hope for continuing prosperity. This is an issue that more than 5 billion of us must recognize. We have invited researchers from 13 countries to this symposium, and to have them seriously discuss from that angle, on behalf of the International Symposium Organization Committee, I once again would like to express my appreciation.

Contributors

Byung-Joon Ahn
Professor, Yonsei University
Seoul, Korea

Satoshi Amako
Professor, Aoyama Gakuin University
Tokyo, Japan

Chen Qiaosheng
Director, Management and
   Administration Research Institute
Shiyan, China

Chen Qimao
President, Shanghai Association for
   International Relations
Shanghai, China

William Cline
Senior Fellow, Institute for International
   Economics
Washington DC, USA

Fumiaki Fujino
Director, Itochu Corporation, Corporate
   Administration Group I
Tokyo, Japan

François Gipouloux
Research Fellow, National Centre for
   Scientific Research
Paris, France

Yutaka Hara
Professor, Aoyama Gakuin University
Tokyo, Japan

Shigeru Ishikawa
Professor Emeritus, Aoyama Gakuin
   University
Tokyo, Japan

Fumio Itoh
Dean, SIPEB, and Chairman of the
   Organizing Committee, Aoyama
   Gakuin University
Tokyo, Japan

Jiang Ping
Professor, China University of Politics
   and Law
Beijing, China

Isao Kaminaga
Professor, Aoyama Gakuin University
Tokyo, Japan

266

Werner Kamppeter
Professor, Friedrich-Ebert Foundation
Bonn, Germany

Ryutaro Komiya
Professor, Aoyama Gakuin University
Tokyo, Japan

Liu Guoguang
Adviser, Chinese Academy of Social
  Sciences
Beijing, China

Fu-chen Lo
Principal Academic Officer, United
  Nations University Institute of
  Advanced Studies
Tokyo, Japan

Lu Xueyi
Director, Institute of Sociology, Chinese
  Academy of Social Sciences
Beijing, China

Tetsuo Minato
Professor, Aoyama Gakuin University
Tokyo, Japan

Mitsuo Morimoto
Professor, Aoyama Gakuin University
Tokyo, Japan

Yasuo Okamoto
Professor, Aoyama Gakuin University
Tokyo, Japan

Hiroshi Okuzaki
Professor, Aoyama Gakuin University
Tokyo, Japan

Dwight H. Perkins
Director, Harvard Institute for
  International Development
Cambridge, Mass., USA

Lucian W. Pye
Professor Emeritus, Massachusetts
  Institute of Technology
Cambridge, Mass., USA

Rong Yiren
Vice-President of the People's Republic
  of China

Helmut Schmidt
Former Chancellor
Federal Republic of Germany

Susan Strange
Professor, University of Warwick
Warwick, UK

Khien Theeravit
Professor, Chulalongkorn University
Bangkok, Thailand

Takeo Uchida
Former Senior Academic Officer, United
  Nations University
Tokyo, Japan

Oleg Vikhanski
Professor and Head of School of Busi-
  ness Administration
Moscow State University
Moscow, Russia

John Wong
Director, The Institute of East Asian
  Political Economy
National University of Singapore
Singapore

Wu Jiajun
Director, Institute of International
  Economics
Chinese Academy of Social Sciences
Beijing, China

Wu Jinglian
Senior Research Fellow, Development
  Research Centre
State Council of the People's Republic
  of China
Beijing, China

Mitsuru Yamamoto
Professor, Aoyama Gakuin University
Tokyo, Japan

Zou Yilin
Professor and Director of the Institute of
  Chinese Historical Geography of
  Fudan University
Shanghai, China

267

Index

3309 028